The Pocket Legal Companion to Trademark

The Pocket Legal Companion to Trademark:

A User-Friendly Handbook

on Avoiding Lawsuits and

Protecting Your Trademarks

BY LEE WILSON

ALLWORTH PRESS
NEW YORK

15 14 13 12 11   5 4 3 2 1

Published by Allworth Press, an imprint of Skyhorse Publishing, Inc. 307 West
36th Street, 11th Floor, New York, NY 10018.

Allworth Press® is a registered trademark of Skyhorse Publishing, Inc.®, a
Delaware corporation.

www.allworth.com

Cover and interior design by Mary Belibasakis

Library of Congress Cataloging-in-Publication Data

Wilson, Lee, 1951-
The pocket legal companion to trademark : a user-friendly handbook on avoiding
lawsuits and protecting your trademarks / by Lee Wilson.
    p. cm.
Includes bibliographical references and index.
ISBN 978-1-58115-909-7 (pbk. : alk. paper)
1. Trademarks—Law and legislation—United States—Popular works. I. Title.
KF3180.Z9W545 2012
346.7304'88—dc23
                                    2012021282

ISBN: 978-1-58115-909-7

Printed in the United States of America

DEDICATION

This book is
dedicated to my
old friend and
business partner
Bill King, my favorite serial
capitalist, whose accom-
plishments in the business
world are proof that
good ideas and hard
work are rewarded
in a free enter-
prise society.

Contents

Appendices

Introduction

As more and more of the wealth of our country becomes embodied in intellectual property, it becomes increasingly important for businesspeople to grasp the basics of intellectual property law. Almost everyone has a hard time remembering the difference between the three major sorts of intellectual property: trademarks, copyrights, and patents. Trademarks are the subject of this book. Before you can completely understand trademarks, however, you need a passing knowledge of copyrights and patents. After we briefly distinguish trademarks from copyrights and patents, we'll consider trademarks in detail.

Although all three protect products of the human imagination, trademarks, copyrights, and patents are distinct but complementary types of intellectual property. Each is governed by a different federal law. The copyright and patent statutes both originate in Article I, Section 8, Clause 8 of the Constitution, which empowers Congress "to Promote the Progress of Science and useful Arts, by securing, for limited Times to Authors and Inventors, the exclusive Right to their respective Writings and Discoveries." Our federal trademark statute originates in the "commerce clause" of the Constitution, which gives Congress the power to regulate interstate commerce. Only our federal government regulates copyrights; copyright registrations are granted by the Copyright Office, which is a department of the Library of Congress. Similarly, only the federal government can grant a patent. However, although the federal government grants trademark registrations, so do all fifty states. And for complicated reasons, the U.S. Patent Office and the U.S. Trademark Office are two halves of the same division of the Department of Commerce, called the United States Patent and Trademark Office.

Confused? It gets easier. In fact, the best way to understand copyrights, patents, and trademarks is to consider them together, in relation to each other.

Copyrights

A copyright is a set of rights that the copyright statute gives to the creators of artistic, literary, musical, dramatic, and audiovisual works. Only the person who created the copyrighted work is legally permitted to reproduce, perform, or display it, distribute copies of it, or create variations of it; any unauthorized exercise of any of these rights is called "copyright infringement" and is actionable in federal court.

Since January 1, 1978, in the United States, a copyright is created whenever a creator "fixes" in tangible form a work for which copyright protection is available. Under most circumstances, a copyright will endure until seventy years after the death of the creator of the copyrighted work; after copyright protection expires, a work is said to have fallen into the "public domain" and anyone is free to use it. Registration of a copyright enhances the rights that a copyright owner gains automatically by the act of creation, but is not necessary for copyright protection. The chief limitation on the rights of copyright owners is that copyright protects only particular expressions of ideas rather than the ideas themselves. This means that several people can create copyrightable works based on the same idea; in fact, there is no infringement no matter how similar one work is to another unless one creator copied another's work.

(For more information about copyrights, see *The Pocket Legal Companion to Copyright,* by Lee Wilson, published by Allworth Press.)

Patents

The word "patent" is used ordinarily to designate the rights granted by the federal government to the originator of a physical invention or industrial or technical process (a "utility patent") or an ornamental design for an "article of manufacture" (a "design patent"). A patent is a monopoly granted by the U.S. Patent Office for a limited time to the creator of a new invention. A utility patent may be granted to a process, a machine, a manufacture, a composition of matter, or an improvement of an existing idea that falls into one of these categories. Utility patents endure for up to twenty years after the application for the patent was filed. Plant patents are issued for new asexually or sexually reproducible plants and similarly last for up to twenty years after the application for the patent was filed. Design patents are granted for ornamental designs used for nonfunctional aspects of manufactured items. A design patent lasts fourteen years from the date it is issued. A patent holder earns the exclusive right to make, use, and sell the invention, process, or design for which the patent was granted. Any un-authorized manufacture, use, or sale of the patented invention, process, or design within this country during the term of the patent is infringement.

(For more information about patents, see *The Patent Guide* by Carl Battle, published by Allworth Press.)

Trademarks

Trademarks are (usually) words or designs that identify products or services to consumers. Unlike copyrights, in which their creators have protectable rights from the inception of the copyrighted work, rights in a trademark accrue only by use of the trademark in commerce and then belong to the company that applies the mark to its products rather than to the person who comes up with the name or designs the logo that becomes the trademark. Roughly speaking, a company gains rights in a trademark in proportion to the geographic scope and duration of its use of the mark. Ordinarily, the company that uses a mark first gains rights in that mark superior to any other company that later uses it for the same product or services. Unauthorized use of a trademark is trademark infringement.

Trademark infringement is a commercial sin. It is one of the more common forms of a large and not-very-well-defined area of the law called "unfair competition." Basically, the law of unfair competition has, over the years and in numerous cases, labeled certain efforts at commercial competition "unfair"—even fraudulent—because they are too aggressive or less than honest. Unfair competition is, generally speaking, competition by dirty tricks, although several forms of unfair competition can result from otherwise innocent blunders. By declaring certain actions "unfair" in commerce, the courts seek to promote both free competition *and* fair competition. Among the types of trademark-related commercial conduct that have been held to constitute unfair competition are:

- trademark infringement;
- trademark dilution;
- use of confusingly similar business names;
- use of confusingly similar literary titles;
- unauthorized use of a distinctive literary or performing style;
- copying a product's trade dress and configuration; and
- infringement of the right of publicity.

Not every action that has been or could be labeled unfair competition is codified, that is, named and written down in a statute. Judges may add to the list of unfair business tactics as new situations are presented that seem to them to entail overreaching by a marketer.

As is the case with copyrights, registration enhances rights in trademarks but does not create them. It is generally easy to register a mark within a state, but federal trademark registration, which confers much greater benefits, is more difficult to obtain. Trademark rights last indefinitely; as long as a mark is used in commerce, its owners have protectable rights in it.

A trademark represents the commercial reputation of a product or service as embodied in, usually, a word or design. Trademark law prohibits certain trade practices that are considered unfair, such as the imitation of another's trademark in order to profit from consumers' mistaken belief that the imitation trademark and the product it names are authentic. This is trademark infringement. Trademark law exists to protect consumers. It ensures, for instance, that when you buy a pair of running shoes marked with the NIKE® name, they are of the high quality you have come to expect in NIKE products because they are, indeed, manufactured by NIKE. (Lawyers use

5

capital letters to indicate the precise verbal content of trademarks. We'll do the same with all trademarks and with all titles, slogans, and names used like trademarks.) And in protecting consumers, trademark law also protects the interests of trademark owners—their understandable desire to market their products without interference from other marketers who seek to trade on their fame.

The two things anyone who markets a product needs to know about trademarks are how to choose them and how to use them.

Choosing a new product name is not a simple undertaking, or should not be. Certain kinds of names are not registrable as trademarks with the U.S. Patent and Trademark Office. The knowledgeable businessperson who christens a new product will take these restrictions into account, since federal registration is, or should be, the goal of every trademark owner. The other major consideration in choosing a trademark is picking one that no one else is using. This process is called "trademark clearance." You ignore it at your peril, since adopting and using someone's established trademark, even innocently, is trademark infringement, and trademark infringement can result in lawsuits that are expensive to settle and hopelessly expensive to defend.

In the United States, trademark ownership accrues by use of the trademark in commerce. Unless a trademark is used in the marketplace, there is no trademark, because there is no commercial reputation that can be symbolized by the word or design. Roughly speaking, trademark owners earn the right to prevent others from using the same design or word to represent or name a product or service similar to theirs in direct proportion to the extent of their use of that name or design, geographically and otherwise.

The owner of the two BIJOU theatres in northeast Idaho can probably keep other theatres and entertainment venues from using BIJOU in their names, but only within the same general area. Unless the fame of the BIJOU theatres—their commercial reputation—has spread beyond the geographic area where they are located, the owner of the BIJOU trademark can prohibit the use of the name only within the same area.

The long-standing and widespread fame of New York's RADIO CITY MUSIC HALL, however, allows the company to stop the use of that or any confusingly similar name for any concert or entertainment venue anywhere in the United States. The RADIO CITY MUSIC HALL name is now understood by even those who have never been there to refer to the famous theatre. Because the reputation of the entertainment destination has spread across the entire United States, U.S. trademark law prohibits any entertainment venue anywhere in the country from appropriating the RADIO CITY MUSIC HALL name, even though, arguably, someone who buys a ticket for a show in Oklahoma is not a potential buyer for a ticket for the same date in New York. What matters in the case of famous marks is that similar or identical names are likely to create the idea in the mind of consumers that two commercial entities are somehow associated even when they are not.

Once a trademark is "cleared for takeoff" and is in use, *how* the mark is used is very important. If a trademark is used as a noun rather than as an adjective ("WINKLES" rather than "WINKLES toy trucks"), it can lose its status as a trademark. That's what happened to "aspirin," "cellophane," and "escalator," all of which once named particular brands of the products for which they are now the generic names.

If the ® symbol is not used properly in conjunction with a federally registered trademark, the trademark owner's right to collect money damages in a lawsuit against a trademark infringer may be diminished.

In the abstract, these may seem like niggling considerations. In actuality, proper trademark usage can be crucial to the overall health of the company that owns the mark, since the trademark may represent the most valuable asset of the company, its goodwill. The Xerox Company thinks so, at least. Otherwise it would not run thousands of dollars worth of ads every year pointing out that photocopiers are not "xerox machines" and that its machines are "XEROX® brand photocopiers."

Xerox doesn't want to end up like the Otis Elevator Company, whose famous ESCALATOR ironically lost its uniqueness because of that very fame, thanks to the popularity and success of the moving stairways marketed under the ESCALATOR name. When the name ESCALATOR became a generic term applicable to all moving stairways, the ESCALATOR moving stairway was demoted to "escalator" and faded into the woodwork, so to speak, becoming so famous it became anonymous. The Xerox ads emphasizing the proper use of the XEROX trademark have been joined in recent years by similar protests (in the form of "cease and desist" letters to journalists and others who use name as a lower-case verb: "google") pointing out that GOOGLE®, is a trademark rather than a synonym for "to use the Google search engine to gather information on the Internet."

The chapters that follow contain the rest of the story. I hope I have told it well, because trademarks and the law and their interaction have been a major focus of my practice for more than half my working life. Like many English majors, after graduation from college I looked for areas of commerce where my love of language could be useful. I tried most of the usual ones. I was a newspaper reporter. I wrote and produced advertising for several years. And I supported myself—badly—during law school by working as a freelance writer. But I had missed one interesting area of the law that is especially suitable for anyone who cares about the effects of language (and symbols) on human behavior—trademark law. Then, during my second and third years of law school, I clerked for a crusty but kind intellectual-property lawyer named Edwin Luedeka, who one day pointedly told me "trademark law is a good field for a woman." And for English majors, I found.

Trademark law is more like linguistics than any other area of the law. Once you grasp the real nature of trademarks, the intricacies of trademark law seem logical. And the importance of trademarks is hard to overstate, because nearly every dollar spent in our capitalistic society is directed into one corporate pocket rather than another because of the reputation of the product or service purchased, which is represented by its trademark.

9

This book is designed to be a primer for anyone who creates or uses trademarks, which is just about everyone employed in any management position in American business, whether that business is a one-person, headquarters-at-home, cottage industry or a giant corporation that employs thousands of people. Since I have nibbled several of the edges of American business and have practiced trademark law for nearly thirty years, I believe I am well suited to talk about the issues, concerns, and problems of both trademark owners and of those who encounter trademarks in their business life and must know how to choose, handle, and protect them.

My long-time tutor in matters of business, especially start-up businesses, is my friend and former business partner Bill King, to whom this book is dedicated. I am also indebted to another friend and lawyer, Larry Woods, for some of the ideas and insights in chapter 6; his years of experience helped me expand my own observations beyond the one-person-one-viewpoint barrier that faces anyone who writes on topics as broad as the legal profession.

I enjoy trademarks, although they sometimes make *my* head hurt. Trademarks are one variety of intangible creations of the human imagination that have a very tangible, dollars-and-cents effect on both our commercial and personal lives. I hope you find my fascination with trademarks informative and useful. If you live in America, chances are that you will play several innings in capitalism, a game even more characteristic of this country than either baseball or basketball. This book can help you avoid some of the pitfalls that can take out even talented players too early in the game.

Thanks, Mr. Luedeka.

Chapter 1
Understanding
Trademarks

This is a short chapter because, beyond knowing what a trademark is (as you must already know if you live in the United States) and how trademark ownership arises (which is not a very long story) the main thing you need to know about trademarks is how not to infringe them. We'll get to that just as soon as you really do understand trademarks.

The Lanham Act, which is a federal statute governing unfair competition and trademarks, defines a trademark as "any word, name, symbol, or device or any combination thereof adopted and used by a manufacturer or merchant to identify his goods and distinguish them from those manufactured or sold by others." The statute defines a service mark as "a mark used in the sale or advertising of services to identify the services of one person and distinguish them from the services of others." A word or symbol qualifies as a trademark when it is both actually used in commerce to identify the goods or services of a manufacturer or merchant or provider of services and when it functions to identify and distinguish the goods or services from those of other manufacturers, merchants, or providers of services. More than one trademark may identify a product—think of the various logos and versions of the name used to market COCA-COLA® soft drinks.

In a free enterprise society, trademarks are everywhere. Trademarks are the guideposts of commerce. They embody the commercial reputations of products or services in the marketplace. Manufacturers use trademarks to communicate to consumers the origin of the products they market. Consumers use trademarks to help them find the particular products and services they want. Economists have declared that trademarks perform at least two market functions: 1) they encourage the production of quality products and 2) they make shopping easier by facilitating purchasing decisions. It seems clear that as long as you can't thump a television set like a watermelon to decide whether to buy it, but must rely instead on what you know about the television manufacturer, trademarks will remain an important part of life in America.

We all rely on trademarks every day. Almost everything you use, from the coffee you drink to the mattress you sleep on, was bought by brand name, which is another way of saying "trademark." Nobody shows up with a checkbook at the nearest auto dealer and asks, simply, to buy "a car." You drive a TOYOTA® or a FORD® or a VOLVO®, and you bought your car by name because of the reputation, for prestige or economy or reliability, that attaches to that car by its name. We avoid products we dislike, by name, and we seek out the ones we want, by name. These names come to mean something to the consumer. When you ask for CHANEL NO. 5® cologne at the perfume counter of a department store, you won't be satisfied by WHITE SHOULDERS® or OBSESSION®, and when you ask for a DIET COKE® at a fast-food drive-in window, you don't want DIET PEPSI®.

In the United States, a trademark owner gains rights in a particular name or logo for a product or service by using the name or the logo in the marketplace. ("Logos," short for "logotypes," are simply design trademarks, as opposed to names, which are verbal trademarks.) Trademarks can also be combinations of names or words and designs or logos. Service marks are the variety of trademarks that name services. (For simplicity's sake, the general term "trademark" or simply "mark," will be used hereafter to refer to both the names or symbols for services and those for products.)

It is very important to understand that in this country trademark rights are gained by use of a mark, not by registration of it. State or federal registration of a trademark enhances the rights of the owner of the trademark and serves as notice to others of ownership of the mark, but a business that uses a trademark in the marketplace owns the right to use that mark *because* of that use—unless some other business has a better claim to it through longer and/or wider use—whether or not the mark is ever registered. Trademark ownership is also determined by *priority* of use: to own a trademark, you must do more than simply use it in the marketplace. You must also be the *first* to use the mark. In other words, a company acquires rights in a trademark roughly commensurate with the length of use, the geographic scope of use, and the variety of commercial uses it makes of the mark. So, for example, a large company that has long marketed a variety of products across the U.S. under its trademark has a much stronger claim to its mark and is much better able to halt anyone else's use of any similar mark for any similar products than does a recently established mom-and-pop company that sells its products only in the city where it is located.

Nor can registration perpetuate the existence of a moribund trademark. If a trademark owner ceases for too long to use a trademark in the marketplace, that owner can lose all ownership rights in the mark, regardless of whether the mark has been registered. Without *use* of a name to market a product or service, there *is* no trademark—the name has ceased to embody a current reputation for the product or service to which it was applied. Think of it this way: a person's reputation dies with him or her—that is, the reputation that remains after someone's death is only the memory of that person's actions in life. Because a person's activities cease at death, his or her reputation does not continue to accrue in the present. The same is true of trademarks, which are simply the reputations of products and services. If there is no use of a trademark in the channels of commerce, the reputation of the product or service formerly marketed under that trademark becomes defunct.

Anyone involved in the marketing process knows what enormous effort and expense go into developing and publicizing new products. Trademark law allows companies that spend time and money developing their market shares to reap the benefits of that effort. Trademark law lets you enjoy the benefits of your own commercial reputation and prohibits anyone else from taking a free ride on your commercial coattails. It also protects consumers by allowing them to spend their money on the products and services they have grown to trust. This is the heart of the concept of "branding" that has garnered so much ink in the U.S. business press in recent years.

When marketers today speak of branding, they are talking about marketing efforts aimed at creating a relationship between their products and their customers. This relationship is a combination of old-fashioned brand loyalty combined with the newer concept of creating a mystique for the product. When such a relationship can be established, it is a very powerful connection. During the early decades of the twentieth century, when American advertising was just beginning to assume the incredible power and ubiquity it has today, people bought products almost solely for their utility. That is, the ability of soap to clean and the durability of work clothes were of prime importance to the buyers of those products. Now, although the utility of many products is still important, the buying decision may be more influenced by the *feeling* the product gives the customer—whether that feeling is the confidence that GERBER® baby food is safe and healthy or the self-assurance that an ARMANI® suit creates. The baby food is evaluated on a different basis than the suit—GERBER® baby food is recognized as healthy and nutritious for infants, but ARMANI® suits are valued as much for their cachet as their style and structure. Every brand that survives has its own personality, a halo of residual goodwill that attaches to it and surrounds any product it names. And in a world where almost all products are sold by brand—by trademark—and practically nothing is sold *without* a brand name, brands and the personalities they exemplify are the keys to the survival of a product in the marketplace.

Almost anything can be a trademark so long as it is used on a product or in advertising a service in such a manner as to indicate the origin of the product or service. In other words, trademarks answer two questions: *who made the product* and *who renders the service*. All the following can and do serve as trademarks because consumers have come to associate them with the products and services they are used to market.

- **Words** — ACE® bandages; PLEDGE® furniture polish; AERON® desk chairs; KODAK® film and cameras
- **Names** — WATERMAN® fountain pens; HARTMANN® luggage; DELL® computers; HEINZ® sauces; TOM'S OF MAINE® for personal care products; JIMMY DEAN® sausage
- **Designs** — the embroidered JORDACHE® jeans hip pocket design; the COCA-COLA® "dynamic ribbon device;" the NIKE® "swoosh" design; the UNITED WAY® outstretched-hand-and-rainbow design symbol
- **Slogans** — "WHEN IT RAINS, IT POURS®" (for MORTON® salt); "SOMETIMES YOU FEEL LIKE A NUT, SOMETIMES YOU DON'T" (for PETER PAUL MOUNDS/ALMOND JOY® candy bars); and "TASTES SO GOOD CATS ASK FOR IT BY NAME" (for MEOW MIX® cat food)
- **Drawings** — the Rock of Gibraltar logo for PRUDENTIAL® insurance; the GERBER® baby for baby foods and products
- **Likenesses of fictitious people or characters** — BETTY CROCKER® for cake mixes; RONALD MCDONALD® for hamburgers; the QUAKER OATS® Quaker man for oatmeal; the Energizer Bunny for ENERGIZER® batteries
- **Likenesses and/or names of living people** — Paul Newman's image used as a logo for NEWMAN'S OWN® salad dressing and spaghetti sauce; Wally Amos's likeness used on packaging for his FAMOUS AMOS® cookies
- **Likenesses and/or names of deceased people** — Colonel Harlan Sanders's image on KENTUCKY FRIED CHICKEN®

containers; a depiction of the SMITH BROTHERS® on Smith Brothers Cough Drops packaging; L. L. BEAN® for clothing and sporting goods

- **Characters** — the main characters in the STAR WARS® movies are trademarks for a variety of goods; so are the characters from the PEANUTS® comic strip; RONALD MCDONALD® and his buddies for restaurant services; the PILLSBURY® Dough Boy for ready-to-bake food
- **Abbreviations and nicknames** — BUD® for BUDWEISER® beer; VW® for VOLKSWAGEN® automobiles; HOG® for large HARLEY-DAVIDSON® motorcycles
- **Initials** — IBM®; CBS®; A&W®
- **Radio and television station call letters and radio broadcast frequency designations** — WSM® radio; WTBS® television; WGBH® television; RADIO 1430®
- **Telephone numbers** — 1-800-HOLIDAY® (for Holiday Inn reservations); 800-SEND-FTD® for florists
- **Numbers** — A.1.® steak sauce; V8® vegetable juice; FORMULA 409® household cleaner
- **Music or songs, and sounds** — the SESAME STREET® television show theme song; the MR. RODGERS® television show theme song; the NBC® chimes; the roar of the MGM® lion
- **Package designs** — the well-known CHANEL NO. 5® perfume bottle shape; the familiar shape of the classic bottle for COKE® soft drinks
- **Architectural features of businesses** — the MCDONALD'S® hamburger restaurants' golden arches; the characteristic orange roofs of the HOWARD JOHNSON® hotels; the design of WHITE CASTLE® hamburger restaurants

- **Characteristics of products** — IVORY SOAP® is "99 44/100 PERCENT PURE®"; BON AMI® cleanser "HASN'T SCRATCHED YET!"; MORTON® salt— "WHEN IT RAINS, IT POURS®"; the shape of LIFESAVERS® candies
- **Internet domain names** — AMAZON.COM® for selling books and many, many other products online; REDENVELOPE.COM® for online sales of gifts; GODIVA.COM® for online sales of chocolate products

Is It a Trademark?

As you can see from the list of established trademarks above, almost anything can serve as a trademark. However, this does not mean that *every* element of a product or of the presentation of services can or does serve as a trademark. Marketers familiar with a variety of offbeat sorts of marks are often surprised to learn that some characteristic of their product that they consider to be unique is not considered by the Trademark Office to meet the minimum requirement for registration, that is, it does not serve as "an indicator of source" for the product. Serving as a source indicator is the most basic function of a trademark and unless a name or other sort of mark does serve as a source indicator, it's not a trademark, no matter how clever or attractive it is. Almost any product element can fail to serve as a trademark, depending on the way it is used in the marketing of the product, but there are three reasons that are commonly cited. They are:

1. **The mark is "merely decorative":** This is an objection that commonly has to be overcome for design marks, especially those that are design elements of the product (think of the NIKE® "swoosh" device, the POLO® polo player design, the COCA-COLA® "dynamic ribbon device"). The application to federally register a design as a trademark may

be rejected if the trademark examiner feels that a design is used more to decorate the product than to serve as an indicator of the product's origin. This is because the federal trademark statute denies registration to any "device . . . that does not primarily serve to distinguish and identify the goods." The "merely decorative" ground for rejection of a trademark registration application is often raised with applications to register clothing marks, especially those that are printed or embroidered directly onto the clothing, but it can also occur with other products.

Obviously, there are many famous design marks that are both decorative *and* registered. Remember that the objection that a design does not serve as a trademark is that the design is "*merely* decorative"—so long as a design mark also serves to indicate the source of the product to which it is applied, it is a trademark, no matter how decorative it may be. Sometimes the question can be resolved by repositioning the mark on the product—i.e., moving the depiction of the sunflower for SUNFLOWER ladies' tops from the front of the T-shirt, where it is the predominant decorative element, to the label sewn inside the T-shirt and to the hangtag for the T-shirt. Or, such a design may appear both as a decorative element on the front of a shirt *and* on the label and hangtag. The Trademark Office just wants to make sure that consumers look for the sunflower design *as a trademark* in addition to whatever ornamental use is made of it on the clothing it helps to sell.

Sometimes marks that were originally "merely decorative" come, over a period of time, to signify a source for the products to which they are applied because consumers get used to looking for them, even on the front of a shirt. Think of the various forms in which the name "Tommy Hilfiger" appears, in whole or in part, on TOMMY HILFIGER®

clothing. There is no question that these marks serve *as* marks. There is also no question that they are to some extent decorative. There are numerous examples of decorative marks that did not function as trademarks until they had acquired "secondary meaning," which means that a mark used to market a product or service has become famous enough to be associated with one particular marketer. All this is true of common geometric shapes and colors, too, which are subject to the same "merely decorative" objection as designs, at least until they become famous enough as signifying a particular product of a particular manufacturer to overcome this objection to registrability.

2. **The mark is "functional":** This is similar to the "merely decorative" scenario. A mark is "functional" when it is part of what the product or service *does,* rather than being merely an indicator of the source of the product or service. A very good example of this is the characteristic roar of HARLEY-DAVIDSON® motorcycles, which is recognizable by motorcycle aficionados. The Harley-Davidson company applied in 1994 to register this sound as a trademark with the U.S. Trademark Office. Its application said: "The mark consists of the exhaust sound of applicant's motorcycles, produced by V-twin, common crankpin motorcycle engines when the goods are in use." Harley-Davidson met with opposition from nine of its competitors who opposed registration on the ground that the sound mark was "functional" and therefore not eligible for registration. Honda said that any motor of the same sort would produce the sound that Harley-Davidson said was characteristic of its motorcycles and indicated their source. After some years of haggling over the issue, Harley-Davidson dropped its application to register its roar.

20

One basis for this principle of trademark law is that the law recognizes that it cannot grant a monopoly, in the form of a trademark, to any truly functional feature of a product because doing so would deprive other marketers of the same sort of product from using that functional feature in their own products. In other words, if it is protectable by patent, it should be protected by a patent rather than a trademark. There is no "back-door" protection for a functional element of a product through trademark law.

3. **The mark does not *yet* serve as a trademark:** This objection is perhaps only applicable to the names of certain sorts of series of products, such as series of books, movies, magazines, etc. The Trademark Office will deny registration of a series name if there is not yet a series. That is, if only one title of a planned series has been published, there is no series yet and there is no series trademark—yet. Before a name is applied to two or more of the series installments, it is viewed as merely a literary title rather than a trademark that indicates the source of the series. For example, the name of the extremely popular HARRY POTTER® series of books would not have qualified for trademark registration in the U.S. Trademark Office prior to the publication of the second book in the series. Trademark owners who want to protect the names of series of books, etc., can get around this restriction to some extent by filing what is called an "intent-to-use" federal trademark registration application just after the publication of the first book (etc.) in the series. This sort of application gives the applicant three years to begin to actually use the mark in interstate commerce—enough time to publish the second series title and qualify for trademark registration.

For more, and more detailed, information about the inherent characteristics of trademarks and how they affect the registrability of trademarks, see chapter 4.

Naming the Baby

Businesspeople often encounter trademarks in what is perhaps the most critical period of their existence—their birth. When this happens, they are being asked to "incubate" brand-new trademarks. Designing a new corporate logo or design trademark is one of the most important business functions you will undertake. Naming a product well is nearly as challenging as naming a new baby. And it's also risky, perhaps more so than any other creative activity undertaken for a business purpose. That's because we are running out of trademarks. The number of applications for new registrations that the U.S. Trademark Office receives annually has mushroomed in recent years. During the last five years, the U.S. Trademark Office has received an average of around 400,000 new trademark registration applications per year. These applications sometimes take a while to be finally denied or granted; during the last few years, there have been about 600,000 applications pending at any given time. The Trademark Office, despite its best efforts, is overwhelmed by the number of registered and pending marks. To some extent, so is the marketplace. Each year nearly 300,000 new registrations are added to the nearly two million currently registered United States trademarks that already crowd the media. With such a deluge of new trademarks annually joining the existing vast reservoir of active marks, it is easy to see why it has become very difficult to avoid infringing an existing trademark when you design a new logo or name a new product. It can be done, however, and the next chapter will tell you how.

Chapter 2
Trademark Infringement

A trademark represents the commercial reputation of a product or service in the marketplace. Trademark owners often expend enormous amounts of money in establishing and promoting their trademarks. Once established, a trademark may be one of the most valuable assets owned by a company. (Think of the Coca-Cola Company. Its various COCA-COLA® and COKE® trademarks are worth far more than the physical assets of the company.) Consequently, trademark owners act quickly against anyone who encroaches upon their trademarks. Adopting the wrong trademark can land you in a lawsuit for trademark infringement, even if you had no knowledge when you chose your trademark that it might infringe another trademark. This means that care in choosing a name for a new product or service is very important. Unfortunately, trademark selection in this country is, for the uninformed, a little like Russian roulette.

Imagine this scenario: After you've made three separate presentations and long after you've given up hope of landing the account, someone from the marketing department of the Omega Corporation calls to say that they have chosen your ad agency to handle all their U.S. advertising. Seems they were impressed with your proposals and have decided to give their business to an agency in your city, where they have their home office. They are happy with their decision. You are happy with their decision. You and your partners hire two more artists and a new copywriter and get to work on your first big Omega assignment, developing an ad campaign to break their new product, a universal television/VCR remote control that will work with all Omega Electronics products and with those of most other manufacturers as well.

But before you can advertise the new remote, you have to name it, so you and your three best creative people retire to your conference room late one afternoon to think of the perfect name. After several loud arguments, two six-packs, and more than three hours of intense brainstorming, you reach a consensus.

You and your staff like the name UNI-TROL. So do the Omega marketing people, when you present the name to them. They give you the go-ahead on the whole project and, simultaneously, a tight deadline. They want to have their product in the stores before the beginning of the new fall television season and they authorize you to do whatever is necessary to complete on time all the packaging and advertising materials they need. You roll up your shirtsleeves, work a lot of late nights, and meet their deadlines.

The new product is a hit. There is no other product like it that is as inexpensive or as simple to operate. Sales are through the roof. You start thinking of buying a new car. Then, out of the blue, you get an outraged call from the head of the Omega marketing department. He's just learned that the Omega Corporation has been sued in federal court for trademark infringement by a big New York law firm representing a German corporation that owns U.S. and Canadian trademark registrations it says are infringed by the name you created.

It seems that the German corporation, Unicorp, markets various sorts of electronic equipment around the world under various trademarks, all of which begin with UNI-. They are asking the court for an award of money damages and the profits from Omega's marketing of the UNI-TROL remote, plus an injunction that would force Omega to recall all its remotes previously distributed under the UNI-TROL name, to destroy all packaging and advertising materials that use or bear the offending name, and to cease using, immediately and forever, the trademark by which the public knows the new product, UNI-TROL. There is no joy in Mudville.

The only people who are not unhappy about the trademark infringement lawsuit are the lawyers hired by the Omega Corporation to defend it. They know that some of the money you thought Omega would spend with your agency is now going to be consumed by their legal fees.

The saddest news of all is hearing that Omega's lawyers have said that Omega's use of the UNI-TROL mark does infringe the Unicorp marks and that, under the circumstances, the best thing for Omega to do is to cut its losses and immediately pull all the UNI-TROL television and print ads and stop distributing the remotes completely until a new name and new packaging and promotional materials can be developed. Which means, of course, that what Omega's dealers will remember about Omega's innovative remote control product is that 1) somebody goofed in naming it and 2) that goof destroyed the momentum the product initially gained in the market, cutting their profits. And what Omega will remember, regrettably, is that you proposed the name that is causing all the trouble.

None of this had to happen. In almost every case, trademark infringement problems can be avoided by the proper attention at the right time to a few simple considerations.

Had you been better informed, you would have made some effort to check on the availability of the UNI-TROL mark when you proposed it to Omega, by recommending to Omega that it conduct a trademark search or by commissioning one yourself on behalf of Omega.

A "full" trademark search, that is, a search of United States federal and state registrations as well as of data regarding valid but unregistered marks, would have turned up the "family" of UNI- marks owned by Unicorp and registered in the United States for various electronic products. The lawyer interpreting the trademark search report would have picked up the phone and called you and recommended that you go back to the drawing board for the new Omega mark. The whole process would have taken no more than ten business days and cost under a thousand dollars, lawyer's fees included.

You could have chosen another good name for the remote. Omega could have liked it. The lawsuit might still be in the back pocket of the Unicorp lawyers. And all those carefully produced UNI-TROL ads and materials could be winning you awards instead of gathering dust in an Omega warehouse somewhere.

But perfect hindsight is poor consolation. What you really need is to know enough about trademark infringement to avoid it. Lots of trademark disputes arise because trademarks are chosen solely on the basis of artistic merit and the image they will create in the advertising media. Those are, of course,

26

important considerations. Coming up with a name that fits the new product and will attract consumers is a hard thing to do. However, the other hard part of naming a new product or service is finding a name that doesn't infringe an established mark. That part of the process can make you wish you'd gone to dental school.

Trademark infringement usually results because someone has chosen a name for a new product or service that is the same as or is very similar to a mark that has been used longer for the same or a similar or related product or service. In the United States, trademark ownership is created by use of a mark. Generally speaking, the first company to begin using a mark owns it. Once a company has established ownership of a mark, anyone else who uses the mark for a similar product or service is said to be "infringing" the rights of the trademark owner. This means that any proposed trademark must be evaluated to determine whether it will infringe an established mark.

The test courts apply in determining infringing similarity between marks is "likelihood of confusion." That is, are consumers likely to confuse the new name with the older, established trademark because of the similarity of the marks? The similarity between marks is gauged by what is called the "sight, sound, and meaning test." This means that you want to avoid choosing for a new mark any word and/or design that looks or sounds so much like and has a meaning so like an established trademark representing a similar product that consumers will mistake the new mark for the established mark. The degree of resemblance between conflicting marks is analyzed by a comparison of the following characteristics of the marks:

1. the overall impressions created by the marks;
2. the pronunciations of the marks;

3. the translations of foreign words that are elements of the marks;
4. the verbal translations of visual elements of the marks; and
5. the suggestions, connotations, or meanings of the marks.

The new mark infringes the older mark if there are enough similarities between the marks that it is probable that the average buyer will 1) confuse the products or services the marks represent, or 2) believe that the new product or service is somehow related to the owner of the older mark. Confusing similarity does not exist when it is *merely possible* that consumers will confuse the similar marks, but rather, when such confusion is *probable*.

Generally, infringement occurs only when similar or identical marks name similar or related products or services. However, this is not always true in the case of "strong" trademarks. Strong marks, because they have achieved broad reputations, enjoy broad protection from upstart imitators who try to capitalize on their fame and distinctiveness by associating themselves with the famous marks. KODAK®, COCA-COLA®, and LEVI'S® are examples of strong verbal marks. The "woolmark" design logo of the International Wool Secretariat, the "Morton Salt girl" character trademark, and the Shell Oil Company logo are examples of strong trademarks that consist largely or only of design or visual elements. It is a very good idea to give famous trademarks a wide berth when naming any product or service, even if the new product or service is very different from those named by the famous marks, since most owners of widely advertised and well-known marks protect their trademarks vigorously.

All this sounds a lot harder than it usually is. Since "confusing similarity" is evaluated as if through the eyes and/or ears of an average consumer, you can function as your own first line of defense against choosing a trademark that infringes another trademark. In other words, if you think your new mark might infringe an older mark, you're probably right.

Keep in mind that it is not necessary that a new mark be identical to an established mark in order to infringe it. In fact, the degree of similarity necessary to constitute infringement varies depending on the similarity between the two products or services named by the marks. When the products or services are directly competitive, less similarity will constitute infringement. When they are not directly competitive and/or are sold in different channels of trade, more similarity is necessary to constitute infringement. A few examples will give you a feel for the degree of similarity between trademarks that constitutes "confusing similarity."

BEARCAT for trucks will infringe BEARCAT for boats or tires or travel trailers, but not for, say, bicycles or hunting boots or police scanner radios.

TWINKLE TOYS for a child's building block set will infringe the famous TINKER TOYS® trademark. Call your new block set TWINKLE BLOCKS, though, and you're probably safe.

ZESTA® for saltines does not infringe SHASTA® for soft drinks. Calling any food item the same name as any other food item, however, is asking for a lawsuit, no matter how different the two varieties of food. The reasoning behind this rule is that consumers can reasonably assume that a manufacturer of one food item has begun marketing another under the same trademark. This sort of association confusion as to the origin of a product is a variety of trademark infringement. For example, the manufacturer of GOLD MEDAL® flour might not like having its commercial reputation confused by being mistakenly believed to be the maker of GOLD MEDAL ice cream, even if the ice cream is very good ice cream.

Bear in mind that the categories of products or services named by the marks are very important in making any evaluation of possible infringement. A breakfast roll named BON JOUR probably won't infringe the mark of a department store named BON JOUR, because rolls are far removed from department store services, both in their consumers and in the channels of trade in which they are offered. However, as we have seen, strong marks transcend the boundaries between categories of products and services. BON JOUR for a brand of breakfast rolls could infringe the trademark rights of the owners of a famous restaurant named BON JOUR, for a combination of the reasons just mentioned. That is, because consumers, familiar with the reputation of the famous restaurant, might believe that breakfast rolls were a new product of the restaurant.

Generally, infringement results when the inherent similarity between two marks is "multiplied" by the degree of similarity of the products or services the marks name and the fame of the established mark. At some point, these factors reach a critical mass and ignite into a trademark infringement lawsuit.

In the case of logos or design marks that have no verbal content, the standard for judging confusing similarity is the same as that used to evaluate the similarity between word trademarks, with the exception, of course, that a mark without any words has no "sound when spoken." With logos or design marks, you must carefully compare the appearance of the proposed logo or design mark with that of all other marks that designate similar products or services, including marks that are combinations of words and design elements. You must also consider the implications of the design elements of your proposed mark. That is, will your star logo infringe an existing mark for a similar product named STAR?

Judging similarity between logos or the design elements of marks is often more difficult than judging similarity between verbal marks because the similarity between visual elements may be much more subtle.

It is hard to talk about design trademarks in print, but a few examples of confusion between design trademarks are possible.

Any white-on-red or red-on-white curve at all similar to the famous COCA-COLA® double-curve design trademark used for any soft drink will infringe COKE'S® famous trademark. However, a similar curve in another color combination used for, say, a brand of farm equipment, might escape challenge.

Similarly, any design of any deer or deer-like animal used for insurance services or related services, such as financial services, would probably infringe the famous hundred-plus-year-old HARTFORD INSURANCE COMPANY® standing-stag design trademark. Use your deer for ice cream, however, and you are safe.

Any clown design or character used to advertise a fast-food restaurant, whether like MCDONALD'S® RONALD MCDONALD® trademark character or not, would probably be viewed by MCDONALD'S® as infringing upon its famous clown trademark. If your clown design or character was very different from our friend Ronald (perhaps a female clown named Pandora who wears a yellow wig and dresses all in pink), you could safely use her picture and an actress dressed like her to advertise and promote children's shoes.

Employ any depiction of a tipped cup perpetually losing the "last drop" of coffee and you will run afoul of MAXWELL HOUSE®. You may even get into trouble by using such a depiction in signage for a chain of coffee shops, since consumers could reasonably believe that the shops serve, or otherwise have some association, with MAXWELL HOUSE® coffee. Set your coffee cup upright on its saucer, however, and it is probably safe to use for coffee shops.

The famous Columbia Broadcasting System "eye" symbol is as effective today as it was when first used in 1951. That means that any abstract or realistic eye design used for any U.S. product or service that is even remotely connected with broadcasting or television or film production is going to be challenged by CBS®. You can use a dissimilar, realistic depiction of the human eye as the logo for franchise optometry shops, however, without looking over your shoulder to see if CBS is watching.

Ignore these analyses at your peril. Owners of established marks are quick to send cease and desist letters to marketers of new products who tread on their marks. An example of a cease and desist letter is reproduced in Appendix A. Names have been faked to protect the guilty, but this is essentially the text of an actual letter sent in circumstances very similar to those mentioned. If you'd like to read the first page of an actual cease and desist letter, sent by an international law firm to a website regarding the "infringement" of one of the National Pork Board's trademarks by a spoof product, canned unicorn meat, go to www.thinkgeek.com/blog/2010/06/officially-our-bestever-cease.html. The spoof was apparently convincing enough to anger the Pork Board or someone at the law firm. The letter supports the conclusion of many recipients of trademark cease and desist letters: trademark lawyers have *no* sense of humor. None. And they are prepared to fight to the death to protect their trademarks from infringement. If you can avoid it, *never* give anyone reason to send you a cease and desist letter, because what follows a cease and desist letter (which is just a threatening letter) is a lawsuit for trademark infringement, filed (usually) in a U.S. District Court. Judges can order you to do a lot of things you may not want to do, including stopping use of an infringing trademark, destroying materials that bear the infringing mark, and paying damages to the plaintiff whose mark you infringed.

Too Close for Comfort

The following pairs of trademarks were held by courts to be confusingly similar when used in conjunction with identical or similar products.

AMERIBANC and BANK OF AMERICA

ARISE and AWAKE

ARM & HAMMER and ARM IN ARM

ARROW and AIR-O

AVEDA and AVITA

BEAUTY-REST and BEAUTY SLEEP

BECK'S BEER and EX BIER

BEEP and VEEP

BLOCKBUSTER VIDEO and VIDEO BUSTER

BLUE NUN and BLUE ANGEL

BLUE SHIELD and RED SHIELD

BLUE THUNDER and BLUE LIGHTNING

BREW MISER and COFFEE MISER

BUST RUST and RUST BUSTER

CAESAR'S PALACE and TRUMP'S PALACE

CAT TRAC and KATRACK

CENTURY 21 and CENTURY 31

CHAT NOIR and BLACK CAT (foreign language equivalent meanings can constitute infringing similarity)

CITIBANK and CITY BANK

CITY GIRL and CITY WOMAN

COCA-COLA and CLEO COLA

COMSAT and COMCET

CRISTÓBAL COLON and CHRISTOPHER COLUMBUS

CYCLONE and TORNADO

DAN RIVER, DAN MASTER, DAN TWILL, DAN TONE, DAN, and DANFRA (a new mark that is even somewhat similar to an established family of marks can infringe those related marks by being mistakenly believed to be merely a new addition to the "family")

DATSUN and DOTSON

DELL and BELL

DERNIER TOUCHE and THE FINAL TOUCH

DOWNTOWNER and UPTOWNER

DRAMAMINE and BONAMINE

EL GALLO and THE ROOSTER

EST EST EST and IT IS IT IS IT IS

FACE TO FACE and CHEEK TO CHEEK

FIRM 'N GENTLE and NICE 'N GENTLE

GASTOWN and GAS CITY

GENTLE TOUCH and KIND TOUCH

GOOD MORNING and BUENOS DÍAS

HERITAGE and HERMITAGE

HINT O'HONEY and HIDDEN HONEY

JOUJOU and JOJO

KAHLÚA and CHULA

KEY and a picture trademark in the form of a representation of a key

KNORR and NOR-KING

LISTERINE and LISTOGEN

LONDON FOG and SMOG

LORRAINE and LA TOURAINE

MANPOWER and WOMENPOWER

MEDI-ALERT and MEDIC ALERT

MENNEN and MINON
MIRACLE WHIP and SALAD WHIP
MOUNTAIN KING and ALPINE KING
NIKON and IKON
OLD FORESTER and OLD FOSTER
ORKIN and ORKO
PHILADELPHIA and PENNSYLVANIA
PIZZERIA UNO and TACO UNO
PLAY-DOH and FUN DOUGH
PLEDGE and PROMISE
PORSCHE and PORSHA
RAIN BARREL and RAIN FRESH
ROCKLAND MORTGAGE CORP. and ROCKWELL
    NATIONAL MORTGAGE
SAVINGS SHOP and THE SAVINGS SPOT
SEIKO and SEYCOS
SILVER FLASH and SUPER FLASH
SMIRNOFF and SARNOFF
SNAPPY and SNIPPY
S.O. and ESSO
SPARKLETTS and SPRINKLETS
SQUIRT and QUIRST
STEINWAY and STEINWEG
TELECHRON and TELICON
TORO ROJO and RED BULL
TOYS "R" US and KIDS "r" US
TRAK and TRAQ
ULTRA BRITE and ULTRA-DENT
ULTRA VELVET and ULTRA SUEDE
WEED EATER and LEAF EATER
YAMAHA and MAKAHA

Close, but No Cigar

Think you've got the hang of it? Maybe not. The following pairs of trademarks were held by courts not to be confusingly similar when used in conjunction with identical or similar products.

ACCUTRON and UNITRON

AFTER TAN and APRÉS SUN

BANK IN A BILLFOLD and BANK IN A WALLET

BOSTON TEA PARTY and BOSTON SEA PARTY

CAR-X and EXXON

COCA-COLA and COCO LOCO

COCA-COLA and THE UNCOLA

CREAM OF WHEAT and CREAMY WHEAT

DAWN and DAYLIGHT

DUVET and DUET

FILM FUN and MOVIE HUMOR

FRUIT OF THE LOOM and FRUIT OF THE EARTH

GREEN LEAF and BLACK LEAF (when applied to plant sprays, the marks have opposite meanings)

HELICARB and HELI COIL

HOUR AFTER HOUR and SHOWER TO SHOWER

100 YEAR NITE-LITE and CENTURY NIGHT LIGHT

L'AIR DU TEMPS and L'AIR D'OR

LONG JOHN and FRIAR JOHN

MARSHALL FIELD'S and MRS. FIELDS

MATCH and MACHO

MOTHER BESSIE'S and MOTHER'S BEST

MR. CLEAN and MASTER KLEEN

PECAN SANDIES and PECAN SHORTEES

REJUVA-NAIL and REJUVIA

SATIN QUICK and SUDDENLY SATIN

SILKY TOUCH and TOUCH O'SILK
SUBARU and SUPRA
SURF and SURGE
TIC TAC TOE and TIC TAC
T.G.I. FRIDAY'S and E.L. SATURDAY'S
TACO TOWN and TACO TIME
THUNDERBOLT and THUNDERBIRD
TORNADO and TYPHOON
VANTAGE and ADVANCE
WHEATIES and OATIES
WINTERIZER and WINTERSTAT

Is It Infringement?

1. **Q.** You have been famous for years among your friends
and relatives for your plum preserves and decide to
market them. You tell the graphic designer you hire to
create the label for your preserves that you really like
the red-and-white "gingham" labels for the popular
MABEL'S line of jellies and jams and you want to
use something similar for your own labels. You love
the label he designs. It is identical to the MABEL'S
labels except that instead of "Mabel's," it says
"Natalie's," and there is a little sketch of a basket of
ripe plums where the MABEL'S labels use drawings of
various fruits on the vine. You show your design to the
lawyer who is helping you meet FDA labeling requirements for your preserves. He frowns when he sees it
and tells you that you need to go back to the drawing
board, since he believes the Mabel's Company will
have grounds for suit if you use your label as it is. You
don't see why he thinks there is a problem. NATALIE'S

37

certainly doesn't sound like MABEL'S, or look like it, or have the same meaning. And you are marketing plum preserves—the Mabel's Company markets strawberry, blackberry, peach, and grape jams and jellies, but no plum preserves, and it has never used a drawing of a basket of plums on its labels. The question is: *Is it infringement?*

A. Sorry, but your lawyer is right. Insofar as it goes, your information as to what constitutes trademark infringement is correct, but, as the saying goes, a little knowledge is a dangerous thing. In isolation, NATALIE'S for preserves does not infringe MABEL'S for jams and jellies because it doesn't sound sufficiently like MABEL'S, or look enough like it, or have a similar enough meaning, to be likely to confuse consumers. However, you are overlooking an important factor in the analysis of possible infringement—"overall commercial impression." If you think about it, you'll have to admit that the overall commercial impression created by your label design would be extremely similar to that created by the MABEL'S labels. Consumers could easily confuse your product with MABEL'S products because the small differences in their labels would not be apparent to a busy shopper who reaches for a familiar red-and-white "gingham" label, especially since your product and the MABEL'S products would be shelved in the same section of grocery stores and both use a woman's given name as a trademark.

If you proceed with your plan to use the red-and-white knockoff label, MABEL'S will sue you for trade dress infringement as well as for trademark infringement, as soon as it notices your products. Trade dress infringement is related to trademark infringement. It is the unauthorized adoption of another marketer's packaging design, colors, typeface, and even container shape. It is presumed to be an effort to pass off the copycat product as the more established product by the use of the established product's characteristic commercial "costume."

Your dilemma is not quite the situation that exists when the names of two vastly different kinds of food products are similar. There is a long-established rule that a name for any food product will infringe the same or a very similar name for any other food product. This is because the original user of the name could easily be presumed to have expanded its line to include the new food product named by the similar name. After all, no one would be surprised if General Mills added, say, frozen prepared cakes to its line of BETTY CROCKER® cake mixes. Here, you must take into consideration more than the name of your product, since consumers recognize products by more than just their names.

39

Ask your designer to create a label with a solid plum-colored background—no gingham checks—and your preserves will get you into stores and keep you out of court.

2. Q. You name your fledgling messenger service FLASH MESSENGER SERVICE and embroider a gold lightning bolt on the caps and shirts your messengers wear and paint it on the sides of your delivery vans. You are very happy with your creativity until you receive a call from the owner of another local messenger service, LIGHTNING MESSENGER SERVICE. It seems that for twenty years LIGHTNING MESSENGER

SERVICE has used a lightning bolt design as its logo. The owner of the Lightning Company is very unhappy that his only competitor in town has adopted what he thinks is his sole property in what he insinuates is a transparent effort to trade on Lightning's good reputation. You tell him you will get back to him and call your cousin Megan, who is a third-year law student. You ask Megan: *Is it infringement?*

A. If Megan was in class the day her intellectual-property law professor talked about trademark infringement, she will answer, immediately and unambiguously, "Yes." One of the factors considered in comparing two marks for the possibility of conflict is the meaning of visual elements of the marks. Here, your lightning bolt logo infringes the trademark rights of the owner of LIGHTNING MESSENGER SERVICE in two ways. First, your use of the same symbol for your logo as the one long used by Lightning is likely to confuse consumers. Secondly, the reasonable verbal meaning of your logo is "lightning." This will certainly add to the likelihood that consumers will confuse the two messenger services. The best course for you may be to immediately retire your lightning bolt caps and shirts and repaint your vans to eliminate the infringing symbol that is on its way to getting you named as a defendant in a trademark infringement suit you are likely to lose. You'll at least save yourself the considerable costs of defending a suit that is a losing proposition. And maybe you can pay Megan for her help by shipping her a dozen or so slightly used lightning bolt shirts. She could probably use them. Law students never get around to doing laundry.

3. **Q.** The day after you celebrate the first anniversary of
   your popular coffee shop, CAFÉ AU LAIT, you get
   a strange call from someone trying to make dinner
   reservations who seems to think that you serve Spanish food. Two days later, you get another such call.
   You decide that the moon must be full and think no
   more about the calls until you notice a new restaurant that has just opened near your favorite shopping
   center. The restaurant is called CAFÉ OLÉ and, upon
   investigation, you discover that it serves Spanish food.
   You are worried. If people calling information for
   the CAFÉ OLÉ phone number are being given your
   number, what is happening to your calls—and customers? You call CAFÉ OLÉ and express your concerns
   to the manager. He dismisses your concerns and tells
   you that your coffee shop and his Spanish restaurant
   are not in competition for customers and that, even
   if the names of your respective establishments sound
   alike when spoken, they don't look alike in print and
   don't have similar meanings. You are unconvinced and
   remain worried. You hang up and call your lawyer.
   You want to ask: *Is it infringement?*

   A. Your lawyer will confirm your suspicions that your
   predicament is a case of trademark infringement.
   Regardless of the difference between CAFÉ AU LAIT
   and CAFÉ OLÉ, the fact that their pronunciations are
   indistinguishable to the average ear is already resulting in what is called in trademark law "actual confusion"—in this case, the misdirection to your coffee
   shop and, possibly, vice versa by telephone information operators of consumers who want CAFÉ OLÉ.
   When proven in court, this is prima facie evidence

of trademark infringement. In other words, proving that the likelihood of confusion between two marks is no longer merely a likelihood, but has become a continuing reality, is sufficient to convince any judge in a trademark infringement lawsuit that the plaintiff's rights are being infringed. Lucky for you that you applied for and were granted a federal registration for CAFÉ AU LAIT, since federal registration is a prerequisite for bringing a trademark infringement lawsuit in federal court and can affect the damages the judge will award you and greatly diminish the costs you will incur to press your case.

4. Q. You and your cousin talk your dad and your uncle into investing in a bakery business you call English Teatime Cookies. You bake yummy cookies made according to your English grandmother's recipes. You start with her Butterscotch Wafers, her Raspberry Jam Tarts, and her Old-Fashioned Shortbread. All three are very popular. You decide to add her delicate little lemon cookies, your personal favorite, which she always called Cheerios. The lemon cookies are as popular as the other cookies made from your grandmother's recipes. People start buying your cookies by the bag and it's not long until your receipts exceed your expenses. You and your cousin consider leasing a bigger bakery.

Then you get a nasty letter from some lawyers for General Mills, the conglomerate that markets the whole-oat breakfast cereal CHEERIOS®. The letter says that because you are marketing lemon cookies called Cheerios, you are infringing the trademark rights of General Mills, the owners of the federally registered CHEERIOS trademark. You think the letter must be a joke—or a mistake. What do lemon cookies have to do with breakfast cereal? And you know for a fact that your grandmother has been baking her Cheerios—and calling them that—for nearly sixty years because she told you so. Further, in spite of your success, English Teatime Cookies is just a small operation—you only sell your cookies in your hometown and in Atlanta and Chattanooga, which are the nearest large cities.

You mention the letter in passing one day to your lawyer (who is your older brother) when you and he have a working lunch to discuss the lease for the new bakery. You think he'll get a giggle out of the ridiculous claims and demands of the General Mills lawyers, but he doesn't laugh. In fact, he insists that you call your cousin immediately and have him fax the letter to his office. Then he tells you that neither he nor you will be staying for dessert, that you both have an urgent phone call to make back at his office. You don't understand, but you do what he says. You wait until the waiter brings the check for lunch to ask him: *Is it infringement?*

43

A. Your brother won't answer any of your questions until he has read the faxed letter from the General Mills lawyers. Then he bends your ear for nearly fifteen minutes, while he waits for a return call from the lawyer who wrote the letter, which he tells you is something called a "cease and desist letter." He says that you have no choice but to do whatever you can to keep General Mills from suing you for infringement of its famous, federally registered CHEERIOS® trademark. That you'll be lucky if General Mills doesn't exact some payment from you to settle what would almost certainly be a winning suit and that the age of your grandmother's recipe has no bearing on whether you have stepped on General Mills' corporate toes and neither does the fact that she has long been calling her cookies Cheerios. What *does* matter, he says, is that you have been calling the cookies CHEERIOS *in interstate commerce*. He ignores your argument that your selling cookies in Chattanooga that were baked twenty minutes across the state line in Georgia is only barely interstate commerce—apparently, engaging in interstate commerce is like being pregnant: a little is enough.

Further, he tells you that if you have any hope of staying in business long enough to repay your (and his) father's and uncle's investment, you've got to start acting like a business person, which means that you need to have him clear any new trademark for use before you use it. You ask why, since there has been absolutely no trouble with the names of your other three cookies, which continue to sell like, well, hotcakes. He tells you that if you knew anything about trademark law you'd know that this is because the names of your other three cookies (Butterscotch Wafers, Raspberry Jam Tarts, and Old-Fashioned Shortbread Cookies) are all generic marks—that is, they simply describe what they name—and that there is much less likelihood that generic marks will infringe another, similar, generic mark because no such mark is granted very much protection by the courts.

However, he adds, it is possible that they could infringe another, established mark that has achieved what he calls "secondary meaning" in spite of its genericness. All this makes your head hurt, and you're afraid that he will shoot down your last, best argument, but you raise it anyway: "What do lemon cookies have to do with breakfast cereal?" He gives you a pitying look and tells you that it is an established principle of trademark law that the name of any food item will infringe a similar or identical established mark, even if it names a dissimilar food item. This is, he says, because it is very common for food companies to branch out and begin offering new items under their popular trademarks. "Think of DANNON® yogurt and bottled water. Think of NEWMAN'S OWN® spaghetti sauce and salad dressings," he says. "General Mills might want to market cookies named CHEERIOS. Or it might not. The important thing is that they don't want *you* to—and have people think that your lemon cookies are somehow related to their oat breakfast cereal."

You tell him you make great cookies and that anyone would be proud to be associated with them. He tells you that the quality of your cookies isn't the issue—the hard-won, longstanding commercial reputation of CHEERIOS is. Then he tells you to keep quiet while he talks to the General Mills lawyer. You hear him promise that you will pull all your existing Cheerios cookies from distribution, that you will destroy any and all packaging with the word "Cheerios" on it, and that you will never again use any name similar to Cheerios. Then, with a happy look on his face, he hangs up the phone. He tells you that you are one lucky entrepreneur, that the other lawyer is forwarding a written settlement agreement to him for your signature and that if you sign it and do what he promised you would do, you won't have to pay a penny in settlement. You aren't happy, but your older brother is usually right, and he *is* a lawyer, so you decide to do what he says. Then you tell him that for Christmas you are giving him a year's supply of lemon wafers. They'll have the name inked out on the packaging, but you know he'll love them.

5. **Q.** You and another freshly minted M.B.A. take the plunge and open your own computer components business. You choose as your logo a sphere divided into stripes in the colors of the visible spectrum (violet, blue, green, yellow, orange, and red), in order. The name of your products is SPECTRUM. That name and your striped-sphere logo appear on your stationery, on every one of your products, on all packaging materials, and in your ads. You have just ordered the production of 10,000 of your popular trackballs to fill your biggest order yet when you get a cease and desist letter from lawyers for Macintosh, who are insistent that your logo infringes the famous Macintosh striped-apple-with-a-bite-out-of-it logo. You are indignant. You think that the Macintosh lawyers are just bullies who want to put a competitor out of business. You do not believe your logo infringes the Macintosh trademark. Your logo is a sphere, not an apple, and your stripes are the colors of the spectrum, in order, while the Apple logo uses those colors in another combination (green, yellow, orange, red, violet, and blue). And you know that SPECTRUM doesn't look or sound anything like MACINTOSH® or APPLE®, nor does it

have a meaning similar to either mark. You put in a call to the lawyer who handles your patent filings to find out if you can simply ditch the letter from Macintosh. What you want to ask him is: *Is it infringement?*

A. Unfortunately, your lawyer is going to tell you that you can't ignore Macintosh's letter because you are, indeed, treading on their trademark. Then he will tell you why. His explanation will sound something like this: the minor differences you can point to between your striped-sphere logo and Macintosh's striped-apple logos are immaterial. In a comparison of marks for infringement, the overall commercial impression created by the marks is determinative. In a proper analysis, the marks are not dissected and their minor dissimilarities tallied and totaled. Rather, the total effect they have on consumers who encounter them in their "natural habitats," i.e., in the environments where the products they name are sold, is judged. This impression is created in a matter of seconds in most settings where consumers encounter trademarks, and it is created primarily by the dominant elements of the trademarks. Any element of a trademark can be the dominant element because dominance can be produced by almost any characteristic of any element of a trademark: the uniqueness of the element, its size relative to other elements of the mark, its color, its visual appeal, its memorability, etc. Your striped-sphere logo and Macintosh's striped-apple logo are more dominant than the verbal marks used with them (SPECTRUM and MACINTOSH®, respectively) because they are more colorful and more visually appealing.

Consumers are not likely to pause in electronics stores to note that the colored stripes in your logo are the colors of the visible spectrum, in order, as opposed to the same colors in different order in the Macintosh logo, which is an apple, as opposed to your sphere. They may, however, decide that since your products bear what they may mistake for the Macintosh logo, the SPECTRUM name refers merely to a new line of Macintosh products. This is, of course, infringement.

Further, products like computer components are marketed worldwide. The visual elements of a trademark are even more important in international commerce since consumers who can't understand or remember an English verbal trademark will have no such difficulty with a memorable visual mark. It is even more likely that consumers outside the U.S. will confuse your logo with the Macintosh apple.

The last thing your lawyer says is that you could have avoided this problem—and the expense of discarding and redesigning everything that bears your old logo, including your stationery, your current ad campaign, and most of a small warehouse full of packaging materials, not to mention figuring out how to stick new logos over the infringing ones on the housings for several thousand computer components—by the simple expedient of a trademark-design search to clear your logo for use. Your protestations that you did clear SPECTRUM are of no avail. In reality, the name of your products, SPECTRUM, and your logo are two separate trademarks, usually used together, but distinct and equally capable of infringing another mark. Real life business teaches harder lessons than business school.

6. **Q.** You and your buddies have formed what you think is
the next big rock band to emerge from an American
garage. You know that trademarks are important in
marketing bands, so you put some time into coming
up with a name. The name you choose, KINXS (pronounced "kinks"), suits everybody but your drummer, a second-year law student who thinks he knows
everything. He likes the name but says that you will be
hauled into federal court by the famous band INXS®
(pronounced "in excess") for trademark infringement
if you use it. You don't believe him because you don't
think the names are similar enough to cause a problem
and, anyway, despite your delusions of rock-and-roll
grandeur, you know that your band is obscure and not
likely to be famous enough for some time to attract
the attention of the lawyers for any other act. Should
you listen to your know-it-all drummer? Or, in other
words: *Is it infringement?*

   A. Sorry, Charlie. KINXS and INXS® are pronounced
differently, at least by those few people who are familiar with your band, and have very different meanings,
but their appearance in print, in ads, and on album
covers is very similar. INXS is an unusual name and
the band that owns it is famous. It is very dangerous
to get too close to unusual trademarks that name famous products or services because the "name recognition" of such marks is so high that people are more
likely to mistake similar marks for the famous ones.

   Further, marks that are similar to famous marks are
likely to run up against the proscriptions of the Trademark Dilution Act, which will only furnish the lawyers
for INXS with further ammunition. (See chapter 4 for

more detailed information about the Trademark Dilution Act.) And your complacent attitude that your band is too obscure ever to come to the attention of those lawyers is only justified to a point, because obscurity will work as a shield only so long. What usually happens with any trademark accused of infringing a more famous mark is that the upstart mark will come to the attention of the owners of the famous mark at about the time it is beginning to gain some fame. This is bad news for the owners of the new mark, because it means a lawsuit that could result in the necessity to abandon the new mark at just the point when it is becoming well-known enough to result in some money. It is always better to adopt a new trademark that you can sink your hard work into without fear that you may be compelled to abandon it.

7. **Q.** You turn your collection of sports memorabilia into a pricey little shop. It seems people are willing to pay much more than you originally paid for autographed baseballs and the jerseys of famous athletes. But jerseys that they buy from you for hundreds of dollars are just too expensive to wear on Saturday errands, so you have the bright idea to manufacture a sports clothing line that only looks like the originals. You order baseball caps and football jerseys in the colors of the teams in your region. When they arrive, you take them to a local screen printer to have the team names and logos emblazoned on them. To your amazement, the printer tells you he is an honest guy and he doesn't want to go to jail. The next screen printer you approach almost throws you out of his office. You don't understand why they are so jumpy until you see this

story (edited from an actual report) in the newspaper the following day.

South Carolina Man Pleads Guilty to Trafficking Clothing with Counterfeit Trademarks

Columbia, South Carolina —— United States Attorney J. Strom Thurmond, Jr., stated today that, William Haskell Farmer, age forty-nine, of Travelers Rest, South Carolina, entered a conditional plea of guilty today in federal court in Columbia, South Carolina, to trafficking in clothing with counterfeit Nike and Tommy Hilfiger trademarks and two counts of money laundering conspiracy, violations of Title 18, United States Code, Section 2320 and 1956(h). The plea came on the fourth day of a jury trial, and after United States District Judge Cameron M. Currie of Columbia ruled that Farmer could not argue his defense to the jury. Farmer will be sentenced after the U.S. Probation Office prepares a presentence report.

Evidence presented during the trial established that Farmer obtained blank tee shirts from mills that manufactured shirts for Nike, and then paid to have the shirts either embroidered or screen-printed with a Nike trademark. Farmer then sold the shirts to Carolina Apparel Trading, an off-price clothing jobber in Hendersonville, North Carolina. Mark Lewis, the owner of Carolina Apparel Trading, has already been sentenced to five months in prison, to be followed by three years of supervised release and five months of home confinement. Roy Steve Sutton, who managed Heritage Embroidery of Camden, has pled guilty to trafficking in counterfeit clothing and is awaiting sentencing. Joe Bolin, who owned Dixie Screen Printing of Gaffney, pled guilty to a conspiracy charge but died before he was sentenced. Farmer's defense was that he did not violate federal trademark law because the shirt on which he placed the Nike trademark had been manufactured for Nike. Judge Currie ruled that it did not matter if the shirt was manufactured for Nike, as long as Nike did not authorize the placing of the mark on the goods, the mark was counterfeit, and thus the Government had established that Farmer violated the law.

Mr. Thurmond stated the maximum penalty Farmer can receive is a fine of $3 million and/or imprisonment for 30 years. In addition, Farmer agreed to forfeit over $500,000.00 in cash and cashiers checks seized by United States Customs Service during a search of Farmer's residence and eight vehicles, including two Mercedes Benz automobiles, two cargo trailers, and numerous pallets of clothing. Finally, all clothing bearing counterfeit trademarks will be destroyed, pursuant to Title 18, United States Code, Section 2320(b).

This case was investigated by the United States Customs Service, and Assistant United States Attorney Eric W. Ruschky of the Columbia office handled the case.

You are jumpy yourself when you finally figure out that you could be prosecuted by the federal government for criminal trademark infringement simply for "re-creating" sports clothing. You had no idea that what you wanted to do could be illegal. Just to be sure, however, you call your lawyer. You want to ask: *Is it infringement?*

A. Your lawyer calls you "rash" and "woefully uninformed," but you think he really wants to call you worse names, especially when he reminds you that he is a civil lawyer and knows nothing about criminal law. He tells you that what you planned to do is trademark counterfeiting and that it is a crime under more than one federal statute. He also tells you that it makes no difference that you didn't realize you would be breaking the law. Then he sends you home to do homework. He tells you to go to the U.S. Justice Department website to read a little more about criminal trademark infringement, the crime you had no idea existed. You do what he says. Then you donate the baseball caps and football jerseys to the homeless shelter in your city. And you never again are tempted to counterfeit *anything,* being very happy to sleep each night in your own nice, soft bed.

   (If you want to read more actual U.S. Department of Justice press releases from the Computer Crime and Intellectual Property Section of the U. S. Department of Justice recounting arrests and convictions related to trademark counterfeiting, go to www.cybercrime. gov/ipcases.html#trademark. These accounts should convince you that it's an excellent idea to stay strictly out of the way of your local U.S. Attorney and that trademark piracy is *not* a viable business approach. Notice that in several cases, potential for harm to the public was created by the infringing use of the names of respected products on inferior and possibly dangerous fake products.)

Chapter 3
Trademark Clearance

The first step in avoiding infringing an established trademark is to consciously avoid choosing for your new product or service a name or design that is identical or closely similar to a nother trademark that is already in use for a similar or related product or service.

This seems too obvious to mention, but it needs to be said. More than a few trademark infringement lawsuits have been filed because someone mistakenly thought that because a name or design worked once it could work again. This means that in developing ideas for a new trademark, you should ask anybody who proposes one where the idea came from. Ignorance of trademark law will not save you from a trademark infringement lawsuit if you step on the toes of a trademark owner determined to protect its established mark. And it doesn't matter that you came up with the proposed new trademark without the knowledge of the established mark that it infringes. If it infringes the older mark, the source of your proposed mark is irrelevant. Nor will changing a few letters or design elements in an existing mark or spelling it differently or even combining it with other words or symbols save you from a charge of infringement, unless the changes you make are so significant that they eradicate the confusing similarity between the old and new marks.

If you make a wrong choice in choosing a new trademark, or fail to jump through all the hoops in the process of clearing a proposed mark for use, you will receive a cease and desist letter. This is a nasty document that demands, under threat of being sued, that you "cease" from doing something that is claimed to violate the rights of the person or company sending the letter and thereafter "desist" from ever doing it again. It is only the start of the troubles that can befall you. (A sample of a cease and desist letter is reproduced at the end of this book as Appendix A.) The next step after a cease and desist letter is a lawsuit that requests that the court order your products pulled from distribution in order to avoid confusing consumers. ("Honey, what's the name of that cereal the kids liked so well? Was it SWEET CRUNCHIES or CRISP SWEETIES?") Such suits are often settled out of court, but a settlement would involve your abandonment of your new mark and, probably, the payment of a sizable amount in lieu of damages the court could award. Neither scenario is likely to make you (or your client) happy about having adopted a new mark. That's why it's important to do whatever you can to make sure that your new mark won't land you in a lawsuit. This means a thorough trademark search.

Searching a Mark

The most important step in developing a new trademark is a trademark search, which is a two-part process. You can perform the first part of the search, the "screening search," without a lawyer. The second and more important half of the search process is called a "full search" and is too complicated for anyone but an experienced lawyer to perform successfully. However, don't doubt the value of a careful screening search. Whether you are creating the new trademark for your own business or for a client business, it's likely that you will save yourself a lot of time by early elimination of any mark that will have to be abandoned. A screening search is also a very good way to reduce the expense of developing a new mark. By eliminating an unavailable name before making it the subject of a full search, you avoid the expense of a full search for that name.

The Screening Search

A screening search is an examination of readily available data on trademarks that are already in use, whether registered or unregistered. By searching for conflicting, existing trademarks when you have narrowed your choices for your new mark to three or four names, you can eliminate names that are already registered, are the subject of pending registration applications, or are in use but unregistered. This saves the expense of conducting a full trademark search for every proposed name and speeds up the selection process by halting your further consideration of unavailable names. Screening searches are also called "knockout" searches because they quickly "knock out" any unavailable mark from consideration.

You probably already have access to the equipment you need for a reasonably thorough screening search—a computer, Internet access, and some reference materials. The resources you need to conduct a screening search are free, so you can preliminarily screen the names on your list yourself without incurring any expense for your company or your client. You can spend your money later, where it will do the most good, when you hire a trademark lawyer to conduct a full trademark search. The extent of your screening search will probably be determined by how much time and energy you have. To be useful, any screening search should include *at least* a search of U.S. Trademark Office records, a domain name search, and a Google search. But don't worry if you can't make it through a search of all the sources of trademark data listed below. Your screening search is a tool to save money and time by allowing you to eliminate any unavailable mark from further consideration before you pay to have a full trademark conducted for it. So don't be afraid to jump right in and do whatever searching you can manage yourself. You can't make any mistake that will get you in trouble if your screening search is only a preliminary to a full search. Grab your list of proposed marks and go directly to the first venue for your search, the U.S. Patent and Trademark Office website.

U.S. Government Trademark Records

The best source for information on established U.S. trademarks is the U.S. Patent and Trademark Office Trademark Electronic Search System (TESS). Go to the U.S. Patent and Trademark Office home page at www.uspto.gov/index.jsp and click on "Search Marks" under the Trademarks heading. This will take you to TESS, which is a searchable online database of millions of pending, registered, and dead federal trademark applications and registrations. (Even trademark registrations that have expired may alert you to marks that are still in use and, therefore, still protectable, even though their registrations have expired.) TESS is intended for use by the general public and is a very good place to *start* to clear a mark.

Since using TESS is free, the best way to figure out how to use it is to wander around through the various search options to educate yourself as to the capabilities of the TESS service. TESS does not contain information on marks that are in use but never registered or on foreign marks that are not registered in the United States. However, it can quickly eliminate as potential new trademarks any U.S. trademarks that are already owned by people sophisticated enough and careful enough to seek registration for them. Owners of registered marks are typically vigilant about challenging infringers, so finding a mark in the TESS database that is very similar or identical to your proposed mark and is used for an identical or closely similar product is a clear signal that you should abandon that mark and move on to the next on your list. (A search hint: the TESS system may be less congested after business hours.)

Let's say you started with a list of three potential names for a new product. Because you found during your TESS search that one of your proposed marks is identical to a mark that is already registered for a similar product and that another one of them is the subject of a pending "use" application for registration (which means that it is already in use and, therefore, someone else has gained protectable rights in it by using it), you have one name left to consider.

Domain Names

Your Internet search effort should examine domain names because even though domain names are not necessarily trademarks, they may be and may represent an ongoing business effort with which your proposed mark would conflict. Search for any domain name that matches your proposed mark by searching the various forms of domain names that could be formed from it. You can do this through a Whosis search on the InterNIC site www.internic.net/whois.html for the domain-name forms of your mark that end with these suffixes: aero, .arpa, .asia, .biz, .cat, .com, .coop, .edu, .info, .int, .jobs, .mobi, .museum, .name, .net, .org, .pro, and .travel. Again, save information on any match for later evaluation by your lawyer. You can perform the same sort of search of domain names with any accredited domain name registrar. For a list of these, go to www.icann.org/en/registrars/accredited-list.html. ICANN is the Internet Corporation for Assigned Names and Numbers. It is the organization that, among other functions, accredits domain name registrars.

Search Engines

After searching the U.S. Trademark Office's online database and registered domain names, you should search your proposed mark using, at least, Google and another big search engine. Your screening search isn't complete until you further examine the availability of your remaining proposed mark by looking at every other source of information about similar or identical marks that you can find. Before the widespread availability of the Internet, it was hard to get a good picture of what trademarks were already in use. Since the advent of Internet search engines, the process of locating competing marks has been simplified. You can find a long list of search engines here: www.thesearchenginelist.com/.

Search using your proposed name as well as the description of the product you want to market: "BEEFY" dog biscuits; "SWEET DREAMS" pajamas; or "CRYSTAL SHINE" dish detergent. Search using quotation marks around your proposed mark. Then search without the quotation marks. Reverse the order of the words in your proposed name. Try alternate spellings of the proposed mark. Search using synonyms, if any exist, for the words in your proposed name. If your proposed name consists of or includes a unique word or coined word, conduct a search of that word only to find any existing uses of the word. Look for similar or identical names used for products or services that are similar or identical to those with which you want to use your proposed mark and for unique or coined marks that may occupy a larger portion of the public imagination simply *because* they are unique. (No one would think of naming *anything* KLEENEX®, no matter how different from paper products.)

Keep printouts of information about any mark that you think even *might* be infringed by your proposed mark and take these printouts to your lawyer later for further investigation. For instance, if you search HUSKY for chainsaws, you will find that Google thinks you mean HUSKY hand saws (sold by Home Depot) or HUSQVARNA® chainsaws. A Yahoo! search further discloses something called a HUSKY chain saw sharpener. Taken together, these three pieces of information probably should eliminate your proposed mark HUSKY for chainsaws from further consideration, but let your lawyer help you decide in cases where there is no exact match of name and product.

Search your proposed mark using Google and at least one other big search engine. If there is a search engine that applies particularly to the sort of product or service you are naming, run your proposed mark through that search engine as well. And if you are naming a product, as opposed to a service, search Amazon.com and price-comparison sites (like FatWallet, CheapUncle, PriceGrabber.com and FindersCheapers) for similar or identical product names. When you enter a proposed name, search the entire site; it may not matter to you that there is a line of electrical supplies with your proposed name for work boots, but finding out someone is already using the name for hunting clothes is a different matter.

Directories and Databases

The fourth stage of a screening search is a search of any non-governmental records, of any sort you can locate, for evidence of trademarks that, although unregistered, are in use and protectable. This can include names that most people don't think of as trademarks. Even if there is no federal or foreign registration for the famous Mark Hopkins Hotel in San Francisco, it has been building its reputation as a four-star hotel since it opened in 1926. Naming any business that offers hotel or hospitality services "The Mark Hopkins" would have the owners of the San Francisco hotel knocking on your door pretty quickly—or saying mean things about you in a trademark infringement complaint in federal court. That's why you must take into account what are called "common law" records— that is, nongovernmental records of every sort that mention the names of businesses and services and products that, because they already exist, represent valuable property rights that are protectable in court.

First look at a nationwide telephone–type directory like Switchboard (www.switchboard.com/) or another extensive "Yellow Pages" directory. In this and other searches, remember to search for dominant verbal elements in your mark—for instance, in screening the proposed mark ASTROWORLD, search for uses of ASTRO and WORLD as well as for ASTROWORLD. Remember that you are looking for closely similar names for closely similar products—RELIABLE for tires would not be infringed by RELIABLE for cough drops but would be infringed by RELIABLE for car batteries. And try to keep an eye out for marks that are spelled differently from your proposed mark but would be infringed by it—DUNKIN' DONUTS® would be infringed by DUNCAN DOUGHNUTS.

Some of the best remaining sources for figuring out if someone is already using the name you want to use are directories of companies and manufacturers. Look for names that would be infringed by your remaining proposed marks in every sort of database you can lay your hands on. You should start with any trade publications or directories of products and services specific to the industry in which your proposed marks would be marketed. This includes any sort of business directory that you or your client have or know about. The venerable *Thomas Register of American Manufacturers*, published since 1898, is now available online in an expanded database form at www.thomasnet.com/. (Thomas stopped producing the print version of its registry in 2006). ThomasNet now provides not only product and company information, but online catalogs, computer-aided design drawings, news, press releases, forums, and blogs. It is a great source for information about U.S. and Canadian companies and their products and services and is available for free to anyone who has Internet access.

Access to other databases, some available only through subscription, will require a trip to the library. The reference section of your local main library or a university library, especially a business-school library, may prove to be a treasure trove of information. Whether you visit one or several libraries, ask the reference librarians for help—they're an amazing resource—tell them why you are searching and what sort of product or service your proposed mark would name. Then let them suggest directories—print or otherwise—that may have information about the names of similar products or services. One reference work of this sort is the *Brands and Their Companies* directory, which is also available as an online database. There are other, similar directories and databases. You may find several at your library or only a few, depending on the size of your library. Look at as many such directories and databases as you can locate.

If you can't decide whether an existing mark would be infringed by your proposed mark, either because your proposed mark is not identical to the established mark or because your product and that named by the established mark are different, print out information on the product or service named by the established mark or any similar company name and save it to show to your trademark lawyer later before you undertake a full search for the proposed mark.

State Trademark Records

There are other sources of information about existing trademarks, but they are harder for the average person to access. One of these is state government records. Many marketers ignore state trademark registrations in evaluating proposed trademarks. It is true that state trademark registration is much less valuable than federal registration in terms of the protection it offers a mark. And registration (or use) of a mark only within a state does not confer widespread rights in the mark. However, from the viewpoint of the owner of a mark registered in a state, state trademark registration is very important because it alerts other marketers to the existence of the conflicting, registered trademark.

Even if an existing mark is used only within the boundaries of one or two states and is registered only there rather than in the U.S. Patent and Trademark Office, it can cause problems for a new, similar product marketed under the identical or a similar name. Procter and Gamble would abandon a proposed name for new bath soap if it discovered that a small company in California produced and marketed soap under the same name because, of course, Procter and Gamble would want to sell its product in California and would advertise through media that would be read or viewed in California.

And even if you operate your restaurant in only two locations in your state, if its name is too close to the name of a famous restaurant, even in a distant state, you could be liable for trademark infringement. Consumers who are familiar with the reputation of the famous more-than-one-hundred-year-old Bourbon Street restaurant Galatoire's, which now has a new location in Baton Rouge, would assume that your new restaurant of the same name, although operating in New Hampshire rather than New Orleans, was simply a new location of the famous New Orleans restaurant. That's trademark infringement.

It's a good idea to take state trademark registrations into account when you are performing a screening search to clear a trademark. Many states offer online databases of the trademarks registered in those states. The U.S. Trademark Office offers a webpage listing the websites for searches of trademark registrations in the fifty states and Guam at www.uspto.gov/trademarks/process/State_Trademark_Links.jsp. Remember that, depending on the use you would make of your proposed mark, you may have to search the trademark registrations in *every* state to make sure that no existing trademark registered in one of those states would be infringed by a proposed mark—information from one or two or even three states is really not complete enough to clear a mark for any use that is, or could become, more widespread than strictly local. However detailed your search of state trademark records, make notes of the information you gather to give to the lawyer you will later hire to conduct a full search.

You are ready to proceed to the final stage of the screening search, in which you will examine trademark registrations outside the United States.

Foreign Trademark Records

If you know or even suspect that the product that will be named by your new trademark will be marketed outside the United States, whether immediately or later on, you should consider that fact at this point in your screening search. You owe it to yourself or the client or company for whom you are developing the new mark to consider the possibility that your proposed marks will infringe marks that are already in use in the country or countries where the new product will be marketed. In deciding whether it is advisable to search foreign marks in your screening search, remember that although trademark laws in other countries vary from the U.S. trademark statute, the criteria for judging infringement elsewhere are basically the same as in the United States and that all it takes to halt plans for marketing a product in another country is an injunction from a court in that country based on a claim that a mark registered there has been infringed.

Even though you may not be able to get complete information about existing marks in other countries from your own screening search, do what you can and make a careful note of any information that you even suspect may present a conflict. What you are looking for throughout your screening search is red flags. Information you uncover can be used by your lawyer (he or she is just over the horizon) to help you evaluate the advisability of adopting your proposed mark. Any trademark that is likely to be valuable enough to cause its owners to challenge your use of a similar or identical mark in the same country is also likely to be the subject of an international trademark registration.

The World Intellectual Property Organization (WIPO) has established an online portal to trademark databases in countries around the world that are party to the Madrid System for the International Registration of Marks. The Protocol Relating to the Madrid Agreement Concerning the International Registration of Marks—the Madrid Protocol—is one of two treaties comprising the Madrid System for international registration of trademarks. It provides a cost-effective and efficient way for trademark holders—individuals and businesses—to ensure protection for their marks in multiple countries through the filing of one application with a single office, in one language, with one set of fees, in one currency. Moreover, no local agent is needed to file the application. While an International Registration may be issued, it remains the right of each country or contracting party designated for protection to determine whether or not protection for a mark may be granted. Once the trademark office in a designated country grants protection, the mark is protected in that country just as if that office had registered it. The Madrid Protocol also simplifies the subsequent management of the mark, since a simple, single procedural step serves to record subsequent changes in ownership or in the name or address of the holder with the World Intellectual Property Organization's International Bureau. The International Bureau administers the Madrid System and coordinates the transmittal of requests for protection, renewals, and other relevant documentation to all members.

You can search records of Madrid Protocol trademark registrations in countries from Albania to Zambia by accessing the WIPO ROMARIN International Trademark Information Database at www.wipo.int/romarin/. (ROMARIN stands for "Read-Only-Memory of Madrid Active Registry Information.") The ROMARIN database, updated daily, contains information regarding all international marks recorded under the Madrid system that are currently in force in the International Register or have expired within the past six months. It also includes data relating to international applications and subsequent designations that are still under the examination process within the International Bureau.

For products produced in the United States and marketed primarily on this continent, existing Canadian and Mexican marks probably present the biggest potential for conflict with proposed marks. Remember that the names of many U.S. products that are not physically marketed in other countries can creep across national boundaries by means of television and print advertising and the Internet. This probably will not be the case for a new doughnut shop that will operate only in your city, but it could well be a problem for a rock band or a toothpaste or kitchen utensils, any of which could reach across borders for sales, whether by means of physical presence or in ads or catalogs or through online sales.

Remember too that French is spoken in Canada and Spanish is spoken in Mexico. A U.S. mark in English could infringe a Canadian or Mexican mark named by a word with the same (or a similar) meaning or sound, even though the U.S. mark varies from the foreign mark when spoken. A Canadian trademark L'ETOILE would be infringed by an identical American product named STAR, as a Mexican trademark CIELO would be infringed by an identical American product named SKY. And don't forget the earlier CAFÉ AU LAIT/CAFÉ OLÉ example of conflicting marks that are pronounced the same way even though they are spelled differently and have different meanings.

Don't worry if you feel that you can't wade through all the various sources of information on existing identical or similar marks that may or may not be infringed by your proposed mark. Your own search is just a preliminary effort to eliminate marks that would be problematic if adopted. Any information you turn up is helpful. Once you've completed your screening search, however comprehensive it is, you should hire a full trademark search, which will fill in any omissions and clarify the information you have uncovered yourself. This is not a do-it-yourself job, whatever Internet ads tell you. It's time to call a trademark lawyer.

The Full Search

If even one of the proposed marks on your list has survived to this stage, you're lucky. As we have seen, we are running out of trademarks—so many products and services are being marketed so widely by all the very effective means of modern communication that it is becoming progressively difficult to find an effective new trademark that does not infringe any existing mark. In other words, almost any new trademark will be, potentially, seen and heard all over the global village.

It is very important to realize that although a screening search can be very useful, it can only short-circuit further pursuit of unavailable marks. It *cannot* finally clear a mark for use. For this, you must hire a "full" trademark search. A full trademark search will cover much the same ground as your screening search, but a full search will be performed by highly trained people who maintain databases that are much more comprehensive than those available to the ordinary marketer. In addition, the results produced by the full search will be interpreted by a lawyer who knows just what weight to give each piece of information produced and what to do about any seeming or actual conflicting marks. At this point, your primary job is to make sure that you hire a qualified trademark lawyer who will select a reliable trademark search firm. Your lawyer will question you about your proposed mark (the one that survived the screening search) and your plans for it. Then she or he will instruct a reputable search service as to the direction and scope of the search when commissioning it, will evaluate the raw data in the search report, and will give a legal opinion assessing the degree of risk, if any, involved if your proposed mark is adopted. Most trademark lawyers will charge you around a thousand dollars to commission a full search, pay the search service fee, and prepare an opinion letter to you that evaluates the information in the search. (The cost of the search and the lawyer's fee for evaluating it will vary based on the breadth of the search you need.) Any marketer will tell you that it's money well spent, especially any marketer who has ever experienced the headaches and expense and lost momentum caused by the necessity to abandon a new mark because it infringes an existing mark.

Caveat Emptor

Don't just randomly hire one of the many search services eager to sell you their services through Internet ads. It is very unlikely that you will be able to determine the proper extent for any such search or that you'll be able to properly evaluate the information produced by it. Trademark search services maintain comprehensive databases and choosing among their many options for searching is confusing to anyone who isn't familiar with the process and practice of trademark clearance. Nobody but a trademark lawyer can reliably decide the extent and character of the search you need to finally clear your mark. And only a trademark lawyer will be competent to evaluate the results of the full trademark search you hire. You need advice from a lawyer who has significant trademark experience—your pal the real estate lawyer is extremely un-likely to be qualified to help you search and register your trade-mark. See chapter 6 for tips on finding a trademark lawyer.

Be prepared to find out that your favorite proposed mark is already being used by someone else. It happens every day to someone who spent weeks developing what she or he believed to be a unique new mark. The good news is that it is much easier and much less expensive to discard a proposed mark before any money is spent advertising it than to abandon a new trademark six months into your first big promotion of it.

Of course, if you own or work for an ad agency or graphic design studio and are given the task of creating a mark for a client, you can't compel your client to hire a trademark search. However, you can make sure that you formally, in writing, advise that your client conduct a search to "clear" the mark you suggest. Your job is to help choose a mark that works for the new product or service and that, above all, doesn't cause problems. At the very least, you want to avoid being blamed for any problems that may result from the new mark. If you routinely recommend trademark searches, you won't lose the confidence of your clients because of what they perceive to be your negligence. Although it is not your *legal* responsibility to determine that any mark you propose to a client will not infringe someone else's mark, a client who has been hit with a trademark infringement suit may fail to make that distinction. Clients will always be fickle, but trademark searches give them one less basis for deciding that you should be replaced.

All this is also true for in-house creative and market-ing people, except that for them the stakes are higher. If you work for a company and are asked to name a new product or service, failing to recommend a trademark search could cost you your job. Unless you know that your company's legal department, if there is one, or an outside law firm is handling a search, recommend at the very beginning of the trademark selection process that your company locate and hire a trademark lawyer to commission a full trademark search. The least that will happen is that you will look like you are doing your job. The best result of your recommendation may be that you save your employer a great deal of money by averting an avoidable problem.

Most experienced marketing people view trademark searches as a necessary part of the process of launching new products or services. It's your obligation to point out the pitfalls inherent in ignoring the fact that adopting a trademark without investigating its availability can result in real trouble. Any professional learns that part of success in business is "encouraging" clients and employers, in a loud voice if necessary, to do what is best. This is your line: "Mr. Jones, I'm sure a man of your experience understands the necessity for a full trademark search to clear this proposed mark for use before you invest a zillion dollars in it. When may I expect to see a copy of the search report?" Nobody is happy with anybody else after any business dispute, and trademark infringement lawsuits are likely to have everyone involved in the creation of the offending trademark pointing accusing fingers at everyone else. Luckily, you can help eliminate much of the risk in adopting a new trademark simply by remembering that the risk exists and advising your client or boss to take steps to avoid it.

Trademark Clearance Checklist

If you carefully follow each instruction listed below, your chances of adopting a trademark that leads to a dispute or lawsuit is very small. Think of the whole clearance process as insurance against trouble that no business needs.

1. **Find out where proposed marks come from.** Ask everyone on the task force you create to select a new trademark to propose one or more names for your new product or service. And ask them to briefly describe the sources of the names they propose. For example, for a fashion doll, "MIRANDA—after the heroine of Shakespeare's play *The Tempest*," or for a stuffed toy dog, "PUPSY—my best friend's dog's name in 1965." Reject any proposed name that derives from the name of *any* commercial product or service, previously or currently in use, or the name of any person alive during the last one hundred years.

   Further, because one of your primary goals in selecting a new trademark should be to select one that is capable of being protected and registered with the U.S. Patent and Trademark Office, eliminate any proposed name that transgresses one of the Ten Deadly Sins of Trademark Selection (statutory bars to federal trademark registration) discussed at some length in chapter 4.

2. **Narrow your list of proposed marks to five or fewer marks.** Pick your favorite marks for further consideration. You can do this by polling your creative team or asking the opinion of the management of the company whose product or service the new mark will name. This is also the time for focus groups or consumer surveys regarding your proposed marks. This step allows you to put your efforts into marks that are likely to succeed from a marketing standpoint. However, don't undertake any test-marketing of the new product or service under any proposed name at this point, since such marketing on even a small scale may lead to liability for the infringement of an established mark.

3. **Conduct a screening search for each proposed mark.** A screening search (described earlier) is a stage of preliminary trademark searching during which you check your list of proposed marks against easily available data on existing marks and halt consideration of any mark that would likely infringe an established mark. Eliminate any proposed mark that is similar to 1) any mark registered in the same class as the one your new mark would be registered in, even if the established mark is used for goods or services that are dissimilar to yours, or 2) any mark used for goods and services that are related or similar to yours, even if the established mark is registered in a different class. The U.S. Trademark Office classification system for goods and services can be found at the end of the Trademark Office publications *Basic Facts about Trademarks* reproduced in Appendix B of this book.

   Further, abandon any proposed mark that is at all similar to any famous mark, since it is possible that such a proposed mark could lead to liability under the Trademark Dilution Act, even if it is used for vastly dissimilar products or services than those named by the famous mark. At this stage of clearing a mark, "famous" can be described as any mark that is immediately recognized by thirty percent or more of your creative team. (See chapter 4 for a detailed discussion of the Trademark Dilution Act.)

4. **Find a trademark lawyer.** Unless an attorney in your company's legal department or your regular lawyer is well versed in trademark law, find a trademark lawyer. Trademark law is a narrow specialty and most lawyers who do not regularly practice trademark law find it confusing and even infuriating. Just by reading this book you will have learned more than many lawyers know about trademark

law. You wouldn't ask an auto mechanic, however competent he is, to fix your stereo—so hire the right kind of lawyer to help clear your new mark. Consult chapter 6 for tips on finding a trademark lawyer. And if you don't have one at the start of the clearance process, move this step in the process to the top of the list and begin there.

5. **Commission a full trademark search.** Have your lawyer hire a trademark search firm to conduct what is called a "full" trademark search for the most promising proposed mark on your short list. A full search is a search of the trademark records in the U.S. Patent and Trademark Office, all the state trademark offices, phone directories, trade directories, and other databases that offer information on unregistered but valid marks, and of foreign records. If you are in a real hurry, commission searches for two or three of your proposed marks at the same time so as to get the news about the availability of these marks all at once rather than searching one mark and then searching another if the first proves to be unavailable. So that your lawyer may instruct the search firm correctly as to the scope of the search, make sure that you give him or her the following information:

a. **A copy of the proposed mark, spelled as you intend to use it.** The actual verbal content of the proposed mark is very important. A word spelled one way may be available while the same word spelled in another way may not be.

b. **An accurate and full description of each product or service that the proposed mark will name.** That is, if you intend to market action figures, comic books, a board game, and children's videos under the mark JUSTICE CRUSADERS, your memo to your lawyer on the subject would describe these products as "toy action figures, named collectively 'Justice Crusaders,' based on the characters of the 'Justice Crusaders' series of comic books, and a board game and videotapes featuring these characters." Because a trademark naming these products would have to be searched in four classes to compare it to established trademarks for goods similar to the JUSTICE CRUSADERS products, the search will be more extensive and complicated, and generally more expensive.

c. **A list specifying the anticipated territories where the products to be named by the proposed mark would be marketed.** Most trademark searches are of U.S. records only. This is fine, as far as it goes. However, many marketers, especially those who market easily exportable services or goods, want, at least eventually, to expand their market to other countries. If you have any plans at all for such expansion, let your lawyer know, since clearing a mark for international use involves searches of records in the other countries where it will be used. Failure to clear a mark in another country where marketing is planned can result in a suit for trademark infringement in that country, which is as much of a problem, or more, as a U.S. suit.

d. **All the information that you turned up in your screening search.** Printouts from Web pages and Xerox copies of directory pages or other records work. The information doesn't have to be pretty or even organized. Just make sure that any information you've run across in your preliminary search of your proposed mark makes it to your lawyer. It may influence his directions to the service conducting your full trademark search or send him off in some other direction to investigate a possibly conflicting mark.

6. **Follow your lawyer's advice.** Lawyers' fees buy not only legal services, but also the informed judgment that good lawyers develop over the years of their practice. Your lawyer's evaluation of the likelihood that your proposed mark will conflict with an established mark is the heart of the opinion letter that he or she will write after carefully reviewing your search report. In formulating this evaluation, your lawyer will weigh many factors, large and small, gleaned from the information in the search report. Your lawyer should try to accurately assess the chances of conflict, but most lawyers will be conservative in this assessment. If you feel that your lawyer is being overcautious in recommending that you abandon your plans to use a proposed mark, get another trademark lawyer to evaluate the search report that is, since you pay for it, yours.

Whatever you do, however, don't just ignore your lawyer's reservations and cautions about a mark. This is reportedly what the marketing department at Reebok did when it named a new women's running shoe INCUBUS. The Reebok legal department had apparently advised the marketing department that the word "incubus" means "an imaginary demon or evil spirit supposed to descend upon sleeping persons, especially one fabled to have sexual intercourse with women during their sleep" and had recommended that another mark be chosen. Marketing ignored the advice. After the INCUBUS shoe was introduced, somebody noticed that Reebok had chosen a bad name for the shoe and stories started appearing in the press. The shoes were renamed at some expense. Reebok was embarrassed. It's a safe bet that the folks in Reebok's marketing department wished that they had not ignored the advice of the company's trademark lawyers.

7. **Register your proposed mark(s)**. After you have cleared one or more of your proposed marks for use, file an intent-to-use application to register any mark that you think you may use. This serves several purposes:

   a. Filing an intent-to-use application, in effect, "reserves" any mark for which you file such an application. As soon as you file, your application becomes a part of Trademark Office records and will begin to turn up in other people's trademark searches, resulting in their avoidance of your proposed mark.

   b. Filing an intent-to-use application extends your rights in your trademark. Once you have begun to use the proposed mark and your registration application is granted, the date of first use of the mark is presumed to be the date you filed the registration application, even if that is months or even years before you actually began to use the mark. And because you can postpone the deadline for filing proof of your actual use of the mark for up to thirty-six months after the filing date of your application, you can take your time developing the new product or service the mark will name, as well as the marketing campaign for it, secure in the knowledge that no one else can register your mark before you begin to use it. If you file to register more than one mark and end up using only one, you can simply abandon the applications to register those you do not intend to use. When you decide to abandon a mark that you have previously filed to register, you will have lost only your filing fee and the fee your lawyer charges to prepare the application.

c. Filing an intent-to-use application negates the biggest unavoidable drawbacks of trademark searches. Because trademark searches report the status of the trademarks they include as of the date the search was conducted, they become outdated quickly. This cannot be helped. Like a weather report, a trademark search that is accurate today may be inaccurate tomorrow. However, if you file an intent-to-use registration application as soon as your trademark lawyer lets you know that a proposed mark appears to be available for use, you negate the danger that the report will soon be "stale." Filing to register your proposed mark gets your name in the hat as the owner of that mark ahead of anyone else who may decide to adopt it because, when your application is eventually granted, you will be able to use, as your date of first use of the mark, the date you filed the application to register it. Priority of use is usually determinative in questions of trademark ownership, so filing an intent-to-use application can effectively eliminate any competition for ownership of your mark.

Design Trademark Clearance

A trademark can be a symbol or a name or word. The best trademarks are visually memorable, even if they are primarily verbal. Think of the familiar, distinctive-typeface trademarks for COCA-COLA®, KLEENEX®, and L'EGGS®. As famous as these marks are, even more effective are the symbols that immediately communicate, without words, that the products to which they are applied originated with their manufacturers. A good example of this is Apple Computer's striped apple-with-a-bite-missing logotype. Computer consumers in any part of the world are likely to recognize the Apple logo and to know that it guarantees high-quality products. In an era when many marketers aspire to market their products internationally, symbol trademarks are more important than ever before. Unfortunately, the continuing proliferation of trademarks has made it difficult to create a trademark that is safe to use.

As we have seen, in order to avoid creating trademarks that infringe existing marks, you must know something about the standard used to judge trademark infringement. Trademark infringement is evaluated by applying the "sight, sound, and meaning test." That is, the proposed mark is compared to established marks for similarities of appearance, sound when spoken, and meaning. If there are enough similarities between the proposed mark and an established mark that consumers are likely to confuse the two marks if they are used for similar goods or services, the proposed mark is said to be "confusingly similar" to the established mark and cannot be used without the risk of a lawsuit for trademark infringement. While it is easier to compare verbal marks for confusing similarity, it is equally important that the evaluation of similarities be made for trademarks whose impact is primarily visual. This group of marks includes marks that consist of a name or word that is rendered in a distinctive typeface and marks that include or consist of logotypes.

Available for Use

Obviously, when comparing design marks for similarities, the "sound when spoken" part of the three-part infringement test does not apply. However, the absence of this part of the infringement evaluation test makes the other two-thirds of the test proportionately more important. With design marks, whether you will face a federal lawsuit for trademark infringement after just spending most of your advertising budget for the year to introduce your new logo depends equally on what the logo looks like and what it "means."

The evaluation of a proposed logo starts with a consideration of the broadest possible group of established marks that are similarly configured. For instance, if Texaco were only now considering adopting its familiar T-in-a-five-point-star-in-a-circle logo, all established T and star and star-in-circle marks would be examined to determine if the "new" Texaco logo infringed any of them. All marks that included other prominent visual elements besides Ts and star designs could be eliminated from the universe of marks examined for confusing similarity because such additional elements would eliminate any real probability that consumers would confuse the Texaco mark with them.

Similarly, all star marks that consisted of realistic drawings of stars could be dropped from the ongoing comparison. All such logos would be dissimilar enough to the highly stylized Texaco T-in-a-star-in-a-circle design to eliminate any real chance of consumer confusion. Any remaining star marks would be scrutinized carefully to judge whether the "proposed" Texaco logo would be likely to be confused with them. If such marks were used to market products or services that were remote from petroleum products or gas station services, any similarities that existed would be of less concern. However, if the products or services named by an established mark were close to Texaco's, the established mark would be a more serious impediment to the adoption of the Texaco mark. Even if the "proposed" Texaco mark were nearly identical to an established mark used to market sophisticated medical apparatus to hospitals and physicians, the hospital-equipment star trademark could be of very little concern to the petroleum company.

This would depend largely on whether there was any overlap in the marketplace between the two marks. If not, they could coexist comfortably in American commerce without bumping into each other.

Image Plus Word

These same evaluations would be made in clearing for adoption and use a mark that consisted of a name or word rendered in a distinctive typeface. The difference, of course, is that there would be an additional important element in the search—the verbal content of the mark. The verbal content of a mark is usually considered to be its dominant element for purposes of comparing it to existing marks to determine confusing similarity. However, the visual impact of such a proposed mark is by no means immaterial, especially in a situation where the verbal content of the mark is not so different from that of other marks used for similar products.

For example, if a shoe manufacturer adopted the name SWEET FEET for its new line of ladies' shoes and printed the mark in a script typeface in navy blue ink on the insoles of its products, it might encounter some opposition, in the form of a cease and desist letter, from the marketer of the SUGAR FOOT line of women's footwear, especially if the SUGAR FOOT mark were applied to SUGAR FOOT products in the same location and with the same color ink in a similar typeface. The verbal elements of these two marks do not sound alike when spoken and do not have identical meanings. However, the products they name are identical. The choice of a script typeface for the new SWEET FEET mark is all that is necessary to push SWEET FEET into "confusing similarity" territory, where the SUGAR FOOT manufacturer will have no choice but to challenge it.

The good news for the SWEET FEET graphic designer is that, although the designer may not have been consulted about the name of the new shoe line, which, of course, contributed to the problem with the SUGAR FOOT people, the designer is not helpless when it comes to protecting the Sweet Shoes Company from a trademark infringement suit. The designer can insist on seeing the report for the full trademark search that the Sweet Shoes marketing department had performed before it chose the name SWEET FEET. (And the SWEET FEET designer wants the *report*, which consists of fifty to one hundred pages of data, including reproductions of design marks, produced by a trademark search firm on similar marks already in use, *in addition to* the opinion letter, based on the search report, written by the trademark lawyer who interpreted the report data but only in terms of the verbal elements of established marks versus those of the proposed mark.) And the designer can, using what can be learned by looking at the existing, established design trademarks in that report, steer clear of any design for the SWEET FEET name that is at all similar to any established mark with any similar meaning.

SWEET FEET, rendered in a block, serif typeface with each letter in a different bright color, may be dissimilar enough to the SUGAR FOOT mark to avoid any potential problem with the SUGAR FOOT folks, who may ignore it and never even think of calling their lawyer. This depends in part on factors that no one connected with the new mark can really predict. One such factor is the plans its owners have for the SUGAR FOOT mark. (Do they plan to expand their use of it or is it an old mark for an unprofitable line of shoes that they intend to phase out?). Another is the vigilance of the SUGAR FOOT lawyers, who may be in the habit of suing any competitor who adopts any mark that is at all similar to the SUGAR FOOT mark or may, instead, take a more laissez-faire approach to the inevitable elbowing between competitors that occurs in a free market economy. The same clearance process is possible for design trademarks that include no verbal elements, but the evaluation of similarities is a little more difficult because confusing similarity may result from more subtle similarities between proposed marks and established marks.

Searching Design Marks

The time to perform a trademark search for a design-only mark is after the field of proposed designs has been narrowed to three or fewer logotypes. The U.S. Trademark Office has categorized design marks in a system that assigns numbers to various elements of design marks. For example, a five-pointed star logo would be coded in category 01 (celestial bodies, natural phenomena and geographical maps), division 01 (stars, comets) and section 03 (stars with five points) (the complete design code is 01.01.03). In conducting a design search, you can focus on an extremely narrow group of similar design marks by using a six- or even eight-digit code or at broader categories or divisions of marks by using either a two-digit or four-digit code.

Searching to clear a design trademark (including design marks that include or incorporate words) can be complicated. Go to the Trademark Office's online Design Code Search Manual (http://tess2.uspto.gov/tmdb/dscm/index.htm) to start your search. The General Guidelines for Coding Design Marks may be found at http://tess2.uspto.gov/tmdb/dscm/dsc_gl.htm. Then, start searching. You may get confused, but there is no charge for wandering around in the design database and whatever you find is likely to be helpful in steering you away from existing marks and avoiding trite designs.

But don't rely too much on what you can find out from the Trademark Office's design mark database. Even if you can figure out how to use the search system well enough to completely avoid stepping on any of the design marks it includes, remember that the database includes federally registered marks only. That means that while your newly created design mark may not infringe any federally registered design mark (this is good!), you still have the rest of the design marks in the world to worry about and you can't get information about the others out there without a full trademark search. So create your mark, check it out online, and, if it looks all right to you, call your trademark lawyer for a full search before your new design mark makes its first public appearance.

A full search for a design trademark may cost a little more than that for a word mark, but the extra expense is definitely worth it. If you don't hire the trademark lawyer yourself, ask whoever does to furnish you with a copy of the search report and the trademark opinion letter. Whether or not your proposed mark proves to be too close to an existing mark, you will gain valuable information about other existing marks already in use for similar goods or services by looking at the search report. You may be able to modify your proposed mark by changing typefaces, colors, or design elements enough to eliminate any chance of conflict. However, show the modified mark to your lawyer and if your lawyer deems the design you create unavailable for use, move on to the next proposed mark on the short list of those under consideration.

And don't forget to have ordinary consumers as well as experts review your proposed design mark if there is any doubt about whether it may inspire undesirable or erroneous associations. Design marks can be powerful, which means if they go wrong, they go wrong in a big way. Some years ago

Nike introduced a new line of shoes that bore a logo on the heel of the shoe that resembled the word "Allah" in Arabic. The logo was intended to represent a flame, but the Council on American-Islamic Relations didn't see it as such. After a year of negotiations, Nike agreed to recall the shoes, to apologize to Muslims for any unintentional offense they had committed, to build three playgrounds in U.S. Islamic communities, and to investigate how the design came about. The Council on American-Islamic Relations agreed to tell Muslims around the world not to boycott Nike products. Someone should have realized that the logo resembled Arabic and that an association between the name of God and a shoe was highly offensive to Muslims. If the Nike team who developed the logo had been more attuned to the international nature of its market, Nike would not have had to additionally divert thirty thousand existing pairs of the offending shoes from Muslim countries to "less sensitive" markets.

Chapter 4
Trademark Selection

In addition to coming up with a new trademark that will grab the attention of consumers of your product and determining that it will not infringe an established trademark, it is important to consider whether the name or symbol you choose will be eligible for federal trademark registration.

There are two types of trademark registration: 1) state trademark registration, which is cheap and easy to obtain and confers some benefits, and 2) federal trademark registration, which is not easy to obtain, but which confers much greater benefits. Since most trademark owners want to be able to register their marks federally, that is, with the U.S. Patent and Trademark Office, we will discuss federal trademark registration.

The federal trademark statute, which governs trademark registration, imposes certain restrictions on which marks can be granted federal registration. The inherent characteristics of the mark determine whether these restrictions will prevent the eventual registration of the trademark. The problem of these restrictions can be largely eliminated by careful avoidance of a few varieties of marks that can cause the Trademark Office to deny a registration application.

The Ten Deadly Sins of Trademark Selection

There are ten reasons the Trademark Office will deny federal registration to a trademark (other than defects in the form of the application or some other procedural problem). They are the following:

1. **The mark is confusingly similar to a trademark that is already federally registered.** The test the Trademark Office uses to determine whether your mark is "confusingly similar" to a registered mark is the same "sight, sound, and meaning" test used by judges in trademark infringement suits to decide whether the plaintiff does indeed have grounds to complain about the defendant's use of its name, but the only thing the Trademark Office will do to you if you adopt a name that's too close to a registered trademark is deny your application to register your name. Any liability that may be incurred by the infringing use of the previously registered mark is beyond the purview of the Trademark Office. It remains the job of the owner of the registered mark to sue you.

2. **The word or, more typically, the symbol for which registration is sought does not function as a trademark—that is, does not act in the marketplace to identify the source of the goods or services to which it is applied.** This basis for refusing federal registration is most often cited in applications for design marks that the Trademark Office

believes are being used on goods merely for purposes of ornamentation rather than in any way that indicates the source of the products. In other words, the famous JOR-DACHE® jeans hip pocket embroidery designs may not have achieved federal trademark registration if they had not become "distinctive of the goods," that is, if they had not begun to function to indicate to consumers that the jeans that bore them were manufactured by Jordache.

3. **The mark is "immoral, deceptive, or scandalous."** To be rejected for registration on this ground, a name has to be blatant. Some marks that are slightly risqué make it to registration, but none that are really off-color or offensive will be granted registration. Usually mild double entendres, obscure sexual slang, and all but the most shockingly vicious phrases or symbols will pass muster with the trademark examiner who reviews your registration application, even though it is the examiner's job to try diligently to figure out why it should not be granted. Before you cry "First Amendment" and "government censorship," bear in mind that the Trademark Office will not, no matter how much it hates your trademark, tell you not to use it. The government just draws the line at *registering* any immoral, deceptive, or scandalous name. In any case, you should avoid any really offensive name for your product or service because consumers may object to it and may have an aversion to requesting it from retailers. Moreover, some advertising media may refuse to air or publish ads that include the offending name.

The "deceptive" part of this restriction is usually not much of a problem unless your mark is going to get you in hot water anyway. For instance, if you get the bright idea to call your line of cubic zirconia jewelry BUDGET

TIFFANY because you intend to copy the famous jewelry retailer's designs and to use the same famous robin's-egg-blue packaging, the Trademark Office will deny your application to register the name on the ground that, because you have no connection whatsoever with the famous jeweler, your name is deceptive. But by the time the Trademark Office's rejection of your application reaches you, you will already be in litigation, initiated by the lawyers for Tiffany's, for the offenses of trademark infringement and trade dress infringement.

Ordinarily, trademark infringement is a civil offense, which means that infringers are sued in civil courts, not brought up on criminal charges by the district attorney. Infringers pay for their transgressions in dollars, not days in jail. Which is funny, if you think about it. If someone breaks into your apartment and steals your stereo, he can be imprisoned, but if he infringes your hard-won trademark, which is like stealing your reputation, he won't go to jail, even though his infringement of your trademark may have cost you a lot more than your stereo was worth. However, remember that wholesale counterfeiting of products that bear a famous name or mark is, potentially and under a handful of state and federal statutes, a criminal offense that can result in jail time and large fines, in addition to the destruction or impoundment of the counterfeited products. (See the end of chapter 2 for information on online Department of Justice reports of criminal trademark infringement prosecutions.)

4. **The mark disparages or falsely suggests a connection with persons, institutions, beliefs, or national symbols, or brings them into contempt or disrepute.** This restriction is similar to the "immoral, deceptive, or scandalous"

89

restriction. For example, if you want to call your rock band TRICKY DICK in honor of the only U.S. president ever to resign from office, that's your business, but the Trademark Office may deny your application to register that name on the ground that it disparages Richard Nixon. It doesn't matter that TRICKY DICK is merely a nickname for Richard Nixon initiated by a political opponent early in Nixon's (tricky) career. It doesn't even matter that he is now deceased. And your arguments that Mr. Nixon's reputation would be hard to hurt aren't going to make the slightest difference to the Trademark Office.

Applications that imply nonexistent connections with particular well-known institutions will also be denied. For instance, the Trademark Office would not grant a registration to a home-security company called F.B.I. SECURITY. Call your company LAW ENFORCEMENT ALARMS, though, and you may be able to register the name. Ditto for HARVARD for scholastic aptitude tests or a restaurant jokingly named SEARS AND ROEBUCK.

And no matter how clever you think it is, the Trademark Office will refuse to register any name or logo that disparages any belief or national symbol.

If you're a group of Jewish cantors who sing traditional Jewish songs at wedding receptions, you may be able to call yourselves STARS OF DAVID and convince the Trademark Office to register the name, since your use of it would not be disparaging. However, you wouldn't be able to register that name for any rock band without running into some trouble from the Trademark Office, which could reasonably interpret your use of the name or symbol as disparaging.

The same goes for crucifixes. If you manufacture and sell white chocolate crucifixes under the name IMMACULATE CONFECTIONS, don't expect the Trademark Office to allow you to register that mark. In fact, the same obstacle will be encountered by anyone who attempts to register any name or symbol dear to the adherents of any religion, including Eastern religions as well as more familiar Western belief systems.

All this is also true for "national symbols." If you apply to register as the trademark for a night club a logo depicting Uncle Sam wearing red lipstick and rouge, white theatrical makeup, and blue eye shadow, the Trademark Office will turn you down, even if your only goal in depicting Uncle Sam in such a manner is to make him look like the female impersonators who appear at your club. Your manner of using the famous American symbol will be interpreted by the Trademark Office as bringing it into contempt or disrepute.

5. **The mark consists of, or simulates, the flag or coat of arms or other insignia of the United States or of a state or municipality or a foreign nation.** The American flag, for instance, belongs equally to every American citizen. Since trademark registration gives the registrant the exclusive right to use the registered mark, the trademark statute prohibits the registration of any mark that consists of the American flag. This doesn't mean you can't use the American flag as a part of your logo. You just can't register your flag logo as a trademark. (If your logo includes the American flag only as a small part of a larger design, you may be able to register the entire design by disclaiming any exclusive right in the flag portion of it.)

The same holds true for other official symbols from just about everywhere. The manufacturer of a line of women's dresses named LA FRANCE cannot register the French flag as its trademark. Nor can a restaurant called THE LONE STAR CAFÉ register the state flag of Texas as its logo.

6. **The mark is the name, portrait, or signature of a particular living individual who has not given his or her consent for use of the mark; or is the name, signature, or portrait of a deceased president of the United States during the life of his or her surviving spouse, unless that spouse has given consent to use of the mark.** The Trademark Office cannot grant exclusive rights in the name or likeness of a living person without the consent of that person. This is an easy restriction to understand. How would you feel if you woke up one morning and found that the Trademark Office had given somebody else the exclusive right to use your name for a product or service without your permission? You'd be upset, right? Well, everybody feels the same way, which is why you have to prove to the Trademark Office that any living person whose name you use as a trademark consents to that use before you can register the name.

However, you can call your outdoor-equipment shop DR. LIVINGSTONE, I PRESUME, after the famous English missionary who explored Africa, or name your line of women's cosmetics CLEOPATRA'S SECRET or bottled olive oil DA VINCI. David Livingstone, Cleopatra, and Leonardo Da Vinci were all real people, but "were" is the operative verb. They are no longer living and are, therefore, no longer in a position to object to your use, without permission, of their names or to profit themselves from such uses. (Consider, for example, SHAKESPEARE fishing rods. No one had to ask the famous bard for his permission to use his name as a trademark.)

A caveat, however: There is something called the "right of publicity" that famous people acquire with their fame, and sometimes it can be inherited by descendants. Basically, the right of publicity is a celebrity's right to be the only person who profits from the use of her or his famous name. This means that you should not only avoid choosing as a trademark the name of any living person but should also be very careful about adopting the name or even the nickname of any famous figure who died after, say, 1900.

Remember that this restriction applies even if you own the company that owns the trademark. Honest. Dolly Parton had to give her written consent before the trademark used to market the DOLLYWOOD® amusement park could be registered. Ditto for Oprah Winfrey and the popular OPRAH® television show.

So much for living people. The dead presidents' restriction is sort of a leftover from when companies were likely to name their products after popular politicians in an effort to appeal to the people who made the politicians popular—you know, "TEDDY ROOSEVELT MOUSTACHE WAX." This restriction is of less concern to marketers than many of the others in the Trademark Office's long list of types of unregistrable marks, but it could play a role in your choice of a name for a new product. For example, during the lifetime of Jacqueline Kennedy Onassis you could not have registered the name JFK for rocking chairs similar to the one used by the late president without her permission. The trademark statute doesn't say what happens if the dead president is female—presumably, her widower would have to consent to any use of her name. Apparently the men (they were men) who wrote our trademark statute decades ago thought that the possibility of a woman being elected president was so slender as to be nonexistent, so they specifically worded the statute in terms of deceased male presidents.

7. **The mark is "merely descriptive" of the goods or services it names.** Many marketing people hate this restriction and make rude noises when their lawyers remind them of it, since they believe that the more a new product name describes the product or service it names, the better a trademark it is. If you think about it, you will realize that this is not the case.

In actuality, the best trademarks are fanciful, that is, they don't mean anything much. They just capture the imagination and come to signify the particular product they name rather than being equally applicable to any product of the same kind, which is the case with marks that are descriptive. Think of KLEENEX® or EXXON® or WISK®. None of those marks mean anything as ordinary English words, but they each immediately bring to mind the specific products marketed under them.

Besides this important consideration, there is the fact that the Trademark Office almost always disallows an application to register a descriptive mark. It will not allow, by virtue of a federal trademark registration, one company to bar all others from using what are simply ordinary words to describe a product or service. If you ask yourself whether a proposed mark would tell consumers what a product or service is, or in the case of names for publications, by whom the publication is intended to be read, you can ferret out descriptive marks before they are adopted and later turned down for federal registration.

Now, it must be said that there are many trademarks that are very descriptive that are currently registered in the U.S. Patent and Trademark Office. These marks, for the most part, started out as unqualified for registration because of their descriptiveness but later, because of the fame they acquired as the names of well-known products or services, the trademark came to signify to consumers the products or services of their particular companies. In short, after a while the Trademark Office will reconsider allowing registration of descriptive marks that have achieved some fame. But at the trademark-selection stage in the history of a product, this exception to the descriptiveness restriction should not make any difference to anyone who wants to come up with a mark that won't have to work at becoming eligible for federal registration.

8. **The mark is "deceptively misdescriptive" of the goods or services it names.** This restriction on registration is akin to some of those mentioned that are designed to deter the adoption of misleading or distasteful trademarks. "Deceptively misdescriptive" means a mark that falsely suggests that a product or service has some characteristic that it does not indeed possess—in other words, the mark describes what it names, but falsely.

For example, LAPIS for a line of blue glass-bead jewelry would not be granted registration, since the Trademark Office would hold that the word "lapis," when used for blue jewelry not made of the semiprecious stone lapis lazuli, was a "deceptively misdescriptive" name that could mislead consumers. The same argument would apply to, say, TOP GRAIN for vinyl luggage, SILKSHIRT for women's polyester blouses, or PURE GOLD for jewelry that is merely gold-plated.

This restriction against registering deceptively misdescriptive marks is intended primarily to discourage actual attempts to mislead consumers, but it should not be disregarded if you consider choosing an ironic name. You may appreciate the joke in your new mark, but the Trademark Office will not be persuaded to register it by the mere fact that the name is funny if it transgresses one of the trademark statute's restrictions on registrability. For example, DR. FEELGOOD'S HEALTH TONIC used for bottled beer may not be registrable, no matter how much you or consumers like the name for its wackiness.

9. **The mark is "primarily geographically descriptive or deceptively misdescriptive" of the goods or services it names.** When the name of a product or service includes a geographic term or place name, such as the name of a river or mountain, that either tells where the product or service comes from or suggests falsely that it comes from a place that it does not, that name will run afoul of this restriction when its owner seeks to register the mark federally. The general rule has long been that if the Trademark Office can find a geographic term in any atlas or gazetteer, registration will be denied to the mark that contains it.

The reasoning behind the first part of this restriction is that if a product comes from the geographic region named in the mark, registration for one mark that includes a geographic term that is equally applicable to all products of the same sort produced in that region would unfairly deny other manufacturers the right to use the term to describe their products. For example, CARRARA STONE for marble from Italy would be unregistrable because more than one company markets marble building materials quarried from the famous deposits at Carrara and the phrase "Carrara stone" applies equally to all such products.

The reason for the second part of the restriction—that registration will be denied to any mark that suggests a nonexistent geographic origin—is similar. If the marble were not quarried in Italy at Carrara, the name CARRARA STONE would be geographically deceptively misdescriptive because it would lead consumers to a false conclusion about the origins of the stone. This restriction has more application to manufacturers of cheese, wine, bottled water, and other products tied to certain regions than it does to the marketers of most other products, but it can have an unexpected effect on the uninitiated.

The restriction on registration of geographic marks also applies to graphic representations of a state or country. If your entire logo is the map of a state or some other recognizable representation of a piece of the world, the Trademark Office will deny it registration.

Now bear in mind that you can make up fictitious place names all day long and register them as trademarks. EMERALD CITY for mobile homes or BIG ROCK CANDY MOUNTAIN for sugar cubes would be registrable. And you can use actual place names in purely fanciful ways because no one will be likely to believe that they are used to indicate the origin of a product or service. KENYA for safari-style sport clothing would be registrable and BLUE DANUBE® has long been used for a china pattern.

And remember that, as is the case with some other restrictions on registration, famous marks enjoy different rules. (Consider the country music stars, the group ALABAMA®, for example.) When a geographically descriptive name that the Trademark Office considers unregistrable comes to signify only the product or service it names, it becomes registrable because, in effect, its fame enables it to escape the anonymity inherent in a geographic name and to function as a trademark. But trademark fame is not always easy to achieve and it is a much better idea, when adopting a new mark, to choose one that won't have to outshine competing marks before achieving registrability.

10. **The mark is primarily a surname.** Personal names have long been considered not to be inherently distinctive when used as trademarks, which is another way of saying that they are descriptive or generic and can't, in and of themselves, point to a particular source for a product.

Think of this example: there are four zillion people in the United States named Smith, so the source of SMITH'S SOCKS for children could be anyone in the country whose name is Smith. Moreover, until one SMITH'S SOCKS became well-known enough to transcend the anonymity of most surname marks, all the Smiths in the United States could market socks using their mutual surname without infringing each other's trademark rights. In other words, surname marks do not work as trademarks until they have achieved something called "secondary meaning," which is a term trademark lawyers use to mean "Everybody knows that trademark because it's so famous."

Now, obviously, there are many famous surname trademarks that have been granted federal trademark registration by the Trademark Office. That is because WATERMAN® for fountain pens, SMITH BROTHERS® for cough drops, CAMPBELL'S® for soups, LIPTON® for tea, WILSON® for sporting goods, HOOVER® for vacuum cleaners, and CRANE® for stationery are all trademarks that have risen above anonymity by virtue of having achieved strong reputations in the marketplace. Since a trademark represents the reputation of a product or service in the market, this is just a way of saying that over the years these surname marks have achieved trademark status sufficient to persuade the Trademark Office to allow their registration.

In addition to the potential for difficulty in registration, surname marks sometimes present an additional problem: Before naming a product for a real person, determine whether the founder of the company who wants his name on the product is a discreet and honorable person. All it takes is one brush with the law or the tabloids to diminish the credibility—and market share—of a surname mark. Think of Martha Stewart and what happened to the value of stock in Martha Stewart Living Omnimedia, Inc. when she ran afoul of the law.

Marks formed from first names are equally problematical. Whether any name mark succeeds is largely a matter of chance, even if the mark is the name of the CEO's child— SARA LEE® baked goods and WENDY'S® hamburgers immortalized those two little girls, but not even Ford likes to think about EDSEL® automobiles anymore.

Design Elements of Marks

It is important to remember that all the restrictions on registration listed above can also apply to design trademarks or trademarks that combine graphic elements and words. You may be able to get away with registering BON VIVANT for a "parfum" that is actually manufactured in New Jersey without running into the geographically misdescriptive restriction on registration, but use a map of France as the background for the words BON VIVANT on the perfume bottle labels and the Trademark Office will reject the application to register the mark.

Similarly, although ASTRONAUT for children's pajamas would, alone, be registrable, the use of sketches of Alan Shepard and Sally Ride in conjunction with the word ASTRONAUT, without their permission, would cause the registration application to be rejected. (In addition, this use would probably result in a suit for infringement of the astronauts' right of publicity.)

Another caveat—despite having a whole book of written-down rules to operate by, the Trademark Office, like God, often moves in mysterious ways. This means that all of the above statements about what are and are not registrable trademarks are subject to some Trademark Office exceptions, whims, and inconsistencies. However, it is important to choose a trademark that can be registered, because many unregistrable marks are also all but unprotectable. That is, if you adopt an unregistrable mark, it may be next to impossible to prevent someone else from using your mark, depending on the characteristics of the mark. Use the "Ten Deadly Sins of Trademark Selection" list as a guideline in selecting proposed marks and leave the final opinion as to the registrability of any proposed mark to someone who pays for malpractice insurance, your trademark lawyer. You don't have to function as a trademark lawyer in order to do your job, but you can forestall a great many problems if you know a little about what you are doing when you create a new trademark.

Naming Names

Because a trademark may be unregistrable on the basis of any of the ten registration restrictions mentioned above, it may seem unreasonably difficult to find a trademark that will work.

It is really easier than you think, especially if you keep in mind a few principles of trademark creation.

This is what the Trademark Manual of Examining Procedure (the TMEP) has to say about the several gradations of effectiveness and originality in trademarks:

Matter that is generic for the goods or services is not registrable on either the Principal or the Supplemental Register under any circumstances. *See* TMEP §§1209.01(c)–(c)(iii).

- 1209.01(a) Fanciful, Arbitrary, and Suggestive Marks
  - ○ Fanciful marks comprise terms that have been invented for the sole purpose of functioning as a trademark or service mark. Such marks comprise words that are either unknown in the language (e.g., PEPSI, KODAK, and EXXON) or are completely out of common usage (e.g., FLIVVER).
  - ○ Arbitrary marks comprise words that are in common linguistic use but, when used to identify particular goods or services, do not suggest or describe a significant ingredient, quality, or characteristic of the goods or services (e.g., APPLE for computers; OLD CROW for whiskey). *See, e.g., Palm Bay Imports, Inc. v. Veuve Clicquot Ponsardin Maison Fondee En 1772*, 396 F.3d 1369, 1372, 73 USPQ2d 1689, 1692 (Fed. Cir. 2005) (VEUVE—meaning WIDOW in English—held to be "an arbitrary term as applied to champagne and sparkling wine, and thus conceptually strong as a trademark"); *Nautilus Grp., Inc. v. Icon Health & Fitness, Inc.*, 372 F.3d 1330, 1340, 71 USPQ2d 1173, 1180 (Fed. Cir. 2004)

(defining an arbitrary mark as "a known word used in an unexpected or uncommon way").

○ Suggestive marks are those that, when applied to the goods or services at issue, require imagination, thought, or perception to reach a conclusion as to the nature of those goods or services. Thus, a suggestive term differs from a descriptive term, which immediately tells something about the goods or services. *See In re George Weston Ltd.*, 228 USPQ 57 (TTAB 1985) (SPEEDI BAKE for frozen dough found to fall within the category of suggestive marks because it only vaguely suggests a desirable characteristic of frozen dough, namely, that it quickly and easily may be baked into bread); *In re The Noble Co.*, 225 USPQ 749 (TTAB 1985) (NOBURST for liquid antifreeze and rust inhibitor for hot-water-heating systems found to suggest a desired result of using the product rather than immediately informing the purchasing public of a characteristic, feature, function, or attribute); *In re Pennwalt Corp.*, 173 USPQ 317 (TTAB 1972) (DRI-FOOT held suggestive of antiperspirant deodorant for feet in part because, in the singular, it is not the usual or normal manner in which the purpose of an antiperspirant and deodorant for the feet would be described). Incongruity is a strong indication that a mark is suggestive rather than merely descriptive. *In re Tennis in the Round Inc.*, 199 USPQ 496, 498 (TTAB 1978) (TENNIS IN THE ROUND held not merely descriptive for providing tennis

facilities, the Board finding that the association
of applicant's marks with the phrase "theater-
in-the-round" created an incongruity because
applicant's tennis facilities are not at all analo-
gous to those used in a "theater-in-the-round").
The Board has described incongruity in a mark
as "one of the accepted guideposts in the evolved
set of legal principles for discriminating the
suggestive from the descriptive mark," and has
noted that the concept of mere descriptiveness
"should not penalize coinage of hitherto unused
and somewhat incongruous word combinations
whose import would not be grasped without
some measure of imagination and 'mental
pause.'" *In re Shutts*, 217 USPQ 363, 364–5
(TTAB 1983) (SNO-RAKE held not merely descriptive of a snow-removal hand tool); *see also*
In re Vienna Sausage Mfg. Co., 156 USPQ 155,
156 (TTAB 1967) (FRANKWURST held not
merely descriptive for wieners, the Board finding that although "frank" may be synonymous
with "wiener," and "wurst" is synonymous with
"sausage," the combination of the terms is incongruous and results in a mark that is no more
than suggestive of the nature of the goods); *In
re John H. Breck, Inc.*, 150 USPQ 397, 398
(TTAB 1966) (TINT TONE held suggestive for
hair coloring, the Board finding that the words
overlap in significance and their combination is
somewhat incongruous or redundant and does
not immediately convey the nature of the product); *cf. In re Getz Found.*, 227 USPQ 571,

572 (TTAB 1985) (MOUSE HOUSE held fanciful for museum services featuring mice figurines made up to appear as human beings, the Board finding that the only conceivable meaning of "mouse house," i.e., a building at a zoo in which live and/or stuffed mice are displayed, is incongruous). Suggestive marks, like fanciful and arbitrary marks, are registrable on the Principal Register without proof of secondary meaning. *See Nautilus Grp., Inc. v. Icon Health & Fitness, Inc.,* 372 F.3d 1330, 1340, 71 USPQ2d 1173, 1180 (Fed. Cir. 2004). Therefore, a designation does not have to be devoid of all meaning in relation to the goods/services to be registrable.

104   Trademarks that are coined out of thin air or consist of existing words used in uncharacteristic ways are referred to as "fanciful" or "arbitrary" marks. Fanciful or arbitrary marks are the most registrable and the most effective as trademarks. Marks that are what the Trademark Office calls "suggestive" are nearly as desirable. This is not the kind of "suggestive" you think. Suggestive marks are marks that call to mind—or suggest—an association related to the product they name. They imply strength or softness or freshness or flavor, depending upon the product. They are subtle marks, created by marketers and ad people who are very skilled at making artful associations. Think of TORO® lawn mowers, DOWNY® fabric softener, IRISH SPRING® deodorant soap, and ZESTA® saltine crackers. None of these marks is obvious, but we perceive nonetheless the strength of TORO lawn mowers, the softness DOWNY fabric softener imparts to laundry, the fresh scent of IRISH SPRING soap, and the zesty taste of ZESTA saltines.

The least protectable and effective marks are "descriptive" or "generic" marks—they merely describe what they name. For example, THE HOT DOG SHOPPE for a café that specializes in hot dogs will immediately let everyone who sees its marquee know what sort of dinner he or she can buy there, but it is hardly memorable or distinctive. HOT DOG HEAVEN would be somewhat less descriptive. THE DOG HOUSE would be better still. HOT DIGGITY DOG would be the most memorable and registrable of all, since it would incorporate the "incongruity" the Trademark Office says indicates a "suggestive" mark. If you think up a proposed mark that is too descriptive to register, start substituting words for some of the elements of the descriptive mark. You may be able to move the mark from "descriptive" to, at least, "suggestive" by simply using one different word.

Twelve Steps to Creating a Winning Trademark

Now that you know what to avoid in creating a new trademark, you're ready to actually begin. Any method for coming up with new trademarks that works, works. However, the steps listed below are a good place to start in your quest to create a memorable and effective trademark.

1. **Assemble a creative team.** A study of four hundred U.S. companies by Rivkin and Associates, Inc., a New Jersey marketing and consulting firm, found that the most commonly used and most effective method for finding new trademarks is a task force assembled for the purpose. These committees usually consist of someone from the company's administration, someone from marketing, a PR person, someone from sales, maybe a trademark lawyer, etc. If no one proposes such a committee, be a hero and suggest that one be formed. Several heads are better

than one, and people from different disciplines bring different talents to the task of choosing a new name.

2. **Think up a name that has never existed before.** Nobody had ever heard of EXCEDRIN® or CRAYOLA® until somebody named pain relief tablets and crayons those now-famous names. One way to create this sort of mark is to compose a long list of English-language syllables, each with a vowel and at least one consonant. Include some standard English prefixes and suffixes. Divide the list into three or four sections. Combine a syllable from the first section with any syllable from each of the other sections. Scramble the combinations you don't like, or flip them back to front. Replace syllables with others to make new combinations. Substitute a new vowel for one in a syllable that is not euphonious. Add syllables or whack them off. Be bold. It is a rule of physics that you will come up with approximately forty-seven bad combinations for every good one you stumble onto. Ignore the prevalence of bad combinations and look for the pearls. Your working list will look like this:

RE	GO	WAN	VA
SAR	SI	CO	LA
CO	WET	MA	EY
FA	SIR	RA	MAX
DEN	SO	VA	CAM
PRO	BEN	MO	EX
NO	TA	RON	TER
BE	TAR	NAM	MA
XE	WES	ER	DOM
YO	WA	TOM	WAN
SO	CA	RAK	AL
EM	VEN	PO	SON
(etc.)			

Your list will look like so much nonsense, and so will most of the combinations of syllables you come up with. However, play with the combinations that best roll off your tongue until you create some promising ones, and then post a list of two or three over your desk and look at them for a while. Remember, the combination CO-CA-CO-LA would seem strange to anyone who had never heard of COCA-COLA®.

You can buy software programs that can help you create potential new trademarks. To find available programs, search for "naming software" or "branding software" on the Web. No naming programs will tell you which of the many names they generate is the best—your own taste and marketing savvy will have to do this—but they can provide you with a multitude of possibilities. These programs are cheap enough that you may want to try two or three of them—spending even a hundred dollars or so to help you generate a list of potential new trademarks is much cheaper than hiring a consulting firm at $25,000 or more.

3. **Use a common word in an uncommon way.** "Apple" once meant only a kind of fruit. Now we know it also means a particular, famous brand of computer. The word "windows" has gone through a similar transformation. It now signifies a particular brand of computer software while retaining all its previous meanings. Be creative. Be silly. Mine your dictionary.

4. **Use an uncommon word in a new way.** "Oreo" is the Greek word for "hill." The original plan was to market mound-shaped cookies as OREO® cookies. The cookies were flattened in the process of development, but the name stuck—enough so that every kid in America, and most adults, ask for these particular cookies by name. There are other familiar uses of unfamiliar words: VOLVO® means

"I roll" in Latin. REEBOK® was the name of a particular kind of fleet-footed African gazelle before it became a brand name for running shoes. And NIKE® was the name of the Greek goddess of victory long before it was the name of one of Reebok's competitors.

5. **Marry two or more words.** Some of the most famous marks in the world were formed by constructing a new word by combining others, usually descriptive terms, either as whole words or in a truncated form. NABISCO® was formed from "National Biscuit Company" in this manner. Other examples include CITIBANK® ("city" plus "bank"), SPAM® ("spiced ham"), and NYQUIL® ("night" plus "tranquil"). One way to begin creating a mark of this sort is to list all the words you can think of that favorably describe the product you are naming. Then stick them together in combinations of two or three. Eliminate syllables here and there to create snappy combination words that are easy to say, spell, and hear.

6. **Look at the forms, shapes, and inhabitants of nature.** Inspiration for a new trademark or logo may be as close as the seashore, the woods, the skies, or your backyard. The Texaco T-in-a-five-point-star-in-a-circle logo is one of the simplest commercial designs on the cultural landscape, but it has also outlasted a lot of fussier, more pretentious logos and has for a long time signified only that company and its products to most Americans. Consult field guides and nature encyclopedias. Look at books on symbols. Study reproductions of cave paintings and hieroglyphics. Look at maps of the constellations.

Think, too, of the traditional meanings or mythological significances of certain natural objects and animals. Tradition has it that owls are wise, bulls are aggressive, lions are proud, bees are busy, turtles are slow, ants are industrious, dogs are faithful, cats are aloof, mice are quiet, and monkeys are playful. An owl logo could serve as the trademark for a textbook company. A bee logo would signify the busyness of the personnel of a housecleaning service. A monkey logo could signal visually to kids and their parents that there is fun to be had at an amusement park or a fast-food restaurant. Read Aesop's fables and the Uncle Remus tales. Peruse books of folk tales from other cultures.

7. **Study world cultures**. Study English heraldry or Scottish tartans or Celtic symbols. Get a book on origami or Japanese art or Chinese symbols. Read Shakespeare or Chaucer (that's where Toyota got CRESSIDA®) or Bullfinch's mythology. Ask your librarian for books on African art. Find out about the Olmecs, the Toltecs, the Aztecs, the Mayas, and the Incas. Study Inuit art. Read up on other native cultures of the Americas. More than one product has successfully borrowed the symbols or legends or literature from another culture or the past to create a memorable trademark. The famous automobile trademark THUNDERBIRD® had its origins in the name some Native American peoples gave to the bird that embodied the spirit of thunder, lightning, and rain in their mythology.

8. **Consider meanings, translations, and cross-cultural meanings**. Browse your biggest dictionary and check your thesaurus. Both may give you ideas for names. But make sure you know the meaning and all the connotations for any word you consider using as a trademark. Remember Reebok's INCUBUS? Enough said. (However, INCUBUS did apparently work as the name of a rock

band, which presumably didn't mind its connotations.
Go figure.) The (apparently apocryphal) famous example
of a mark that worked in English but failed spectacularly
in another market is NOVA®. "Nova" means "a star
that suddenly becomes very bright"—in English. This is
certainly an acceptable association for an automobile,
which is what the NOVA mark named when it was introduced some years ago. However, "no va" in Spanish,
means, unfortunately, "it doesn't go," which is certainly
a less-than-wonderful name for a car south of the border
and in other countries where Spanish is spoken. Suppos-
edly, consumers in Spanish-speaking countries refused to
buy a car whose name indicated that it wouldn't work.

The urban-legend nature of the NOVA story doesn't
diminish the truth it imparts: it is essential to have someone who knows languages translate any proposed mark
before you start printing up your packaging materials.
And don't assume that your proposed mark is safe to use
because it won't be used outside the United States. More
than one language is spoken here and this country shows
every sign of becoming more multilingual in the future.
You don't want to end up with a successful product named
by a trademark that offends any segment of this society
or subjects your company to ridicule. If your mark will be
used in other countries, call the languages department of
the nearest large university and enlist the help of a couple
of professors to check your proposed marks for hidden
meanings. Better still, ask a native speaker of the languages
in those foreign countries to review your mark for connotations that may not be apparent to even a scholar of that
language. And if you are adopting a symbol from another
culture or from history, check it out with historians of that

culture and religion professors. After all, once upon a time even the swastika had no evil connotations.

9. **Choose a name that fits your commercial personality.** No hot new club is going to be called ETHEL'S NITE CLUB. Not anymore. An evaluation of the "personality" of a proposed mark should be made for any product or service name. If the product is fun and friendly, choose a fun and friendly name. But nobody wants a bank to be too funny or too friendly—reliability and convenience are the qualities that sell bank services. Figure out the commercial image your product or service must project and then make sure your new mark matches it. And make sure that the vibes your name conveys are distinct *enough*. There are lots of cowardly marks in the marketplace that are so worried about sticking out that they fade into the background. This is related to the "dilute verbal element" problem (discussed below) and presents the same sort of difficulty. You may remember a STARBUCKS® coffeehouse after hearing of it or seeing it only once, but is BREWS a coffeehouse or a microbrewery? Coffeehouses are hip, casual, fun, and friendly. Try JAVA or CUPPA JOE or BUZZ instead.

10. **Avoid "dilute" verbal and visual elements and stay away from initials and numbers.** Some words that may have once implied something to the consumer are today so diluted by overuse that they now mean, essentially, nothing. Try for a memorable mark that is, by its verbal and visual content, distinctive.

Who can distinguish one "NATIONAL" company from another? Think of ACE, ACME, BEST, CONSOLIDATED, EXCELSIOR, FEDERATED, PREFERRED, etc. Verbal elements like this will sink without a trace in the ocean of mass communication. Design elements of marks can be as mundane—the American flag used as the background for a product name disappears into invisibility in most marks.

IBM®, AAA®, and CBS® are certainly well known and successful trademarks, but before those companies bowed to common usage and adopted and began to use these alternate forms of their names in addition to their more formal names, they were called INTERNATIONAL BUSINESS MACHINES®, the AMERICAN AUTOMO-BILE ASSOCIATION®, and the COLUMBIA BROAD-CASTING SERVICE®. The point is that trademarks comprised of initials really only work when they are derived from actual company names that have been shortened in common parlance. J&T TOWING is, by comparison, a less distinctive mark because no one knows, of course, who "J" and "T" are and were before they were reduced to their initials. The exception to this is acronym marks. Consider MADD® (Mothers Against Drunk Driving), VISTA® (Volunteers In Service To America), and NOW® (National Organization for Women). However, acronyms must be memorable to be good trademarks. This means that they should have some meaning as acronyms that relates to the cause or goals or product characteristics of what they name. Only the most talented marketing people can create acronym marks that are not strained or obscure.

The same goes for numbers. There are well-known number marks, but their fame may attest to the excellence of the products they name rather than to the memorability of the marks. FORMULA 409® and X-14® have established profiles in the market as names for household cleaning products, maybe because they are advertised widely. You would do less well with "1234 BAR-B-Q SAUCE," however, especially if you didn't have the money to advertise and distribute it nationally.

11. **Misspell it in an engaging way.** Every kid—and parent—knows TOYS "R" US® (even though the company will never win an award for grammar and it is impossible to render the backwards R correctly using an ordinary font). JELL-O® is a fractured form of "gelatin." NYTOL® is a creative rendering of "Night, all." And L'EGGS® is a "French" form of "legs."

    Marks that are spelled in unusual ways can be memorable because they approach the novelty of coined marks. However, there is nothing more old hat than a too-cute misspelling used as a brand name. No examples of these marks are necessary. You can see them in any grocery store. And don't let your enthusiasm for your clever misspelling lead you to choose a name that is hard to understand, to spell, or to say. A good recent example of a difficult trademark is VAIO® for computers. It means nothing in particular, which isn't necessarily bad, but how do you spell it and how do you say it? And the stylized typeface in which the name is rendered is cool looking but not immediately obvious as English-language letters. Sony should have gone back to the drawing board on this. Your product may be so popular that no one cares that it is hard to spell or write—it happens, but usually only after a lot of heavy lifting from the marketing departments that get stuck with them.

12. **Choose a name that can become an Internet address.** You've lost half the battle if your new trademark can't become an identical Internet address. This criterion was once of *some* importance. It is now critical for the success of any product or service marketed to

113

consumers. Determine early in the selection process whether a proposed mark is available as a domain name; if it's unavailable, abandon it as a possibility. Aside from the unavailability of the domain name you want, you face the potential for infringing the rights of whoever already owns the domain name if you adopt a similar mark. (You can read more about trademarks in cyberspace in chapter 10.) You can check the availability of a domain name through any Internet registrar. And remember that having to insert an extra word or so in order to secure a domain name is like having two names in any context—confusing for anyone who must remember which name applies when.

New Protection for Famous Marks

Owners of famous trademarks gained substantial new protection from the federal Trademark Dilution Act of 1995, which was signed into law by the president and became effective in January of 1996. The act formalizes and makes a part of the federal trademark statute a principle of trademark law that had been available as a ground for suit in only about half the states. It allows the owners of an existing "famous" trademark to ask the court to enjoin the use of the same mark by another company—even if there is no likelihood of confusion between the marks—on the ground that the defendant's use of the mark, even for noncompeting goods or services, "dilutes" the distinctive quality of the famous mark. This allows the owners of truly famous marks to stop the use of their marks by the marketers of noncompeting goods and services as well as by competitors.

One of the first lawsuits brought under the new act was initiated by Hasbro, Inc., which owns the trademark CANDY LAND® for the famous children's board game, against a company that had adopted the domain name *candyland. com* for a sexually explicit website. Hasbro was successful in having the domain name enjoined on the basis that its use would dilute the strength of the CANDY LAND mark. Other, similar cases have followed. One example is the suit brought by Federal Express to halt the use of FEDERAL ESPRESSO as the name of a Syracuse coffeehouse.

The act defines "dilution" as "the lessening of the capacity of a famous mark to identify and distinguish goods or services, regardless of the presence or absence of 1) competition between the owner of the famous mark and other parties, or 2) likelihood of confusion, mistake, or deception." Although most really famous marks are registered in the U.S. Patent and Trademark Office, federal registration is not a prerequisite for protection of a mark under the act, which protects registered and unregistered marks equally, given an equal degree of fame.

The Trademark Dilution Act enumerates several factors to be considered in evaluating whether the mark owned by a plaintiff in a suit under the act really is distinctive and famous enough to be protected under its provisions. These include the following:

1. the degree of inherent or acquired distinctiveness of the "famous" mark;
2. the duration and extent of use of the "famous" mark;
3. the duration and extent of advertising and publicity for the "famous" mark;
4. the geographical extent of the trading area in which the "famous" mark is used;
5. the channels of trade through which the product or service named by the "famous" mark is sold;
6. the degree of recognition of the "famous" mark in the trading areas and channels of trade used by both the

owner of the "famous mark" and the defendant against whom the injunction is sought;

7. the nature and extent of any use by third parties of marks that are the same as or similar to the "famous mark"; and

8. whether the owner of the "famous" mark has a valid federal registration.

These factors are not exclusive; that is, they are specifically not the only factors that may be considered.

For most trademark owners, the Trademark Dilution Act will not offer any more protection than the federal trademark statute offered before the new act was passed. This is understandable; very few marks can hope to reach the level of fame required to trigger protection from trademark dilution under the new law. For an understanding of the sort of fame that courts are likely to require before invoking the penalties of the new law, we have only to look to the LEXIS® case, decided not long before the new act was passed. The manufacturer of the automobile LEXUS® was sued by the owners of the online legal research service LEXIS on the ground of dilution. LEXIS lost. The court held that LEXIS was not well-known enough outside the legal community to have suffered dilution at the hands of the automobile manufacturer.

In other words, the sort of fame necessary to support a claim of trademark dilution is what used to be known as becoming "a household word." When the great majority of consumers are aware of a mark and the products or services it names, it is "famous" in the sense meant by the Trademark Dilution Act. If only some people are aware of the mark, or if almost everyone in a certain profession or industry is aware of it but practically no one outside that group is, the mark has not (yet) achieved the degree of fame necessary to command this very broad protection under the law.

Most marketers need only remember that a long-standing guideline for trademark selection is even more important since the passage of the Trademark Dilution Act. "Stay away from famous marks" is better advice than ever. Now owners of famous marks have a more direct and powerful way to stop you from naming your motor oil COORS® or your new detergent CLEAN-X (KLEENEX®).

The statute specifies several legitimate uses of famous trademarks that will not create any liability under the law. These exclusions from the proscriptions of the act are a response to legitimate First Amendment concerns. The Trademark Dilution Act expressly exempts:

1. fair use of a mark in comparative advertising;
2. parody, satire, editorial commentary, and other noncommercial uses of a mark; and
3. any form of news reporting or commentary that mentions a mark.

(See chapter 9 for a more detailed discussion of the use of trademarks that belong to others.)

Chapter 5
Trademark Protection

Once you have settled on a mark, chosen from a list you or your ad agency proposed after careful consideration of the aforementioned dreaded Ten Deadly Sins of Trademark Selection, and have conducted a full trademark search to determine whether the mark is available for use, the next step is the registration of the trademark. Every trademark wants to be registered after it is born. There are two options for trademark registration, state trademark registration and federal trademark registration.

State Trademark Registration

We will consider state trademark registration only briefly, for two reasons. First, state trademark registration offers much less protection to a mark than federal registration. Second, state registrations do not involve nearly so many rules and regulations as federal registrations and are usually easy to obtain.

You can almost certainly handle state registration of your trademark without a lawyer. The first thing to do is to call or write the trademark department of the state in which you want to register your mark. (State trademark departments are usually part of the secretary of state's office; you can find links to these state agencies at www.uspto.gov/trademarks/process/State_Trademark_Links.jsp.) Request a printed trademark registration form, print it from the state's website, or fill it in online. Carefully read the form and the accompanying instructions, fill in the blanks, sign it, send it back with the proper application fee (fees vary from state to state; most are less than a hundred dollars) and with the specimens of use of the mark required. You will have to specify in what class of goods or services you want to register your mark. The state in which you apply for registration will specify this list of categories, which may be identical to the one that the U.S. Trademark Office uses.

All the states have some sort of trademark statute; most are based on a model trademark statute. The provisions of state trademark statutes largely echo those of the federal statute. However, the federal trademark statute only applies to trademarks that are used in interstate commerce. The state statutes are designed to regulate the use of trademarks and protect the rights of trademark owners within each state.

Although some states offer more protection to trademark registrants than others, it is never a bad idea to apply for and secure a state registration for your trademark. Among other benefits, state trademark registration:

- documents your ownership of your mark before you have used it in interstate commerce and are able to apply for federal registration;

- offers protection against infringement within the state where your mark is used; and
- causes your mark to show up in the trademark search reports other people commission.

You can apply for state trademark registration only in the state or states where you are *currently* using the mark. As with federal registration, "use" of a mark in a specified territory is defined as the offering for sale of the product to which the mark is applied or the advertising of and readiness to offer the services the mark names. The difference is that you may apply for state trademark registration based on your use of a mark *within* a state; federal trademark registration requires use of the mark in *interstate* commerce.

A good strategy is to apply for state registration for your mark as soon as you begin using it. This may be before you have begun to use the mark in interstate commerce or concurrent with your use of the mark in interstate commerce. You should file a federal use-based application or intent-to-use application at the same time. File to register the mark in every state where you are using it; apply to register your mark in additional states when you expand your use of your mark to those states. This plan will give you as much protection as possible as early in the life of your mark as possible, at the lowest possible cost.

Most state trademark registrations endure for ten years, but some last for only five. As with federal registrations, you must renew state registrations prior to the expiration of the initial term of registration. If you have secured federal registration for your mark since filing for state registration and the federal registration is current and in effect at the end of the initial term of state registration, you can safely let your state registration lapse, since a federal registration offers much broader protection.

Even if your mark is only registered in one or more states, you should be careful to follow the rules for proper use of trademarks discussed in chapter 7. However, *do not* use the ® symbol or any other form of notice that indicates federal trademark registration until and unless your mark is registered federally. Ignoring this restriction on the use of notice of federal registration can seriously damage your right to stop infringers or later register your mark with the U.S. Trademark Office. Use the ™ (or ᔆᴹ) symbol freely; neither has any legal effect but can act a "no trespassing" signs. However, be sure to stay away from the ® symbol unless you have earned the right to use it by virtue of having been granted a federal registration—that is, a trademark registration granted by the U.S. Trademark Office.

Federal Trademark Registration

Any company that is serious enough about a new mark to spend any time or money developing it and clearing it for use will want to file as soon as possible for federal trademark registration, which means registration of the trademark in the U.S. Patent and Trademark Office in Washington, D.C. (Ignore the fact that the name of the office includes the word "patent"; the Trademark Office and the Patent Office are entirely separate government departments that were mistakenly joined at the hip by a Congress that got confused and thought that they had something to do with each other.) The Constitution gives Congress the mandate to regulate interstate commerce. In the federal trademark statute, the Federal Trademark Act of 1946 (also called the Lanham Act), Congress gave to the U.S. Patent and Trademark Office, as a division of the Department of Commerce, the power to regulate the registration of trademarks that are used in interstate commerce or commerce between the United States and another country. The Trademark Office consists of several divisions, each of which handles a different function; most trademark owners will be concerned with only one of the various offices that reviews, or "examines," applications to ascertain whether registration will be granted—the office that examines applications for the particular goods or services that the trademark owner offers under its trademark.

There are now two types of federal trademark registration: 1) the use-based application, which is based on current use of the trademark in interstate or international commerce, and 2) the intent-to-use application, which is based on a "bona fide intent" to use the mark in interstate or international commerce. At one time, every U.S. trademark application was based on current use of the mark; since a change in the law, this is no longer the case.

Use-Based Applications

There are several requisite elements for a use-based federal trademark registration application. These include the following: the written application in proper form; a "drawing" sheet, on which the mark is reproduced according to the Trademark Office's specifications; your declaration, made under penalty of perjury, that you believe that you (or your company) own your mark and are entitled to register it; a date of first use of the mark anywhere; a date of first use of the mark in interstate or international commerce; a description of the goods or services marketed under your mark; specimens of ads, packaging, labels, etc., proving your use of your mark; and the proper filing fee, which is (at this writing) $325 per class of goods or services for an electronic filing or $375 for a paper application.

When your registration application is received by the Trademark Office, it is preliminarily reviewed for its sufficiency as an application, i.e., whether it includes all the components necessary to allow the examination process to proceed, and is given a serial number. (If you have omitted one or more important elements of your application, you will be notified.) This serial number remains the way the application is identified throughout the process of examination to ascertain whether a trademark will be granted. After assignment of a serial number, your registration application is forwarded to the correct law office within the examining section of the Trademark Office and is assigned to an examining attorney.

The Trademark Office classifies all goods and services according to the International Schedule of Classes of Goods and Services. The descriptions of goods and services may seem unfamiliar. For example, the REVERE WARE® trademark for cookware is registered in International Class 11, which includes "apparatus for lighting, heating, steam generating, cooking, refrigerating, drying, ventilating, water supply, and sanitary purposes." The lists of goods registered in other categories are sometimes longer. You can read the International Schedule of Classes of Goods and Services classifying products and services from Chemicals (class 1) to Personal Services (class 45) at the end of the Trademark Office publication *Basic Facts about Trademarks*, reproduced as Appendix B at the end of this book along with notes about just what is and is not included in any given class. Read the list to figure out where your product or service would be classified and what products or services fall into the same class. You may not think that personal deodorants and scouring powder belong in the same class, but the Trademark Office does and it will deny your application to register FRESHEN for a new antiperspirant if it already has a registration for FRESHEN for a bathroom cleaner.

The Trademark Office examining offices are numbered: Law Office 1, Law Office 2, etc. Each law office handles all the applications made in the classes of goods or services assigned to that office. Each application is handled by one examiner, who is a lawyer, according to the provisions of the Trademark Manual of Examining Procedure (TMEP). The examining procedures are logical and are designed to carry out the intent of the Lanham Act, but the logic of examiners' decisions is not always apparent to applicants. If you are curious, you can read the TMEP—even download it—at http://tess2.uspto.gov/tmdb/tmep/. Any correspondence between the trademark examining attorney and your own trademark attorney will refer to a specific section of the TMEP for every action taken by the Trademark Office.

Other than a communication that notifies them of the serial numbers assigned to their applications, most applicants will receive no word from the Trademark Office for several months. (The progress of a use-based application to register a trademark will follow, more or less, the timeline set out at www.uspto.gov/trademarks/process/tm_sec1atimeline.jsp on the Trademark Office website.) The first substantive communication you receive after filing will be from the examining attorney who has been assigned your application file; this may be an Office Action or a Notice of Publication. An Office Action will either reject your application for registration or will ask you to furnish more information or correct or clarify statements made in the application. A Notice of Publication will notify you that your mark will be "published for opposition," which means that it will be published so that other trademark owners will know that your mark is being considered for registration.

It is an extremely common occurrence that an examiner will, at least initially, reject an application on one or more bases.

The simplest is that the examiner points out a small technical problem with the form of the application and suggests a small change in the language of the application to correct some technicality, such as asking for a clarification of the description of goods or services named by the mark; sometimes this sort of small amendment can be authorized by the applicant's attorney in a phone call to the examiner.

A more difficult sort of rejection to overcome is a substantive rejection based on the failure of the mark to meet one or more of the legal requirements for registration. Substantive rejections are commonly based on the trademark examiner's decision that a mark embodies one of the statutory grounds for denial of registration. For example, the most common reason for refusing registration is a likelihood of confusion between the applicant mark and an already registered mark or one that is the subject of a prior application. The examining attorney will search the USPTO database to determine whether there are any marks that are likely to cause confusion with your mark. The principal factors considered by the examining attorney in determining whether there would be a likelihood of confusion are:

- the similarity of the marks; and
- the commercial relationship (e.g., channels of trade or class of purchasers) between the goods/services listed in the application and those listed in the registration or pending application.

The marks do *not* have to be identical and the goods/services they name do not have to be the same in order to conflict. It may be enough that the marks are *similar* and the goods/services are *related*. (See the Ten Deadly Sins of Trademark Selection in chapter 4 for the entire list of statutory grounds for rejection of an application.) The reason or reasons for the rejection will be described, and one or more Trademark Office rules or court decisions in trademark cases will be cited to support the examiner's rejection of the application. Whatever the examiner's objections, the applicant has six months to respond to the rejection. Such responses answer questions the examiner may have raised and present counterarguments to the grounds cited for rejection of the application, as well as amending the application to clear up technical problems. Even if your application is initially rejected on a substantive ground, it is possible to persuade the examiner that registration should be granted. However, this can be difficult or impossible, depending on the ground for rejection. Further, this is not a do-it-yourself job.

Like all documents filed with the Trademark Office in the process of pursuing a registration, responses to rejections must fulfill strict requirements in order to suffice. Filing an application to register a trademark is like appearing in a regular court and asking the judge to rule in your favor. The applicant states that he or she believes the mark that is the subject of the application is entitled to registration under the law, presents evidence sufficient to prove that to the Trademark Office, and answers questions and presents arguments to support the granting of the registration. These are difficult procedures that take lawyers years to master. Even an application that is eventually granted can require several carefully composed replies to the Trademark Office.

If, even after your lawyer presents arguments to overcome the examiner's denial of registration, your application is "finally" rejected by the examiner, there are several courses open to you. You can simply abandon your effort to register your mark, which will not affect whatever rights you have or will gain in it. You can file an appeal with the Trademark Trial and Appeal Board, which is a complicated formal undertaking somewhat like appealing an ordinary court case after an adverse verdict of the trial court. Or you can amend your application to ask that registration be granted on the Supplemental Register rather than the Principal Register (see the discussion below for an explanation of the difference between the two types of registration).

If your application is not rejected or if you overcome the examiner's initial rejection of your application, the trademark examiner is satisfied that your trademark is entitled to registration. Your trademark will then be subjected to the next step in the process of qualifying for registration. It is "published for opposition." This means that your mark is reproduced (in the case of purely verbal marks, this means only that it is printed to show its exact verbal content) in the *Official Gazette for Trademarks*, which is published weekly. (You can view the last fifty-two weeks of the *Official Gazette for Trademarks* at www.uspto.gov/news/og/trademark_og/index.jsp.) Anyone who believes that registration of your mark will harm him or her has thirty days to file an objection to the registration, called an "opposition." Many opposition proceedings are settled; some are fought hard through the Trademark Office's in-house court, called the Trademark Trial and Appeal Board. If no one objects to the granting of your registration within the prescribed period, the Trademark Office will issue a certificate of registration about three months after your mark is published. If the Trademark Office has to be talked into granting your registration application or if someone opposes your application, the registration process can literally take years. The Trademark Office moves slowly; even applications that encounter no big problems routinely take year or eighteen months to result in a registration.

There are two varieties of federal trademark registrations: an applicant may be granted a registration on either the Principal Register or the Supplemental Register. Principal Register registrations bestow the most benefits and are the goal of every federal trademark applicant. (When the term "federal registration" is used in this book, registration on the Principal Register is meant.) However, if a mark is unable to qualify for the Principal Register, a Supplemental Register registration also has its uses. Most marks on the Supplemental Register are descriptive, surname, or geographic marks that do not yet function as trademarks in the eyes of the Trademark Office. That is, they do not point to *one* source for the goods or services they name because they are not distinctive and have not yet acquired the degree of fame necessary to result in "secondary meaning." Marks registered on the Supplemental Register are entitled to use the ® notice of registration and gain some benefits of federal registration, such as access to federal courts, and are presumed, after a period of five years, to have gained enough fame to qualify for an upgrade (upon request by the registrant) to the Principal Register.

Intent-to-Use Applications

Once upon a time in America, it was necessary for trademark owners to have used their trademarks in interstate commerce before applying for federal trademark registration, and trademark rights began to accrue from the date a trademark owner actually began to use a mark in the marketplace. However, it is now possible for a trademark owner to apply for registration before actually beginning to use the new trademark, so long as the trademark owner has a "bona fide intent" to begin to use the mark in interstate commerce within six months of the date the registration application is filed. (The period of time for beginning use of the mark may be extended, in six-month increments and upon making the proper filings, to a total period of thirty-six months.) Registration may then be granted after use of the mark is made in interstate commerce.

This system of registration represents a big change in the law. It is not quite the same as the system that exists in certain European countries, which allows marketers to "reserve" a trademark for use before actually adopting it, but it is close, since now U.S. companies can put everyone on notice that they intend to use a mark before they actually do so. This change should eliminate the situation that formerly existed, where two companies that had to begin using their new marks before applying for trademark registration began to use the same mark for similar products—each discovering the existence of the other only upon filing their applications, after they had expended the time and money necessary to launch their new marks. In this situation, only one of the two companies could end up owning and registering the mark—the company that began using it first.

Now, when a company files an intent-to-use application to register a mark, stating that it will begin using the mark within six months, its intentions become part of the official records maintained by the Trademark Office and are included in the data searched by trademark search firms. This means that when a second company conducts a search to ascertain the availability of the mark, the first company's application for that mark, indicating that it has already "staked a claim" to the mark, will appear in the search report and warn the second company away from the mark.

Intent-to-use applications confer one other benefit on trademark owners that was not formerly available: when a registration is eventually granted to an intent-to-use applicant, the date of the applicant trademark owner's rights in the mark is deemed by the new rules to commence from the filing date of the application to register, rather than just from the date of the applicant's first actual use of the mark. This means that early filing of a trademark registration application can now give additional months or even years of ownership rights, on the front end of the ownership period, to a trademark owner who had not even begun to use the mark on the date of filing.

All this complicated stuff boils down to this for business-people: you should know that it is possible to file for federal trademark registration just as soon as a full trademark search has cleared a new mark for use. Speed is important because the earlier the date of filing, the sooner ownership rights in the mark will, eventually, be deemed to have begun. In addition, early filing removes some of the danger that two companies will be competing for registration and ownership of the same mark.

Intent-to-use applications require essentially the same components as use-based applications. However, instead of a declaration that the mark that is the subject of the application was first used in interstate commerce on a certain date, the statement in an intent-to-use application is that the applicant has a bona fide intent to use the mark for the goods or services specified. Further, there is no requirement that specimens of use of the mark be furnished until the applicant is able to file a "Statement of Use" attesting to the fact that the mark has begun to be used in interstate commerce.

Maintaining Your Registration

Federal trademark registrations endure for a term of ten years. However, because all trademark rights are based on use of the mark, between the fifth and sixth anniversaries of the date a registration is granted, the registrant must formally attest to continuing use of the mark by filing an affidavit describing that use and furnish a new specimen of use of the mark. Further, at the end of the initial ten-year registration period, but no sooner than six months prior to the end of the period, you may file to renew your registration. You may renew the registration for your mark at ten-year intervals as many times as you want, so long as you continue to use the mark. In theory, a trademark can live in perpetuity in the marketplace. There are some trademarks that are still active after a hundred years or more of service in commerce.

Apply at Your Own Risk

It is one thing to know that federal trademark registration is desirable and to know something about the registration process, but filing for federal trademark registration is, like searching a trademark (other than a screening search, which you can conduct yourself) to clear it for use, not a do-it-yourself project. The Trademark Office allows trademark owners to file their own applications for registration, without the help of a lawyer, but satisfying the complicated filing requirements imposed by the Trademark Office is not easy and filing without the help of a trademark lawyer is likely to result in the rejection of the application.

This is what the Trademark Office says on its website about hiring a trademark attorney:

> For advice about trademarks and the USPTO registration process, you should consider hiring a private trademark attorney (not associated with the USPTO) to help you. Although [hiring an attorney is] not required, most applicants use private trademark attorneys for legal advice regarding use of their trademark, filing an application, and the likelihood of success in the registration process, since not all applications proceed to registration.

A private attorney may save you from future costly legal problems by conducting a comprehensive search of federal registrations, state registrations, and "common law" unregistered trademarks. Other trademark owners may have protected legal rights in trademarks similar to yours that are not federally registered; therefore, those trademarks will not appear in the USPTO's Trademark Electronic Search System (TESS) database.

A private attorney can also assist in the policing and enforcement of your trademark rights. The USPTO only *registers* [emphasis added] trademarks. You as the trademark owner are responsible for any enforcement.

The Trademark Office now prefers the electronic filing of trademark registration applications rather than the paper applications that were formerly the norm, so it may seem that filing for trademark registration is easier than ever. (Go to the Trademark Office home page at www.uspto.gov/trademarks/index.jsp and click on "TEAS" in the dark blue box on the left to see the beginning page for the Trademark Electronic Application System (TEAS).) Reading the *Basic Facts about Trademarks* publication in Appendix B will also give you an idea of what the registration application process entails. Remember that with electronic filing, as with paper applications, it is hard for an applicant, without the advice and help of a trademark lawyer, to create an application that will not present obstacles to the registration process. A trademark registration application is not a long or complicated form, but what is said and where is important and unless you understand the rules and reasons behind each representation you make on an application, it is very likely that your application will be denied, for one or several reasons. Lawyers do have their uses; filing for trademark registration is one of them.

However, for the brave, you can now file for registration online or print out forms to file a paper application. Directions for filling out registration applications are included with each question on the registration form and in *Basic Facts about Trademarks*.

Most experienced trademark lawyers would tell you that filing for federal trademark registration is not a do-it-yourself job. Even if you manage to meet the requirements of the Trademark Office for a registration application, you may still be confronted with the need to keep your application on track by filing a response to some complicated objections to registration raised by the trademark examiner who reviews and evaluates your application. That is, even if you manage to file a proper application without a trademark lawyer, you still may need one, because almost no one who has not done it before can successfully respond to a complicated Trademark Office rejection of an application. Failure to respond will result in the abandonment of your application; failure to respond fully will result in a final rejection of your application.

Federal trademark registration offers several important advantages to trademark owners; among these advantages are:

- A federal registrant has rights in the registered mark superior to anyone else except prior users of the mark.
- The owner of a federally registered trademark is in a much better position to quash infringers than if the mark were not registered, since federal registration offers immediate access to a federal court, where a federal registrant can obtain an injunction with nationwide effect to stop infringers.
- A federal trademark registrant who sues an infringer in federal court may be entitled to recover profits, damages, and court costs, including attorney's fees. In

133

some circumstances, the registrant may be awarded "treble damages," which are damages three times the amount that would ordinarily be awarded.

- Moreover, because a federal registration gives the registrant the benefit of the presumptions that the registrant owns the registered mark and that the registration is valid, registrants who end up in court have a powerful advantage over any challenger who also claims ownership.

- A federal registration serves as "constructive notice" to any subsequent user of the registered mark that the registrant claims ownership of it. In other words, the presence of the registration in the public records of the Trademark Office is presumed to make any other would-be user of the mark aware of prior ownership claims of the registrant. This eliminates any defense raised by an alleged infringer that the mark was adopted in good faith.

- After five years, a registered mark may become "incontestable"; that is, the registration becomes conclusive evidence of the registrant's right to use the mark.

Even better, federal trademark registration helps trademark owners avoid the necessity of bringing suit to stop trademark infringers in two important ways. First, once a trademark is registered in the Trademark Office, any other companies that conduct searches to clear proposed new marks will know that the registered mark is already in use for the goods and services it names and will stay clear of it or any confusingly similar mark. Secondly, even if some company does infringe the mark, it is likely to agree to stop using the mark immediately upon the receipt of a cease and desist letter from the trademark owner's lawyer, since the infringer will know that the owner of the registered mark does, indeed, have the clout to prevent the continued infringing use of the mark. These circumstances have the effect of stopping trademark infringement lawsuits at the optimum time—before they start.

International Protection

The Protocol Relating to the Madrid Agreement Concerning the International Registration of Marks (Madrid Protocol) is one of two international treaties that allow a trademark owner to seek registration in any of the countries (eighty-four as of 2011) that have joined the Madrid Protocol by filing a single application, called an "international application." The International Bureau of the World Intellectual Property Organization in Geneva, Switzerland administers the international registration system. Since late in 2003, a United States trademark owner can submit an international application to the United States Trademark Office for forwarding to the International Bureau in Switzerland. The U.S. Trademark Office does not *grant* the international registration but, rather, certifies the suitability of the application before forwarding it to Geneva. Once the International Bureau registers the mark (a result that is not guaranteed), the International Bureau will notify each country that is a party to the Madrid Protocol and that is designated in the international registration of the request for an extension of protection to that country. Each of these countries will then examine the request for an extension of protection the same as it would a national application under its laws. If the application meets the requirements for registration of that country, then the country will grant protection of the mark in that country. The Madrid Protocol is an efficient way to file for trademark registration, with one application, in multiple countries. U.S. trademark owners can save time and money through this registration mechanism. There are other such systems for trademark protection in multiple countries, but they involve fewer countries.

135

Why do you need to know anything about international trademark protection? Commerce is increasingly international and the commercial efforts of even ordinary citizens can reach into the markets of the world. However, remember that if filing a United States trademark registration application is too tricky for the average businessperson to accomplish successfully, international trademark registration is even more complicated. Remember that international registration is now possible with less effort and expense than formerly and educate yourself, if you wish, to the steps in obtaining such registration, but call your trademark lawyer to guide you through the process of registering your mark through the Madrid Protocol or other international trademark protection systems.

Chapter 6
Trademark Lawyers

In a world where people find their mates through newspaper ads, it is not surprising that businesspeople sometimes select their lawyers from the Yellow Pages. Like marriage, the relationship between lawyer and client is often contracted with too little thought. Of course, your relationship with your lawyer isn't as important as marriage, but when you choose a lawyer to handle a legal matter, you do entrust an important part of your life to him or her for a while. This means that you should use at least as much care in selecting your lawyer as you devoted to buying your last car.

This is especially true with regard to any legal matter related to trademarks. Trademark law is a narrow area of the law about which most lawyers are content to remain ignorant, because it is confusing and sometimes even infuriating and resembles semantics more than it does other areas of the law.

Very few lawyers who do not regularly practice trademark law are competent to handle even the most minor trademark matter. This means that you will need a *trademark* lawyer in any of the following situations:

- when you choose a new trademark;
- when you expand the use of an existing trademark to additional products or services;
- when you file for federal or international trademark registration;
- when you believe that someone is infringing your trademark rights;
- when you are accused of infringing someone else's trademark; or
- when you want to license your trademark to someone else.

And finding a good lawyer means just that—a real, live, licensed attorney who has your interests at heart. This does not mean hiring one of the proliferating Internet "trademark mills," most of which explicitly state that they are not lawyers and do not render legal advice and some of which tell you that they will furnish you (at additional cost) with a trademark lawyer "if necessary." Although you may file a trademark registration application *yourself,* only a lawyer can represent you before the Trademark Office. That means that you will essentially be on your own unless a problem arises and you have to then hire an attorney. These services promise to help you search and register your trademark for low fees. They may perform the services they advertise, but those services may not be sufficient to help you reach your goal: a viable trademark that does not conflict with an established mark and is eligible for federal registration. Internet trademark mills are *not* the equivalent of a knowledgeable and experienced trademark lawyer. If you think they are, read this disclaimer from the website of one of the most prominent trademark mills, LegalZoom:

> Disclaimer: The information provided in this site is not legal advice, but general information on legal issues commonly encountered. LegalZoom is not a law firm and is not a substitute for an attorney or law firm. Communications between you and LegalZoom are protected by our Privacy Policy, but are not protected by the attorney-client privilege or work product doctrine. LegalZoom cannot provide legal advice and can only provide self-help services at your specific direction. Please note that your access to and use of LegalZoom.com is subject to additional terms and conditions. LegalZoom.com, Inc. is a registered and bonded legal document assistant, #0104, Los Angeles County (exp. 12/11) and is located at 101 N. Brand Blvd., 11th Floor, Glendale, CA 91203.

No such "legal document assistant" can help you much if there is any hitch in the registration process and none will help at all if you run up against a conflicting mark. Stay away from Internet trademark-filing services. Look for your own lawyer instead.

The first thing to know about finding a lawyer is that the lawyer referral services offered by local bar associations are practically worthless. These services include many fine lawyers in their listings, but they also include more than a few lawyers who are badly educated, inexperienced, predatory, unethical, or all of the above. This is because these services ordinarily refer callers, on a rotating basis, to lawyers who are members of the bar associations that sponsor them, without attempting to evaluate the abilities of the attorneys who are listed. You may be referred to a lawyer who has signed up for the referral service as a "trademark lawyer," but that is probably the lawyer's own evaluation, so you really won't know how extensively the lawyer has practiced trademark law or what level of competence he or she has reached. In other words, these services really offer no more information to the consumer than the Yellow Pages.

Most bar associations are like clubs; usually, such an association will accept as a member any lawyer who will pay the association's annual dues and is licensed to practice law where the association is located. The fact that a lawyer possesses a license to practice law is *not* enough to ensure that he or she will give you the help you need in handling a particular matter or treat you fairly. A law license means only that the lawyer who holds it graduated from a law school, passed a character review and the bar exam for the state that issued the license, and has not been disbarred since.

There's a big difference between being the kind of lawyer everyone wants to hire and simply avoiding disbarment. A lawyer with a valid law license may have graduated at the bottom of his class from an unaccredited law school and have passed the bar exam only on the third try. She may be inexperienced, inept, ignorant, and disorganized. He may be an alcoholic or a drug addict. She may be dishonest or greedy. However, unless these failings have so harmed a client that the client filed a formal complaint with the licensing body in the state where the lawyer practices and that body found, after investigation, that the lawyer should be suspended or disbarred, he or she can hang a valid law license on the wall and continue to accept new clients.

Another poor method for finding a lawyer is lawyer advertising. Some good lawyers advertise. However, many lawyers who hawk their services through Internet, broadcast, and print advertising run their practices like factories. You are unlikely to get much individual attention from one of these lawyers. And although the content of lawyer advertising is regulated to some extent, ads for lawyers are really no more reliable than any other sort of advertising. And representations made on blogs may be as bad. That is, either an ad or a blog *may* publicize the services of competent, trustworthy lawyers, but there's no way to tell whether they actually do.

Compiling a list of trustworthy, qualified lawyers requires some work, but, after all, either the matter for which you need a trademark lawyer is important enough to approach seriously, with some forethought, or it isn't. If you are not willing to expend the time and effort that such an initial screening process requires, you should reconsider whether you really want to insert a new trademark into interstate commerce or would rather just forget the whole thing. There are several ways to come up with a list of good trademark lawyers; none of them is especially difficult.

Perhaps the best way to find a competent, ethical trademark lawyer is to call a lawyer you know and trust for help. If you already have a relationship with a lawyer you like who doesn't practice trademark law, ask that lawyer to recommend three other lawyers who *are* qualified to help you. Most lawyers within a city know, or can find out, which other lawyers are considered able, honest, and experienced in their fields, even if they are not familiar with the specialized work of those other lawyers. And a lawyer whose client you have been and who you trust is likely to be careful in making such recommendations; in fact, if you ask a lawyer for three or four names and he or she responds with only one or two, he or she is being scrupulous by refusing to refer you to someone about whom he or she knows too little.

The best referral is from a lawyer who personally knows the lawyers to whom he or she refers you. This is because most lawyers will be especially careful of their treatment of a client when they know—or think—their actions are likely to be judged by another lawyer. However, a subclass of lawyer referrals to watch out for is the referral to another lawyer in the same firm. It is very possible that the lawyer to whom you are referred under such circumstances will be a paragon of skill and knowledge. It is also possible that you will be referred to a lawyer in the same firm simply because the referring lawyer is more concerned with the firm's income than with your getting the best possible recommendation. Don't reject such referrals out of hand, but make your own judgments. Nothing obligates you to engage the services of any lawyer to whom you are referred—lawyers speak of "their" clients; in reality, the clients should think of "their" lawyers, because the client is the person who calls the shots, although many lawyers forget this fact of capitalism.

If you don't know a lawyer who can recommend one or more trademark lawyers to you, ask several other people whose opinions you respect for a similar list of lawyers. But don't *only* ask your friends; even if they are true-blue, they may have very little information concerning trademark lawyers. Instead, ask other businesspeople in your town, especially those who own or manage businesses similar to yours. They may have had to solve trademark problems themselves.

Ask three questions of everyone you approach for names of lawyers: 1) "How do you know these lawyers?" 2) "What do you know about them?" and 3) "Why do you think one of them could help me?" Enter the name of any lawyer who is recommended by a reliable source on your master list. After you have three or four names of trademark lawyers, start investigating them.

142

You probably want to hire a trademark lawyer near you. Although it is easier to work with a local lawyer, trademark lawyers are urban creatures and are seldom found outside sizable cities. You may not be able to find one near you. However, since trademark practice is mostly a matter of specialized paperwork, it is likely that you can successfully manage your lawyer's work on the phone and by email. It is also possible that you will need to hire a lawyer in the same locale as that where suit has been brought against you or where you want to sue someone else. The matter of venue in trademark lawsuits is influenced by several factors, so if you are involved in a trademark dispute, one of your first questions to any lawyer you interview is whether he or she is located and licensed in the right place to defend or bring a suit for you. Any trademark lawyer can handle trademark searches and registrations or other matters in the Trademark Office in Washington, D.C., from anywhere in the United States. This means that a trademark lawyer you hire to advise you in these matters can live near you or in another city altogether—it really doesn't matter.

Your primary tool for investigating the lawyers recommended to you is Martindale.com. This is a free online lawyer-locator service; listings are organized by lawyer name, law firm name, area of practice, and state and city. This database is very reliable and complete; any lawyer who is actively engaged in practice in the United States will be listed in the Martindale.com database. Lawyers use the Martindale.com database to investigate their adversaries. But there's no reason you can't use it, too. The Martindale.com database is not the best *starting* place for someone in search of a lawyer. However, it is a very good place to gather information on lawyers.

When you go to the Martindale.com home page, you can search by entering just the lawyer's name at the top left of the page or by filling in one or several of the blanks in the "Advanced Search" form that appears on the page. When you click "search," you'll be taken to listings that match your search terms. The listing for each lawyer will tell you something about that lawyer. Look especially for the "peer-review rating" for any lawyer—a high rating is the sign of a very good lawyer. You can choose to email the lawyer by hitting the "contact now" button on the search results page, but a better practice is to simply call the lawyer directly, leaving a message that you are considering hiring that lawyer and want a brief phone consultation. All but the busiest lawyers will return your call or have an associate call. If the lawyer you call doesn't call back, move to the next lawyer on your list of recommendations.

If you want to search by practice area, first specify a city or a state on the Advanced Search form as the geographical area for your search. Under the "practice area" question, select "choose from a list" and then select "trademarks (all)." You'll end up with a list of trademark lawyers in your area. Look for names on this list that match your recommendations, then click on the lawyer's name for more information about him or her.

When you access the Martindale.com website, plan to spend an hour researching the lawyers on your master list and printing out their listings. Take your time. You're on a mission to perfect and protect your trademark, potentially one of the most valuable assets of your business, or to avoid being bested by the plaintiff who is suing you or the defendant you want to go after.

There is one other good online resource for finding trademark lawyers, though the information given is more limited. This is a publication called *Intellectual Property Today,* which publishes the results of an annual survey called Top Trademark

Firms. Go to the home page (www.iptoday.com/) of this publication, which is geared toward patent and trademark professionals, and click on the heading in the upper left-hand corner of the page: "2012 [etc.] Top Trademark Firms." You will be taken to a PDF-format list of names of the top twenty-five trademark law firms; you can buy the whole list for twenty-five dollars. Compare your list of recommended lawyers with the *Intellectual Property Today* list of "Top Trademark Firms."

Remember, though, that you don't have to hire one of the top trademark firms in the country in order to get good service from a trademark lawyer—what you most need is competent advice regarding your trademark concerns at a reasonable price and with reasonable convenience. However, finding that one of the trademark lawyers or firms you have been considering was voted one of the top trademark firms in the country by a group of trademark professionals (other lawyers, business executives, etc.) is a reliable indication that you will be in good, if perhaps costly, hands with that lawyer or firm. This is also a very good place to look if you want to file an infringement suit or if, heaven forfend, you have to defend one—litigation may take all the muscle you can hire to help you.

After you do your online research, you're ready for the next step in finding a trademark lawyer—the screening interview.

Employment Interviews

Clients often forget that their lawyers need them just as much as they need their lawyers. The practice of law is, after all, a way of earning a living. Almost any lawyer, given an appropriate case, will accept you as a client and be grateful for the fees your legal problem creates. This means that you should recognize your first meeting with each of the lawyers on your list of prospective lawyers for what it is, an employment interview.

You won't be the only employer of the lawyer you hire, but you will be *an* employer of that attorney and should expect to be treated like the prospective source of revenue that you are.

The first thing to do is call for an appointment with each of the lawyers on your master list of prospects. (You should have narrowed your list to two or three lawyers by now.) When you call, make sure that you mention two things to the people who answer the phone: 1) that you are a prospective client and 2) that you have been referred to the lawyer you are calling. These statements will get most of the lawyers you call to the phone. You can probably eliminate some of your prospective attorneys from consideration on the basis of these initial phone calls. If you like the sound of a lawyer during your first phone call to him or her, ask for a brief in-person interview. It may seem to you that it would be more efficient to interview the lawyers on your list by telephone (and geography may dictate this), but you'll find out more about them and get a better feel for which one you want to hire if you visit their offices.

Any lawyer you call, or the lawyer's secretary, will tell you at the time you make the appointment whether there will be a charge for this initial consultation meeting. Don't interpret a fee for your first meeting as a sign that the lawyer who charges it is not for you. It is likely that any lawyer with whom you meet will give you some useful advice during the course of the meeting and, in any event, lawyers make money by selling their labor by the hour and some of the best charge for *every* hour they work. However, just as many good lawyers do not charge for initial meetings, regarding such meetings as a necessary predicate to a new client relationship rather than actual billable time.

Your screening interviews should be both short enough to be efficient and long enough to determine the answers to a few basic questions.

If you are involved in any conflict between two marks, it may be inevitable that your dispute will ripen into a lawsuit. Any lawyer who practices trademark law should be able to help you clear a new mark, file to register it, and use it properly. However, not all trademark lawyers have significant experience in trademark litigation, especially if they have been in practice only a few years. This means that you should hire a lawyer who has the ability to represent you in litigation or, at least, one who can call on the more extensive litigation experience of another lawyer in the same firm.

And although you should arm yourself for war, your goal should be a treaty; that is, you should try to settle any dispute on a satisfactory basis before it becomes a lawsuit. Litigation should be avoided because its costs so often outweigh its benefits, even for plaintiffs who prevail in court. To ensure that you will be able to achieve the results you want with as little expenditure of time and money as possible, you will want to hire an attorney who is open to the idea of settling your dispute without full-fledged litigation. Because litigators, like surgeons, often see the most extreme remedy available as the only one, you should also ask what success any lawyer you interview has had in settling disputes out of court, either by means of settlement agreements negotiated between lawyers or through some variety of alternative dispute resolution. Remember Ambrose Bierce's definition of litigation: "A machine which you go into as a pig and come out of as a sausage."

After you briefly describe the matter with which you need help, you should ask each lawyer you interview for a brief preliminary assessment of your chances of success. Pay attention to their answers; lawyers learn to make pretty reliable judgments even in on-the-spot evaluations. And remember that if a lawyer tells you that your mark is unregistrable or infringes another mark or that you are not likely to prevail in a dispute or lawsuit, he or she is obligated to give an honest opinion. You can do whatever you like with the information, but no lawyer can tailor an opinion just to tell you what you want to hear.

Besides what you can learn about a lawyer from the Martindale.com website, there are several other indicators that you will be pleased with an attorney. Keep the following guidelines in mind when you interview the lawyers you consider hiring.

Remember that many of the best lawyers do not practice in big firms with luxurious offices in ritzy buildings. Before you are too impressed by a lawyer's fancy office, remember that it is the clients of that lawyer who pay for the oriental rugs and original art.

Remember, too, that the standards for membership in most bar associations are lenient; i.e., any lawyer who is licensed in the locality for which the bar association is organized and will pay the requisite dues can become a member. This means that a lawyer's memberships in his or her local, state, and national bar associations mean very little as far as establishing whether he or she is the better-than-average attorney you want to hire. Lots of the framed certificates indicating membership in organizations with fancy names that you may see in the offices of the lawyers you interview mean absolutely nothing to you as a consumer of legal services. However, certificates that indicate further training past law school or certification by some national association show, at least, a lawyer who is concerned with keeping current and developing the abilities necessary to adequately represent his or her clients.

Pay attention to the support staff you see in each lawyer's office. Past a point, it is immaterial to most people who need a lawyer's services whether the lawyer commands a platoon of secretaries, paralegals, and associates, since no client except a big corporation that needs mountains of paperwork churned out before next Wednesday is likely to need the services of all those other people. However, a good secretary, a skilled paralegal, or a sharp associate can make a client's life easier and diminish legal fees by making or returning phone calls that would otherwise be billed by the lawyer and handling—without charge or at a reduced rate—the more routine work performed for a client. Ask any lawyer you interview which other people in the firm would be working on your case and what their qualifications are. Try to meet these people before you terminate the interview. Give the lawyer points for friendly, intelligent subordinates who look and act like professionals.

Even if you are impressed with an attorney after your meeting, don't hire him or her on the spot. Most successful lawyers are skilled at selling themselves to prospective clients; an honest lawyer won't make promises he or she can't keep, but you should make allowances for the mild sales pitch any lawyer who is interested in your business will make, if for no other reason than that lawyer enthusiasm has been known to wane after a client has been "landed"—like a fish. This means that you should give yourself time to reflect on the substance of your meetings with the lawyers on your list and to compare your impressions of all of them and their evaluations of your trademark problem. The bigger the problem, the longer you should consider how to handle it and who should help you. Even if you like a particular lawyer, things may look different after you meet with the next one.

Give yourself at least a week for your round of interview meetings. Your time and money will be well spent. By the time your meetings are completed, you will have had the advantage of the preliminary opinions of several lawyers about the cost of the work you need help with or your chances of success in settling or winning your dispute and will be considerably more educated about the issues involved. You will also have completed a crash course in Lawyers and Their Habitats.

When you make up your mind which lawyer you want to hire, call that lawyer to tell him or her that you want to engage his or her services. If you didn't like any of the lawyers you interviewed enough to hire one of them, repeat your research and start interviewing again. If you are faced with any matter that is too complicated for you to handle or settle on your own, it is important to get the right lawyer to help you, since the wrong one may be no help at all or even impede your progress toward your goals.

After you have hired a lawyer, you must know how to recognize common failings of lawyers to protect yourself against them. Regrettably, lawyers, as a class, are subject to most of the failings to which the rest of humankind is prey. Since lawyers are only human, you may never find one who doesn't displease you in some way. However, because lawyers *are* human, put up with your lawyer's foibles if his or her work is good and he or she seems truly concerned with your best interests. Good lawyers share most, if not all, the following characteristics.

Eight Signs of a Good Lawyer

1. **Your lawyer returns your phone calls promptly.** Lawyers are like dentists; they are paid only for the work they perform. This means that your lawyer tries to turn every moment of the workday into billable time and that he or she probably really is "on the phone" or "in a meeting" or "in court" when you call. Moreover, as a time management technique, many lawyers never *take* telephone calls but, rather, return their calls only during the periods of the

day they set aside for *making* calls. Don't be offended if you can't get your lawyer on the line every time you call.

However, pay attention and complain if your lawyer does not get back to you promptly. "Promptly" usually means a return call the same day you call. It certainly means a return call within twenty-four hours. It also means that your lawyer's secretary will call to let you know that your lawyer is traveling or otherwise unavailable if he or she cannot call you back within twenty-four hours.

2. **Your lawyer keeps you informed.** One of a lawyer's more important duties to his or her clients is to keep them well informed of the progress and status of the matters they entrust to him or her. Lawyers are simply skilled agents who act on behalf of their clients only to the extent that those clients direct and authorize them to do so. Therefore, the entire lawyer-client relationship is premised on the assumption that the client will be kept informed by the lawyer. This means that you should receive copies of any trademark searches conducted for you, any Trademark Office filings and correspondence, all of your lawyer's substantive communications with your adversary's attorney, and any documents such as court filings, depositions, responses to interrogatories, etc., as well as an occasional phone call or update letter. No important transaction should occur without your prior knowledge and consent.

This does not mean that your lawyer must check with you every time he or she picks up the phone or writes a letter, but, rather, that he or she should act only within mutually agreed parameters. If your lawyer seems to have forgotten that he or she works for *you*, complain about it. If he or she doesn't reform after your complaint, get another lawyer.

3. **Your lawyer keeps commitments.** Every lawyer must reschedule a meeting or ask for an extension of a deadline occasionally, but there is no excuse short of being hospitalized or stuck in a blizzard that will suffice to explain away a lawyer's missing an important deadline or failing to show up for a meeting, deposition, or court appearance. Lawyers who miss deadlines and can't be relied on to show up when they say they will lose the respect of other lawyers and of judges, their credibility is damaged, and, consequently, they may be less able to successfully negotiate on your behalf. You can lose important rights because of your lawyer's disinterest, disorganization, or overbooking.

   If your lawyer misses (as opposed to rescheduling) any important commitment without a really good reason, view him or her as an unexploded hand grenade; that is, get as far away from him or her as possible, as soon as possible, to avoid the injury that *will* result from his or her inability or unwillingness to handle your business carefully.

4. **Your lawyer follows your instructions.** The word "attorney" means simply "agent." Lawyers stand in the place of their clients and speak and act for them only to the extent that they are authorized to do so. Any lawyer who loses sight of this fact has ceased to act as an agent for her or his clients and has become, at least potentially, a loose cannon. Don't expect a lawyer who views you only as a vehicle for exercising his or her bag of professional tricks to miraculously change. Cut your losses and find an attorney who will take instruction.

   However, don't view your lawyer's resistance to particular directives as mutiny. Lawyers are supposed to exercise their own informed judgment and any lawyer who blindly follows the orders of a client has abdicated a large part of a lawyer's professional duty. Expect that your lawyer will, in any given situation, enumerate for you the alternatives available to you, evaluate the wisdom of each of those alternatives, and make recommendations for action. The final decision in any such situation should be yours.

You should expect that your lawyer will frankly tell you what is objectionable about any instruction that you give to which he or she objects, and you should know that any ethical lawyer will resign from representing you if you insist that he or she participate in any dishonest strategy. Watch out for a lawyer who doesn't object strongly to any suggestion that he or she stretch the truth or engage in any sort of monkey business. People seldom direct their dishonesty in only one direction; you may find that you are on the receiving end of your lawyer's lack of scruples if you expect or tolerate ethical corner-cutting from him or her.

5. **Your lawyer never makes inflated claims regarding his or her abilities.** As much as lawyers wish otherwise, no lawyer can really predict with certainty the outcome of any legal proceeding or negotiation. Regardless of how skilled your lawyer or how just your position, there are factors in any matter before the Trademark Office or in any trademark dispute over which neither you nor your lawyer has any control at all—the judgments of the Trademark Office or the attitudes and agenda of your adversary and of your adversary's attorney. No amount of skilled lawyering can persuade the Trademark Office to grant a registration when the trademark statute or the *Trademark Manual of Examining Procedure* dictates otherwise. And a really determined bad guy can derail even the most reasonable and competent attorney's strategies for a fair settlement of a dispute.

If you are in court, the number of important factors out of your attorney's control increases. Among the things that are uncontrollable, there is no more unpredictable and unassailable factor than the judge who hears your case. Many judges are wise and fair and struggle to mete out the justice that they are supposed to dispense. Others make arbitrary and unfair rulings that are, seemingly, based more on what they had for breakfast than on any reasoned interpretation of the law.

All this is by way of saying that no lawyer can make reliable claims of success. During the course of a dispute or lawsuit, events can occur that no one can predict or control or mitigate; such events can defeat any lawyer. If you hear the words "I've never lost a suit," or "I've got that judge in my back pocket," or "This case is a cinch," issue from the mouth of your lawyer, pin him or her down before any such rash statement has evaporated. Your lines are "Is that so? It seems impossible that you've never lost a suit," and "What, exactly, makes you think you can persuade that judge to see things our way?" and "Really? If our winning is a foregone conclusion, then why didn't the defendant settle out of court?" Get another lawyer if you find that any large percentage of your lawyer's discussions embody such delusions of grandeur. One of the primary jobs of a lawyer is to communicate with precision. Your lawyer's routine overstatement of his or her abilities is likely to cause problems; at the least, such behavior makes him or her an unreliable advisor. Look for a sober, serious, careful lawyer instead. A serious lawyer may not be as entertaining, but he or she won't lead you down the garden path or out on a limb, either.

6. **Your lawyer is never overly aggressive or hostile.** Anyone who thinks that every good lawyer eats nails for breakfast

should reconsider that assumption. Actually, there are very few lawyers for whom a consistent posture of aggression or hostility is effective for anything other than giving clients a false sense of security. As a practical matter, a lawyer who is always aggressive is not an effective representative for his or her clients. Lawyers should be fearless enough to ask for what their clients want, clever enough to figure out how to get it, and bold enough to engage in the occasional bluff. However, they also should keep in mind, *at all times*, the best interests of their clients. A lawyer who only knows how to fight and intimidate his or her adversaries is a hack who is lacking several of the tools a good lawyer knows how to use. The abilities to negotiate and strategize are at least as important to most lawyers as the ability to fight. Think about it. If your lawyer's actions only operate to activate the defenses of your adversary, it is much more likely that you will find yourself in a full-blown fight than able to make a reasonable settlement. Unless you want to spend your retirement fund paying the fees of an attorney who loves a good fight, expect your lawyer to control his or her temper and to expend his or her aggression in some manner other than useless sparring on your behalf.

155

7. **Your lawyer is always frank when answering your questions.** Sometimes lawyers, who are prone to get carried away on the wings of their own oratory, forget the value of plain statements of fact. This sort of tin-pot eloquence will never be eradicated completely from the repertoire of most lawyers, and it is unlikely in the extreme that it will vanish from the armory of litigators, many of whom are hams at heart. Further, some of your lawyer's windy explanations may be necessary to convey the information

you request. Clients always think that anything can be explained briefly; in reality, a long, confusing explanation may really be the best answer possible to a question, even though the necessity for its length may not be apparent to the client.

However, you should pay attention if the answers you get from your lawyer are always too vague to satisfy your inquiries. If this long-windedness is chronic, ask your lawyer to respond to your questions more plainly and with more brevity. If he or she won't or can't change, consider whether the long-windedness is really intentional obfuscation. Long, complicated answers may be simply an occupational trait of lawyers, but mendacity should not be. Regardless of this, some lawyers do engage in various sorts of prevarication, ranging from hedging to outright lying, even with their clients, to whom they owe *at least* the truth. Any evasion of the truth by a lawyer in any statement to a client is the sign of an incompetent lawyer who is covering up her or his inadequacies or a lawyer who, like a cat with a mouse, is manipulating the client for selfish ends.

Don't allow your lawyer to toy with you or the matter that you have entrusted to him or her. But don't discharge him or her until you have asked for an explanation of what you think is a lie. If your lawyer's explanation is not convincing, get another lawyer.

8. **Your lawyer never overbills you.** Because lawyers must make judgment calls at every turn in handling almost any client matter, it is often difficult to know when a lawyer is billing you for make-work. However, it is important to question your lawyer if you think you are being billed for unnecessary work, because an uncomplaining client who pays excessive bills without question can count on

receiving more and bigger bills from his or her lawyer, who may view the client as a fatted calf.

No fee statement should come as a surprise to you. When you engage your lawyer's services, you should receive a letter or be asked to sign a short agreement that specifies your lawyer's hourly rate and billing policies. If the matter you entrust to your lawyer involves a trademark dispute or lawsuit and your lawyer agrees to work on a contingency-fee basis, you should receive a detailed fee agreement specifying 1) what share of any award or settlement amount your lawyer will be entitled to; 2) what expenses you will be expected to pay; and 3) whether other expenses will come off the top of the judgment or settlement or will be deducted *from your share* of that amount.

Question any fee or expense you think is excessive. If your lawyer does not answer your questions frankly and to your satisfaction, don't pay the disputed amount until you are satisfied that the charge is fair, or offer to pay only what you believe is fair under the circumstances. Any lawyer with your interests at heart should be willing to explain any legitimate fee or billed expense that puzzles you and, within reason, to modify any billing practice to which you object.

Unless a lawyer has abandoned all pretense of living up to his or her professional and ethical standards, even a polite complaint letter or phone call from a client is likely to produce better behavior. In fact, any complaint, except one about truly outrageous behavior, should be polite and, to the extent possible, non-accusatory. Despite occasional evidence otherwise, most lawyers will conduct themselves professionally if their clients make it obvious that they expect good treatment. The alternative, of course, is that a lawyer you reprimand, even mildly, will refuse to reform. If this happens and the transgression is substantive, find another lawyer. You get the behavior you put up with.

Off With Their Heads

And then there are the sins of lawyers that require summary execution, without discussion, without possibility of a reduced sentence. It may be unlikely that any lawyer you investigate before hiring will ever commit any of these sins, all of which are major breaches of a lawyer's duty to his or her client. However, although lawyers don't like to admit that any such breaches ever occur, they sometimes do. In the burgeoning population of American lawyers, there are bound to be some who are truly corrupt, because of alcoholism or drug abuse or gambling, because of ineptitude, because of depression or some other mental illness, or because of simple, garden-variety venality.

For lawyers, these mortal sins are failing to keep a client's secrets, stealing from a client, and lying to a client.

If at any time you find that your lawyer has committed any of these sins, terminate his or her services immediately by means of a hand-delivered letter in which you demand prompt delivery to you of your file and the return of any retainer or deposit against fees for legal work that has not yet been performed. Threats seldom produce the desired results and, if they are too rash, diminish the force of the threat, but you should include in your letter a measured statement that you will take your complaint to the lawyer-licensing board for your state if your lawyer fails to comply promptly with your demands. Then, if your lawyer's transgression was serious enough, or has caused you significant harm, file your complaint anyway. You will find that the lawyer-licensing board will take your complaint very seriously and that the only lawyer who will criticize your action is the one who will become the subject of the board's investigation.

Managing Your Lawyer

One important factor in obtaining satisfactory legal work that clients often overlook is that almost any lawyer's work will better satisfy his or her client if that person knows how to be a *good* client. Being a good client is part technique and part attitude.

Even a principled lawyer will represent you more satisfactorily if you know how to manage his or her work. There are several techniques that clients can employ to get the best services from their lawyers. Ordinarily, clients learn these lawyer management skills only after they have been through a few battles with the aid of several lawyers. Experience is a good teacher, but when it comes to figuring out how to manage lawyers, learning from experience is a bad method, because the information you need comes only after the fact and because your lawyer's meter is running while you learn.

Fortunately, many techniques for managing a lawyer's work can be employed as easily and effectively by anyone who understands them as by an "experienced" client—a category you may, in any event, want to avoid. Four of the most important lawyer management techniques are as follows:

1. **Give your lawyer the necessary information.** Your lawyer needs accurate information in order to represent your interests. The first thing your lawyer will do is ask you a long list of questions. The more pertinent information you can give your lawyer, the less time he or she will have to spend ferreting out the information, and the smaller your fee bill will be. Try to give your lawyer complete information in an organized form as soon as it is requested. If you

don't have the information your lawyer needs but can get it as easily as your lawyer can, gather it yourself to save legal fees.

A corollary to the principle that your lawyer needs information in order to represent you is that he or she does not need a file cluttered with extraneous information. Points that you think are important may be, in actuality, beside the point. If your lawyer doesn't ask about some topics that you think are pertinent, ask whether the information will help. Save your tale to recount to your friends if your lawyer isn't interested, because the information you considered important is either immaterial, unreliable, inadmissible, or available in some better form elsewhere.

2. **Call your lawyer only when necessary.** It is important to remember that the mere fact that the telephone on your desk is connected to the one in your lawyer's office doesn't mean that it is a good idea to call your lawyer every time you have a question or think of something he or she needs to know. Among other drawbacks, if you are paying your lawyer on an hourly basis, calling him or her every time you have the urge is likely to result in much higher legal fees. Most lawyers bill a minimum amount of time, usually a quarter hour, for any phone call and the time it takes to draft a file memo concerning the phone call. If your lawyer is working on a contingency-fee basis, too many calls from you will exasperate him or her, since he or she will not earn any more for the extra work you create by calling too often than the agreed-upon share of the settlement amount or judgment paid to you that he or she is already due.

One good technique for reducing time on the phone with your lawyer is to put your thoughts in a concise memo for your file. You don't have to hire a secretary to produce such memoranda—an orderly e-mail memo or even a legible handwritten memo will work. Even if your lawyer reads every word of your memo, less billable time will be consumed than if you furnish this information in the course of several phone calls.

Another good approach is to keep a running list of your thoughts and questions and look over and organize these notes before you call. Then, call your lawyer's secretary and make a phone appointment for fifteen minutes or half an hour in order to ensure that your lawyer will be waiting, with your file open, when you call. This saves endless games of telephone tag and won't create more fees than calling without an appointment. Of course, none of this applies to emergency calls, but in most trademark matters or disputes, there *are* very few true emergencies.

And remember that sometimes it is possible to address the questions you have to a lawyer's secretary or a paralegal or associate. These people are less difficult to get on the phone; if they can't answer your question, it may be possible for them to ask your lawyer the question you need answered and call you back with the answer.

3. **Don't quibble over ordinary charges.** It is understandable and appropriate that clients get upset over unreasonable bills from their lawyers. If you receive a statement from your lawyer that you consider excessive, you *should* complain about it. In fact, it is far better for the long-term health of your relationship with your lawyer to question bills you don't understand than to allow them to go unchallenged. This does not mean, however, grilling your lawyer, or your lawyer's secretary, about every charge on your statement.

Part of the responsibility for ensuring that no part of your lawyer's statement comes as a surprise is yours. If your lawyer does not furnish you with a written description of his or her billing practices, including a list of the expenses incurred on your behalf that you will be expected to reimburse, ask for one so that you will know what to expect.

Expect to be asked for a retainer fee to cover the initial work that you hire your lawyer to perform and that you may be asked to make further occasional advance payments against fees and significant expenses. Expect to be charged a minimum of a quarter hour for any phone call made or taken by your lawyer on your behalf, including calls to and from you. Expect that all letters will be billed at a minimum of a half hour. Expect to be billed, at a reduced rate, for the services of paralegals. Expect to be billed for expenses incurred on your behalf, including postage, courier fees, photocopies, travel costs, trademark search fees, Trademark Office and court filing fees, and the costs of court reporters for depositions. In fact, at some firms, expect to be billed for all expenses that are even remotely attributable to work performed for you, including almost everything except the electricity consumed by the lights in your lawyer's office.

But, too, expect that your lawyer or his or her secretary will answer any questions you have about your bills and that, within reason, your objections will be taken seriously and your directions will be followed.

4. **Maintain the right attitude.** Despite what many people may believe, most lawyers don't want passive clients. Such clients often make unrealistic demands on their lawyers, expecting them to pull rabbits out of hats, sometimes in situations where there are no good remedies for the clients' problems. Instead, lawyers want their clients to be,

to a large extent, partners in the effort to reach the clients' goals or the search for solutions to the clients' problems. This means that you should take the attitude that the legal matter or problem belongs to you.

This sounds like a restatement of the obvious, but it really isn't. Once you stop thinking of the legal matter or problem you entrust to your lawyer as a matter that will, by necessity, be satisfactorily resolved by your lawyer simply because you have turned it over to him or her, and begin to view it as a matter that you may be able to accomplish or solve satisfactorily with the assistance of your lawyer, you will have a realistic view of your situation and will be less likely to be surprised by developments or disappointed by results. Your legal concern is *yours*. Your attorney can help you, but only because you hire him or her, furnish the necessary information and direction, and make the correct choices when the available options are presented to you.

Chapter 7
Trademark Usage

Once a trademark is registered federally, and this means registered in the U.S. Patent and Trademark Office, not simply registered in one or more states or in another country, the trademark owner is allowed to use, and should use, a trademark registration notice in conjunction with the registered mark. Use of such notice warns others that the mark is registered and that ownership of it is claimed by the owner, and allows the owner to gain certain advantages provided by the federal trademark statute.

Notice of Federal Registration

The most familiar trademark registration notice is the "circle R" symbol, or ®; the ® symbol should be used "on the shoulder" of the registered mark (in the superscript position), or in the subscript position, very near it. Alternate forms of notice are "Registered in the U.S. Patent and Trademark Office," or

"Reg. U.S. Pat. & Tm. Off."; these alternate forms of notice should be used with an asterisk placed close to the registered mark and a corresponding asterisk preceding the notice itself, which usually appears in a footnote position on the package or label or in the ad, etc.

It is important to know that the forms of trademark notice specified above are the only forms of notice that have the legal effect of proper trademark registration notice. You can't, in short, make up your own.

Not using the ® symbol (or one of the other prescribed forms of trademark registration notice, although they are generally used less often and may, in fact, be less likely to be recognized as notice of registration than the familiar ® symbol) in conjunction with a federally registered trademark will not invalidate the registration, but it can deprive the trademark owner of some very important advantages in the event that the registered mark is infringed.

165

If the Rounder Doughnut Company registers its trademark HOLE IN ONE for packaged doughnuts sold in grocery stores, everyone else in the world who wishes to adopt and use in the United States a confusingly similar trademark for doughnuts is presumed by law to have notice that HOLE IN ONE is owned by Rounder, even if they do not conduct a trademark search and discover Rounder's federal registration. If Burgerama, Inc., adds to the breakfast menu for its fast food restaurants a doughnut it calls HOLE IN ONE, the Rounder Doughnut Company will sue Burgerama, since consumers could easily confuse the fast food restaurants' doughnuts with those marketed by Rounder. By virtue of its federal registration, Rounder will be entitled to an injunction from the court ordering Burgerama to cease use of HOLE IN ONE.

But if Rounder also wants to be awarded an amount of money representing the damages it has suffered because of Burgerama's infringement or the profits of Burgerama attributable to the sale of doughnuts under the HOLE IN ONE name before its receipt of Rounder's cease and desist letter, Rounder must have used the ® symbol (or another prescribed form of notice) on its packaging. If Rounder did not use a trademark registration notice with its mark, the court is allowed by law to award only damages or profits that resulted from actions of Burgerama *after* it received actual, specific notice that the HOLE IN ONE mark was registered.

Now all this may sound like mumbo jumbo, but it's not. It may seem unlikely that something that a commercial artist does or does not do in pasting up the artwork for a new cereal box or an ad for a vacuum cleaner can determine how much money a federal court can award to the cereal company or the vacuum cleaner company, but that is precisely the case.

The responsibility to make sure that a trademark registration symbol is properly used with a registered trademark belongs ultimately to the trademark owner. If you are not the owner of a trademark or responsible for managing a company that owns it, you have no legal obligation to find out whether a trademark owned by your client or your employer is registered or to make sure that the trademark registration symbol is used. However, no client or employer is going to object to your raising the question of the proper use of a registered mark. If you want to keep your clients or employer happy, you must be at least conversant with the basics of proper usage of the trademark registration symbol and notations, since that usage so directly affects valuable rights of trademark owners.

An important related consideration is the improper use of the ® symbol (or another of the prescribed forms of trademark registration notice). If trademark registration notice is used in conjunction with a trademark that is not federally registered, or used with a trademark appearing in advertising for, or in conjunction with, goods or services for which it is not registered, serious consequences can result, including the loss of the trademark owner's right to recover for trademark infringement or to register the mark federally.

Many people, even people who should know better, think that the ™ symbol they often see printed next to trademarks is the equivalent of the ® symbol and has some legal effect. In reality, it does not. The ™ symbol is sometimes used by trademark owners as a "no trespassing" sign to indicate that someone is claiming ownership of the mark. It has no real legal effect but can be useful, since there are no requirements to be met before it can be used and there really is no such thing as misuse of it. In addition, many trademarks are not yet federally registered, or have been denied federal registration, or cannot be federally registered for one reason or another. Use of the ™ symbol, which usually appears in the same locations as those used for placement of the ® symbol, can warn others that the owners of these names consider them to be trademarks and claim ownership of them. (Another form of informal trademark notice, the ᔆᴹ symbol, is often used in the same ways that the ™ symbol is used when the mark in question names services.)

Similar to the ™ symbol is some statement such as "The name DENTAL ASSISTANT'S QUARTERLY is a trademark of the Dental Assistance Association of America." Statements of this sort have exactly the same effect (some) and uses (several) that the ™ symbol does; that is, they are another variety of informal trademark notice.

Use It Correctly or Lose It

Trademarks, whether registered or not, can theoretically last perpetually. As long as someone markets goods or services under a name or symbol, it has a legal existence as a trademark. However, trademarks "die" every day.

Trademark Abandonment

One of the ways a trademark dies is by "abandonment"; that is, the owner of the mark ceases using it. This ordinarily happens to trademarks owned by underfinanced or unskilled marketers and to those that name unsuccessful products or services. Such abandonment is, of course, a result of a decision of the trademark owner. (Does Ford use EDSEL for *anything* anymore?) Sometimes a mark is abandoned because of some spectacularly bad event associated with it. The 1996 Valu-Jet air disaster in Florida may have resulted in the abandonment of the cartoon-plane logo that became familiar to people who had never before heard of the airline through weeks of news footage about the crash; Valu-Jet was sold and merged with another company soon afterward, and the Valu-Jet name and logo fell into what will probably be permanent disuse. When a trademark really has been abandoned—that is, it has fallen out of use for a substantial period of time and its owner has no intent to revive it—it can be used by another marketer because it has ceased to represent the commercial reputation of the products of its original owner. (But remember that it is risky to adopt and use a mark that you believe to be abandoned without some investigation into the intentions of the original owner of the mark. Suspension of use of a mark may occur for several reasons other than the owner's intention to abandon it and, even if the owner does eventually abandon the mark, such intent cannot be deduced merely from a short period of disuse of the mark.)

Trademark Genericness

The second way trademarks die is almost the converse of the first situation, because such deaths often befall very famous trademarks and always occur against the will of the trademark owner. This form of trademark death results when a trademark becomes "generic," that is, when the word that formerly served as a trademark comes to signify to the general public the kind of product or service it names rather than representing a particular brand of that product or service. This form of trademark extinction should be of great interest to anyone who owns a trademark or participates in the marketing of the product or service it names. That is *169* because loss of a trademark through its becoming generic is always a great financial loss to trademark owners, especially considering the fact that many trademarks become generic because they name extremely popular products or services; a mark that names a popular and successful product or service is a valuable mark indeed. Marketing people, graphic designers, and advertising creative people are the first line of defense against genericness.

"Escalator," "cellophane," "trampoline," "shredded wheat," "mimeograph," "linoleum," and "aspirin," all once named particular products of particular companies; they were trademarks rather than, as now, the generic terms for whole classes of goods. Because they became generic, they lost their status as the names of particular products of particular companies; they can now be used by anyone.

Once a trademark,
not always a trademark.

They were once proud trademarks, now they're just names. They failed to take precautions that would have helped them have a long and prosperous life.

We need your help to stay out of there. Whenever you use our name, please use it as a proper adjective in conjunction with our products and services: e.g., Xerox copiers or Xerox financial services. And never as a

verb: "to Xerox" in place of "to copy," or as a noun: "Xeroxes" in place of "copies."

With your help and a precaution or two on our part, it's "Once the Xerox trademark, always the Xerox trademark."

Team Xerox. We document the world.

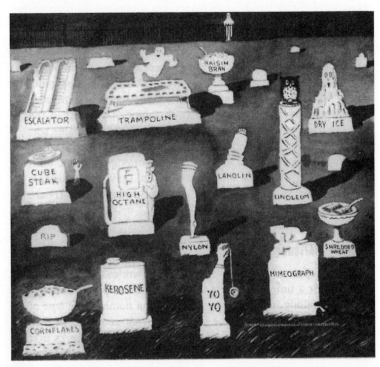

170

This ad reprinted by permission of the Xerox Corporation.

In the case of the former trademark ESCALATOR, a court held that because consumers thought of all moving stairways as "escalators," ESCALATOR had lost its ability to point only to products of the Otis Elevator Company. In the decision that canceled Otis's fifty-year-old trademark registration for ESCALATOR, the court stated that the fact Otis itself had used its trademark in its own ads as "escalator," that is, as a generic term for a class of products, supported the contention that the mark had become generic. Otis and its ad agency goofed, and they paid the price by losing one of the company's most valuable assets, its famous trademark ESCALATOR.

Similar scenarios surrounded the ends of all the former trademarks mentioned above, and others. Ironically, it is the names of unique and innovative products that are most at risk of becoming generic. This is because the name of the first version of a groundbreaking product can come to mean that *type* of product in the minds of consumers, who may refer to all products of the same sort by the trademark of the first one they encountered. XEROX® is one trademark that is presently in danger of becoming a generic term (for photocopy machines and photocopies). LEVI'S®, FORMICA®, GOOGLE®, TUPPER-WARE®, KLEENEX®, ROLLERBLADE®, and POST-IT® may be similarly endangered.

Avoiding Genericness

In some cases, a company may be virtually powerless to prevent its trademark for a unique product that captures the public's imagination from falling into common usage as the name of the *type* of product rather than the name of one particular brand of that product. "Nylon," "yo-yo," and "zipper" may have been marks that no amount of care could have preserved from genericness. However, in almost every case a company can at least put up a fight to halt the fall of its marks into genericness, by care in its use of them and, when necessary, by ads that promote the names as trademarks.

A mark may become generic because consumers and the media begin to use it to refer to a class of products rather than to the products of one particular marketer, and it is important to take measures to squelch such incipient genericness. A bigger problem, however, is misuse of the trademark by its owner or those who use it under the owner's control, since such misuse can be a critical factor in a court's decision whether a mark has become generic, thereby losing its trademark significance.

The very least that is required of any trademark owner is that it police its own use of its trademark and the use of the mark by its licensees and agents, such as ad agencies and retailers. Proper use of a company's trademark can have very real dollars-and-cents consequences for the trademark owner. Trademarks are often considered to be among the most valuable assets of the companies that own them because they often represent a certain steady share of the market for the products they name. If a trademark becomes generic (and therefore available for use by anyone), that market identity and share are lost.

Proper trademark usage, crucial for protecting the exclusive ownership of a trademark, involves a few rules of "trademark grammar" that all marketing people should know and use. Remember that:

- **A trademark is always an adjective, never a noun:** It is "CHEER® laundry detergent," never simply "CHEER"; hence "Get your clothes clean with CHEER® laundry detergent." Think of "CAMPBELL'S® soups," "TOTES® umbrellas," and "HOLIDAY INN® hotels."
- **A trademark is a proper adjective:** It is "ROLLERBLADE® in-line skates," never "I want some ROLLERBLADEs."

Think of "LEVI'S® jeans," "EGG MCMUFFIN® breakfast sandwiches," and "CHANEL® perfumes."

- **A trademark is always singular, never plural:** It is "EASY SPIRIT® shoes," never simply "EASY SPIRITs." Think of CRAYOLA® crayons," "APPLE® computers," and "KLEENEX® tissues."

- **Trademark variations should be avoided:** Trademarks should never be made possessive, i.e., it is never "HEINZ's great taste" but is, rather, "The great taste of HEINZ 57® steak sauce." And if the mark is registered or ordinarily used in one typeface or format, don't change its customary appearance without careful thought; otherwise, how will consumers recognize their old friend? Similarly, avoid changes in the verbal content of the mark at all costs; it is "Fried to a golden brown with CRISCO® all-vegetable shortening!" not "CRISCO-ed to perfection again!"

173

Although these rules aren't really that difficult to remember or follow, not all trademark owners follow them religiously—maybe because they are uninformed or careless or because they think their marks are so famous they can ignore the rules. You, however, should tend to your own mark carefully, in the hope and expectation that someday it will become famous enough that you can hire a dozen or so trademark lawyers to do it for you.

The problem may not be remembering or following the rules in using your valuable trademark, but whether *others* do. If you own a trademark or are in a job that requires you to create or approve ads, packaging, signage, press releases, or other materials that embody a trademark, you owe a duty to yourself, or to your employer or client, to see that the mark is used correctly. There are several ways to do this.

Following the Rules

One of the best ways to avoid trademark genericness is to produce a set of trademark usage guidelines for your company. These guidelines can educate anyone who writes or produces any advertising or public relations materials for you in the proper use of trademarks in general and your mark in particular. It can also be furnished to journalists who write about your product or your company and can be made a part of any agreement to license your trademark to another company (see the discussion on trademark licensing below). Your trademark usage guidelines should include a section on graphic standards for the use of anyone who reproduces your mark in any but purely verbal forms. This section should specify colors and typefaces and should give examples of the proper visual forms of your mark.

174   You can even get creative with these guidelines and print them on T-shirts that you use as trade-show giveaways, style sheets that you furnish to the media, and posters for your retailers. One of the best ways to promulgate guidelines on proper use of your trademark is to post them on your company website. Every big corporation that owns a valuable trademark distributes this sort of trademark usage guide to its employees, advertising agencies, franchisees, dealers, and public relations people. (Go to /www.apple.com/legal/trademark/guidelinesfor3rdparties.html to view Apple's trademark usage guidelines.) To get some good pointers for composing your own trademark usage guidelines, use Google to search "trademark usage guides" and print out the guides that seem to convey the information best. Then, write your own using the guidelines you found as a, well, guide. Don't worry if you can't come up with a document as impressive as those used by big corporations. The main thing is to get the word out to anyone

who has or may have any reason to use your mark in or on anything the public sees.

Another good method for ensuring proper use of your trademark by your company and its agents and licensees is to appoint a trademark czar to review and approve any materials that embody your trademark before they are produced and duplicated. Anyone given this responsibility should be really capable of understanding and carrying out the job. This is not a task that can be delegated to a receptionist who doesn't have enough to do; your trademark enforcer should be a lawyer or senior marketing person who thoroughly understands trademark law and the purposes of correct trademark usage as well as the consequences of incorrect usage. Establish a formal system for review of anything besides internal documents and be consistent in enforcing the rules of usage that you have decreed apply to your mark. Treat the person who is charged with protecting your trademark with at least as much respect as you give your chief financial officer; if you have a hit product on your hands, the trademark that names it will be well worth the attention.

175

Fending Off Infringers

The law imposes upon trademark owners the obligation to police their trademarks. That is, the quid pro quo for the protection the law gives your commercial reputation is the obligation to protect that reputation from those who would damage it and to take action to ensure that the mark continues to point to *one* source for the goods or services it names. The trademark owner's interests are concurrent with those of consumers: if the trademark remains strong and distinctive, it will become more valuable and consumers may continue to rely on the mark as an indicator of a quality product.

Policing a trademark means keeping an eye out for marks that are similar to your mark and acting quickly to stop the use of any that you think infringe it. There are lots of ways to do this, and many degrees of vigilance. Most trademark owners watch the trade publications for their industry. Consciously or unconsciously, one of their reasons for doing so is to discover whether any marketer of a similar product or service is using a name or symbol similar to their own trademarks. If they discover such uses, they will immediately take action, usually by calling their lawyers. All this is obvious. Any businessperson needs to keep up with what is going on in his or her area of commerce and most business people know that a mark that is too similar to their own can present big problems, even if they don't know that what they would be complaining about is trademark infringement.

Finding out about less direct conflicts may be more difficult. Large corporations use in-house paralegals and employ "watching services" to discover the use of any marks that may conflict with their marks. These trademark owners review trade publications, of course, but they also carefully watch the weekly *Official Gazette for Trademarks* (which you can access online, for free, at www.uspto.gov/news/og/trademark_og/index.jsp). Searching the TMOG every week can be a tedious task, but your expenditure of time will be repaid if and when you locate a mark published for opposition that you feel infringes your mark. If you find a mark that is too close to your own, call a trademark lawyer to help you file a Notice of Opposition (to the registration of the mark) with the Trademark Office. This is not an unusual event.

Corporations typically challenge marks that are published for opposition if they seem at all close to those the corporations own. Sometimes big companies challenge marks that are *not* really similar to their own marks by filing or threatening to file opposition proceedings in an effort to halt the granting of registration for the new marks. Many such disputes, especially those involving marks that are not really threats to an established mark, are settled by mutual agreement before the opposition proceeding is actually commenced. The trademark owner's idea, in such a circumstance, may be to give itself time to investigate and to consider whether there *would* be an infringement. It may also be that the trademark owner wants to be able to demonstrate that it acts promptly to stop any threat to its established mark. Courts look at such evidence in evaluating whether a trademark owner has a history of protecting its mark from infringers.

Nevertheless, it must be said that nothing in the law requires a trademark owner to rush to the courthouse to file a trademark infringement suit every time there is a question of infringement. There are effective methods for settling trademark infringement disputes besides slugging it out in court. And quite often trademark owners may be unsure whether the actions of another marketer really do constitute infringement. However, if you "sleep on your rights" long enough and fail to challenge an infringer, a court hearing your tardy trademark infringement suit may rule that your previous failure to object to the actions of the defendant you are suing for infringement has allowed that defendant to depend on your apparent acquiescence to its use of the suspect mark and that to enjoin that use now would be unfair.

All this means that there are two rules for policing trademarks. The first rule is "Rust never sleeps"; that is, vigilance against trademark infringers must be ceaseless and tireless to be effective—you must know what is going on in the marketplace, which is both the birthplace and the stomping ground for trademarks, which do not exist at all if they do not exist there. The second rule is "Walk softly, but carry a big stick"; that is, don't file a trademark infringement suit until you are sure of your facts, have tried to settle the dispute satisfactorily out of court, and have sought competent advice about the probable outcome of your suit, but be ready to act decisively if you determine that you *must* sue to stop the erosion of your own rights.

Although it is important from the inception of your trademark to use it correctly and to see that others do so, the more famous it becomes and the more successful the product it names, the more vigilance it deserves. A viable trademark, that is, a memorable mark that is capable of federal registration, is like a small savings account. If you tend it carefully, it will grow in value. This means that you should watch out for marks that are similar to your fledgling mark and act quickly to stop the use of any that you think infringe it. And if someone uses your mark in a way that could contribute to its becoming generic, take a cue from the owners of the most valuable trademarks and write a letter asking that person to reform—it can be a nice letter, but it needs to be firm and to give specific examples of correct use of your mark. Let them know that you are watching.

Condemned to Anonymity

The following terms were held by the Trademark Office or a court to be incapable of serving as indicators of particular sources for the goods and services they named because they had become, in the minds of consumers, generic terms for those products or services. After being declared to be non-trademarks, these terms became free for anyone to use in describing products or services and ceased to be the exclusive property of their originators.

AL-KOL for rubbing alcohol
ASPIRIN for acetyl salicylic acid
BABY OIL for mineral oil
BATH OIL BEADS for bath oil, water softener, and perfume
BODY SOAP for body shampoo
BRASSIERE for women's bras
BUNDT for a type of ring coffee cake
CELLOPHANE for transparent cellulose sheets
COLA for a soft drink
COMPUTER LEARNING CENTER for computer courses
THE COMPUTER STORE for retail computer sales
    services
CONSUMER ELECTRONICS MONTHLY for a magazine
    for electronics enthusiasts
COPPERCLAD for copper-coated conductors
CUBE STEAK for tenderized steaks
DRY ICE for carbon dioxide in solid form
EASTER BASKET for an Easter floral basket
ESCALATOR for moving stairways
EXPORT SODA for an exported soda cracker
FLOR-TILE for wooden flooring
FLOWERS BY WIRE for intercity floral delivery services
FLUID ENERGY for hydraulic/pneumatic equipment
HAIR COLOR BATH for a hair-coloring preparation
HARD TO FIND TOOLS for a tool mail-order service
HOAGIE for sandwiches
HONEY BAKED HAM for honey-glazed hams
JUJUBES for gum candies
LIGHT BEER for a light-bodied beer
METALOCK for a metal repair method
MONOPOLY for a real estate–trading board game
MONTESSORI for an education method and associated toys

MULTISTATE BAR EXAMINATION for a bar examination given in several states

MURPHY BED for beds that fold into a wall or closet for storage

THE PILL for oral contraceptives

POCKET BOOK for paperback books

PRIMAL THERAPY for a type of psychotherapy

PROM for programmable read-only memory computer systems

RUBBER ROPE for an elasticized rubber rope product

SAFE T PLUG for electrical plugs

SHREDDED WHEAT for baked wheat biscuits

SOCIOGRAPHICS for a technique of management consulting

SOFTSOAP for liquid hand soap

SUPER GLUE for rapid-setting cyanoacrylate adhesives

SURGICENTER for a surgical center

THERMOS for vacuum-insulated bottles

TRAMPOLINE for rebound tumbling equipment

VIDEO BUYERS GUIDE for a magazine for videotape buyers

WORK WEAR for industrial clothing

YO-YO for return tops

Death of a Trademark

In 2000, in a very thorough opinion, a federal district court judge in Manhattan ruled that the name "Pilates" had become a generic term for exercise instruction services and exercise equipment.

Born in Germany, Joseph Pilates began developing the Pilates exercise system while interned in England during World War I. He and his wife Clara emigrated to New York in the 1920s and opened a studio at which they taught his method of exercise. After Mr. Pilates' death in 1976, his wife continued to teach the Pilates method, which became popular with dancers, especially for rehabilitation after dance injuries. They also trained other instructors. The exercise system has since become nationally very popular and prevalent.

The defendant in the lawsuit, a California company named Balanced Body, has since 1976 manufactured equipment for use by followers of the exercise system. The principal plaintiff in the lawsuit, Sean Gallagher, was involved in a business that owned studios that taught the Pilates method and sold Pilates equipment. In 1992, Gallagher acquired trademark registrations for the PILATES service mark and for PILATES STUDIO. Gallagher renamed his exercise studio The Pilates Studio, obtained a Pilates trademark for exercise equipment, started a certification program for Pilates instructors, and began trying to stop use of the Pilates name by anyone else. He sent many cease and desist letters to others who were using the name and brought numerous lawsuits against studios and individuals who taught the Pilates system without having obtained certification from him.

In ruling that Pilates had lost trademark significance, the court based its opinion on several factors, but noted that during their lifetimes Joseph and Clara Pilates had "promoted [the Pilates] method of exercise and attempted to increase its use by the public" and "never did anything to prevent others from using their name to describe what they taught." The court said that since "consumers identify the word 'Pilates' as a particular method of exercise [the] plaintiff cannot monopolize [it]." In consequence, the judge ordered the cancellation of the plaintiff's trademark registrations for the Pilates marks.

In other words, once a trademark has become generic and is used by consumers to denote a kind of product or service rather than a particular product or service, it cannot be retrieved from genericness and restored to trademark status. To some extent, whether a trademark becomes generic is out of the hands of the trademark owner and very much in the hands of those who write, speak, and otherwise use the mark, as the owners of numerous former trademarks, now ruled generic, have discovered.

The winning defendant company in the Pilates case, Balanced Body, has posted the well-reasoned opinion of Judge Miriam Goldman Cedarbaum in PDF format. If you want to read it, go to www.pilates.com/resources/aboutpilates/pilates-decision.pdf.

Chapter 8
Trademark Licensing

One of the best ways to exploit and prof-
it from a trademark is to license it to someone else. Being asked
to license your trademark is exciting. It means, among other
things, that your mark has become famous enough to attract the
attention of consumers and that it stands for a quality product
that consumers desire. Since you, as the trademark owner, are
paid for the use of your trademark and do not put up the money
to manufacture the products or provide the services that you authorize to be offered in conjunction with your mark, trademark
licensing can literally create income from thin air for you.

But the royalty income from any licensing agreement may
be a relatively minor incentive to enter the deal compared to
the added publicity that your trademark will receive; brand
extension is one of the major reasons that the owners of
famous trademarks license those marks for products that
are unrelated to those that the trademark originally named.

Licensing can help you spread the fame of your brand into territories and market segments you would never otherwise have entered. However, if you're not careful, licensing can also result in your killing the goose that laid the golden egg, since allowing anyone to use your trademark whose use of it, for whatever reason, is not controlled by you will result in your loss of your mark.

Because licensing your trademark means letting someone else use it, unless you control that use, you have no way to ensure that your licensee is maintaining the good reputation that your trademark represents. The law views your allowing someone else to use your mark without controlling that use in much the same way it views your acquiescing to use of your mark by infringers who use it without your permission. In either case, your mark has ceased to point to one source—you—for the goods or services it names because you have lost control of how it is used. Where control of the goods and services offered under a mark has been lost by the owner of the mark, the mark may be held to have been abandoned.

Whenever anyone approaches you with a proposal to license your trademark, the first thing you should do after hearing the proposal is to call your trademark lawyer. You can probably create a mark yourself and clear it for use—at least preliminarily. You can figure out how to use it properly and it's even possible that you could register it without the help of a lawyer. This is not the case with trademark licensing. No smart marketer would consider trying to license a valuable trademark without the advice and assistance of a trademark lawyer.

Licensing Agreements

At the very least, a trademark license must be documented in a written agreement. Any attempt at verbal licensing would be viewed by a court as merely "naked licensing," that is, as your having granted permission to someone else to use your trademark without any real effort to control that use. At the least, it is hard to determine just what the terms of any agreement are when they are not memorialized in writing.

And your written trademark licensing agreement must include some very specific language in order to suffice to control the use of your mark. In fact, the word "license" means a permission granted by one person, the "licensor," who owns a right, to another person, the "licensee," who is permitted to exercise some of the rights of the licensor. At a minimum, a trademark licensing agreement should include provisions governing the following important points of agreement:

- **The grant of license:** This provision is the heart of a trademark licensing agreement. It specifies by whom and to whom the right to use the trademark is granted and typically conditions the grant upon the licensee's compliance with the other terms of the agreement.

  The permission to use the trademark is usually exclusive, that is, it is granted only to the person or company specified and the right to use the trademark for the same goods or services is not granted to anyone else during the duration of the licensing agreement. Exclusivity is not, however, mandatory. If a licensor can find more than one licensee willing to pay for the privilege of using a mark for the same goods or services during the same time period and in the same territory, the licensor may make the license nonexclusive.

  What is important is the control maintained by the licensor—that control over how the mark is used may be exercised with one licensee or more than one, so long as it is maintained by the licensor. Further, most good licensing

185

agreements provide that if the grant of license is not exercised—that is, if the licensee fails to actually use the trademark in the whole territory and throughout the entire term of the agreement—the agreement may be terminated by the licensor. This serves to free up the valuable trademark for licensing to another company if the licensee fails to exploit it as agreed; in other words, a licensee must "use it or lose it."

- **The territory:** this provision specifies in which states or countries the licensee is permitted to use the trademark. You may, for instance, license one company to use your mark in the eastern United States, and another in the western United States. The countries of the world may be divided into whatever small or large territorial "slices" the licensor and licensee agree, but the agreed territory for the license should be specified.

- **The term:** this provision specifies the start and finish dates for the licensee's use of the trademark; usually, a renewal period is specified as available to the licensee if certain conditions are met. As with the territory provision, and just as occupying a rental property past the expiration of a lease is trespassing, any use outside the period specified in the licensing agreement is trademark infringement.

- **The product (or services) licensed:** this provision is also very important. It specifies the exact products or services that the licensee may market under the licensed mark. The more carefully drafted the trademark licensing agreement, the more specific this provision. In other words, a good agreement will specify that the licensed mark may be used in conjunction with "boys' red, blue, yellow, and purple four-eyelet, rubber-soled canvas play shoes, up to size 8, manufactured in accordance with the specifications set out in Exhibit C, attached hereto and made a part of this agreement by this reference." Typically and importantly, the licensee is required to obtain permission from the licensor before using the licensed mark on any other product or to advertise any other service or significant variation of the licensed product or service.

- **Quality specifications for the licensed product (or services):** one of the ways the licensor controls use of its mark is to agree that the mark may be applied only to products or services of satisfactory quality. This protects the standing of the licensed trademark and the licensor's investment in it, since just as the good reputation of the product or services to which the mark was first applied will reflect favorably on the licensed product or services, an inferior licensed product would reflect badly on the well-regarded trademark and product. These quite detailed specifications are typically written separately and attached to the licensing agreement as an exhibit, that is, on an attached sheet that is specifically agreed to be part of the agreement.

- **Quality control:** a trademark licensor must be able to determine whether the licensee is living up to the quality specifications for the licensed product in order to protect the licensed mark. All proper trademark-licensing agreements contain a provision allowing the licensor, or the licensor's representatives, access to the manufacturing facilities of the licensee in order to ascertain whether the licensed product or service to meet those quality specifications. The licensor may specify that, in addition to its access to the licensee's facilities, it will have access to the manufacturing records of the licensee and to the personnel who staff the manufacturing operation.

- **Trademark usage:** the actions of a trademark licensee with regard to the way the licensed mark is used accrue to the benefit or detriment of the licensor. This means that the licensor must specify the manner in which the mark may be used on the licensed product or in advertising the licensed services and on or in packaging, signage, advertising, etc. Again, such provisions for use of the trademark often appear in an attachment to the basic agreement; this is one very good use for the trademark usage guidelines that trademark owners write for their own use and that of their agents and retailers.

- **Termination provisions:** all good trademark-licensing agreements give the licensor the right to terminate the agreement if the licensee breaches any of the provisions of the agreement. Typically, small or accidental breaches may be "cured" within a specified short period and the agreement will continue if the licensor is satisfied that the complained-of actions or conditions have been remedied. In the event of really significant and intentional breaches of the agreement (such as using the licensed mark outside the agreed territory), the licensor usually may, at its option, immediately terminate the agreement.

- **Payment of royalties:** this is, of course, another of the most important provisions of any trademark-licensing agreement. Typically, the owner of the licensed trademark is paid an agreed fee per unit of the product that is sold in conjunction with the mark. For services, payment is usually a set fee paid periodically during the term of the agreement. Many agreements provide that if the licensee fails to make to the licensor more than one such payment, the licensor may immediately terminate the agreement.

  As for the amount of royalties that will be paid, there is no single standard for determining what royalty is fair. In fact, the most influential factor in determining the royalties a licensor charges a licensee may be what payment your mark can command. Royalty arrangements vary according to the popularity of the licensed mark, the sort of goods or services licensed to be offered in conjunction with the mark, the territory involved, and the competition from other would-be licensees, if any. Royalties do, however, tend to hover in the neighborhood of ten percent, with some licensors able to command greater royalties and some licensees able to pay smaller ones.

The best way to figure out what royalty is fair is to locate some other licensors and licensees for marks of similar fame and for similar products; a few phone calls to some of the licensing executives involved in licensing deals similar to yours will help you get a feel for what to ask for.

The best way to proceed with any proposed licensing is to ask the would-be licensee to state the basic terms of the offered agreement (term, products licensed, territory, royalty, etc.) in a letter to you. Before you respond, take the letter to your lawyer and ask for advice concerning the fairness of the terms of the agreement. In addition, get some information about the would-be licensee; it's a lot easier to work with a solvent company that can do what it says it can than to find yourself one of the creditors of an insolvent company. Ask for references from other companies that have licensed their marks to the company that wants to license yours. And make sure that your lawyer writes the licensing agreement or, at least, that the first-draft contract offered to you by your licensee is thoroughly negotiated by your lawyer before you sign it. There's a big difference between your paper and theirs—it's often much easier to get the deal you want when you start from a contract your lawyer drafted for you.

Call Your Lawyer

And don't get the idea that you can write your own trademark agreement. Any contract you write yourself is likely to be like an airplane that you build in your basement—you won't know whether it is constructed properly until it crashes and burns. Trademark licensing agreements are highly technical documents that can have dire consequences if they are not drafted properly—you can even lose your trademark by failing to maintain adequate control of its use by someone else. Really. The same goes for a licensing agreement that you buy from an Internet contract mill. Even if you successfully substitute the names, dates, etc., from your own deal for those in one of these prefab contracts that were originally written for who knows whom, will you be confident that the provisions the modified agreement includes are sufficient for your deal? Such agreements may cost only thirty dollars or so (to begin with), but they can ultimately cost you ownership of one of your most valuable business assets, your trademark.

If you want to save yourself some time and money, you can preliminarily negotiate the terms of a licensing agreement yourself and reduce them to a memorandum that your lawyer can use to draft the full licensing agreement. When your discussions with your would-be licensee become definite enough that the potential licensee is willing to specify the offered terms of the license, you can negotiate the essential terms of your agreement: the territory for the license; the term of the license, including any renewals; exactly what trademark would be licensed; exactly what products or services would be offered in conjunction with the licensed mark; and what royalty would be paid and how often. If you can hammer out answers to most of these questions, you will have created the bones of your agreement. However, reserve the right to change your mind about an offered term after you consult your lawyer and don't sign any memo you write or agree in a letter or an exchange of letters to any terms of an offered deal.

Make sure in your discussions and correspondence with any would-be licensee that you neither say nor write anything that can be construed as a definite commitment on your part before you receive the go-ahead from your lawyer. In any communication, make it clear that any license would be reduced to a formal, written document before the license commences. Use contingent language in referring to any offered or expected deal: "I would consider granting a license . . ." "Any licensing offer would have to pay at least . . ." "In the event that we grant a license to use our trademark, we would expect . . ." and so on. It's not a bad idea to end every communication with a paragraph like this: "Thank you for your interest in licensing my trademark. However, it is important that you understand that none of our discussions or correspondence about a possible trademark license represents any commitment from me to grant such a license and that I will make no such commitment until both you and I have signed a formal, written document that includes all the terms of our negotiated agreement." More than one businessperson has been surprised when someone on the other side of a deal thought, prematurely, that an agreement had been reached. Take your time. Then, call your lawyer.

Chapter 9
Other People's
Trademarks

Almost everyone knows that selling toothpaste or sneakers or brokerage services by using a trademark that belongs to someone else is a quick ticket to a federal suit for trademark infringement. The law allows marketers to protect themselves from interlopers who want a free ride on their commercial coattails; they do this by means of lawsuits to preserve the integrity of their trademarks, which represent them to the public. The penumbra of protection granted an established trademark extends to identical marks and to marks that, although not identical, are similar enough to confuse consumers.

Usually, the comparison to determine trademark infringement is made between marks used to market similar products or services. However, the more famous and unusual the trademark, the wider the scope of protection trademark law grants it; no one can use KLEENEX® or COCA-COLA® or EXXON®

for any product without encountering serious opposition from platoons of trademark lawyers who work for those companies, especially since the Trademark Dilution Act became effective in early 1996. (See chapter 4 for a more detailed explanation of the Trademark Dilution Act.)

There are other ways to infringe a trademark besides adopting a name for a product or service that is confusingly similar to an established mark for a similar product or services. Because trademark owners are vigilant in protecting their trademarks, wariness in the matter of other people's trademarks is a very good idea. However, such wariness can lead to an exaggerated fear of trademarks that belong to others and unnecessary maneuvering to avoid any mention or depiction of them. Surprisingly enough, there are some circumstances when using someone else's trademark *is* safe.

Broadly speaking, the law gives a trademark owner protection against any action that creates confusion about that trademark in the minds of consumers. This means that the dividing line between safe and unsafe uses of a trademark is where consumer confusion begins. Determining whether a given use of someone else's trademark will lead to a lawsuit is simply a matter of determining, under all the circumstances, whether that use will confuse anyone.

There are two common varieties of use of someone else's trademark that are usually safe and one that is, by definition, almost never safe. An examination of each of these situations will demonstrate the considerations involved in using other people's trademarks.

Incidental Use of Trademarks

More than one creative director has called in a lawyer to evaluate whether the presence of a COKE® can sitting on a table in a photograph is enough to disqualify the photo for use in an ad that isn't supposed to advertise COKE products. Before the lawyer can answer the question, he or she will have to see the photograph in question and read the ad copy, because the two important factors in evaluating whether the Coca-Cola Company is likely to sue are the emphasis of the photograph and the context of the use of the COKE logo.

Trademarks are a part of our world; they so pervade every environment of modern life that it is next to impossible to walk down a street or visit a public place or sit in a room without being surrounded by trademarks of every sort. This means that any realistic depiction of a street scene or restaurant setting or home or office situation will include representations of the trademarks found in that environment. Even though the trademarks that appear in such depictions are the valuable property of the companies that own them, in a way they also belong to the rest of us because they are a part of our lives. The First Amendment protects commercial speech such as advertising as well as other sorts of speech. This means that, as a matter of free speech, we have a right to "mention" the trademarks around us, either verbally or visually.

Which brings us back to the COKE® can in that photograph. Although free speech gives us the right to talk about or depict the world we live in, including trademarks, trademark law limits that right to some extent by discouraging certain sorts of uses of trademarks. The law would allow the Coca-Cola Company to sue the ad agency and the agency's client for trademark infringement if anything about the photo that included the COKE can implied that there was some connection between COCA-COLA® and the product advertised in the ad for which the photo was used. The same would be true if consumers could

194

infer from the ad that the Coca-Cola Company somehow sponsored the ad or the product it advertised. As a practical matter, it is not likely that either of these grounds for suit would exist unless the COKE logo was legible and the can on which it appeared was a prominent element of the photograph; a background depiction of the can wouldn't create a problem, especially if the can wasn't an emphasis of the photograph.

Similarly, the context of the appearance in an ad of a "borrowed" trademark is important. If the COKE can photograph depicted the scene around the pool at an upscale resort hotel in an ad for that hotel, implying, however obliquely, that COCA-COLA is a favorite drink of carefree, wealthy people who look good in stylish bathing suits, the Coca-Cola Company probably would not object to the incidental appearance of its name and logo in the ad. If, however, the COKE can appeared in an objectionable photograph or if that photograph were used in any unsavory context, the Coca-Cola Company would be inclined to take whatever action was necessary to halt further use of the photo, especially if the COKE can was prominent in the photograph. The Coca-Cola Company, along with everybody else in the world, knows that villains and heroes and every other variety of human being drink COCA-COLA soft drinks. However, it is understandable that no one in Atlanta except the lawyers who earn their keep by guarding the various valuable COCA-COLA trademarks would like to see an ad photo prominently depicting a COKE can lying on a heap of rancid garbage or a broken COKE bottle being wielded as a weapon in a bar fight. Similarly, an identifiable depiction of a COCA-COLA product used in an ad for a topless bar or cigarettes or a personal hygiene product could earn the animosity of the Coca-Cola Company. Any use of a trademark in an unsavory context can lead to a claim of product disparagement,

195

which is comparable to a defamation suit brought to protect the reputation of a trademark.

Comparative Advertising

Strangely enough, there is one variety of calculated, obvious use of other people's trademarks that will seldom cause trouble if carried out carefully. This is the use of trademarks belonging to competitor companies in comparative advertising. Trademark law does not prohibit *non*trademark or informational uses of the trademarks of others but, rather, punishes uses that confuse consumers. Comparative advertising informs consumers by explicitly comparing the merits of one product with those of another. The competitor's product, which always suffers from the comparison, is mentioned specifically in the ad copy and its package is usually pictured beside the advertiser's product in a head-on shot. Such ads require by their very nature that the products compared be carefully identified before the distinctions between them are drawn; only a very clumsy ad would fail to make entirely clear whether JOY® detergent or IVORY® detergent "cuts grease faster in laboratory tests." The test for trademark infringement is whether the public will be confused by the use of the mark. Since the possibility of consumer confusion is eliminated in comparative advertising, so is the likelihood of any charge of trademark infringement.

However, only claims that are truthful and that can be substantiated are safe. Because exaggerated claims or claims that can't be documented can lead to false advertising suits or unfair competition claims, every statement in a comparative advertising campaign should be carefully documented and every element of the campaign should be carefully designed.

Comparative advertisements can safely make use of competitors' trademarks if they are carefully constructed. Using a photo of another company's product or mentioning the product by name in an ad that compares it to your company's product is not an infringement of the trademark rights of the other company if the ad truthfully compares the products named by the trademarks and if the character and arrangement of the visual elements and the content of the ad copy do not create any likelihood that consumers will somehow mistakenly believe that your company's product has some relation to the product of the other company.

Although properly designed comparative advertising does not usually lead to trademark infringement suits, there is one caveat. Whenever you use a trademark belonging to someone else in an ad, it is only prudent to state who owns that trademark in order to emphasize that the mark has no connection with the advertiser's product. This is easily accomplished by means of a "footnote" ownership statement. That is, a short statement should be included somewhere along the bottom margin or up the side margin of print ads and at the bottom of the screen in television commercials to the effect that "DOVE® is a registered trademark of the Lever Brothers Company."

The competitor's trademark should be used in exactly the form it appears on the competitor's product; that is, if it is a federally registered trademark and bears the ® symbol, that symbol should be used in the ownership statement. If the mark is not registered, no such symbol will appear, or the ™ symbol will be used in conjunction with the mark. In this event, the usage as it appears on the product should be duplicated and the ownership statement should read something like this: "CRUNCHIES™ is a trademark of the Toasted Oats Company and is not owned or licensed by the makers of SWEETIES™ brand cereal." A statement that your client's competitor owns its mark should completely eliminate any valid claim that the comparative ad creates confusion regarding the ownership of the mark or the manufacturer of the product it names. However, because not just any such disclaimer will suffice, any such ad and proposed disclaimer should be reviewed, before the ad is published, by a trademark lawyer, who can evaluate the possibility that the ad will result in an infringement lawsuit.

It is important to remember that the laws regarding comparative advertising in other countries may vary considerably from those in the United States. Be especially sure that any ad you prepare that mentions another company's trademark and will be published or circulated outside the United States will not furnish the owner of the other trademark with grounds for suit. Marketers use comparative advertising because it is effective—a comparative ad can lure consumers away from a product they are in the habit of buying on the strength of its convincing claims of the benefits of a rival product that is "new and improved" or simply "more effective in 75% of laboratory tests." This is enough to make the owners of the product that fares badly in such comparisons want to do whatever they can to stop the further publication of the ad. A lawsuit can do this. If a competitor finds your comparative advertising objectionable and the law in one or more of the countries where the ad appears supports that viewpoint, you will be vulnerable in any country where your competitor can, with a straight face, file a suit. Maybe U.S. law, with its predisposition to allow free speech in all possible contexts, can't be used as a club to stop your trumpeting the better performance of your product, but it may be possible to use the laws of other markets for just such a purpose, and every segment of international commerce counts. Japanese or Swedish or German money can fatten the bottom line for marketers just as well as American dollars. It's possible that somebody who works for your competitor wouldn't mind a long trip abroad at company expense to hire and supervise the lawyers who will be suing you under laws that you never heard of. Since you can't keep a tame trademark lawyer in your desk drawer to consult whenever you need advice, put his or her phone number on your ROLODEX® rotary card file (this is an example of correct usage of a trademark) *and* on your speed dial.

Trademark Parody

When a company decides to market a product under a name that is a parody of another mark, it is engaging in trademark parody. Trademark parody is almost always a bad idea, for two reasons. The first reason is that one of the kinds of confusion that trademark owners can legitimately complain about in court is "dilution," which is a claim that someone's use of an established mark is eroding the mark's strength even though the complained-of use is made in connection with a product that is unrelated to the product named by the established mark. If this fact alone isn't enough to convince you that trademark parody is almost invariably a dumb idea, consider this: only very famous trademarks are parodied—a parody of an obscure mark just wouldn't work. This means that the parodist is picking on a company rich enough to finance a trademark infringement lawsuit out of its petty cash. And since the passage of the Trademark Dilution Act, suits for dilution are easier for owners of famous marks to file and win. (The Federal Express suit to stop the use of FEDERAL ESPRESSO for a coffeehouse is a good example of a parody use of a famous trademark that ran afoul of the Trademark Dilution Act's proscriptions soon after the Act became effective.)

Another factor in trademark parody that often contributes to the problems that parodists face is that the parodied mark is

199

often the butt of a joke, which may be an off-color joke. Nobody likes wise guys. The owners of the parodied mark may be so enraged by the parody of their mark that they will rush to file a trademark infringement suit and ask for an injunction against the parodist. Courts are usually sympathetic to the interests of the owners of famous trademarks; as a result, trademark parodists are routinely enjoined from pursuing their bad jokes at the expense of the well-known marks they parody.

You can understand trademark parody better by considering a few trademark parody cases in which the parodists were ordered by the court to give up making jokes at the expense of the plaintiff trademark owners. The pairs of marks that were the subjects of these suits tell the story in themselves; if reading the list makes you wince, you're getting the right idea about trademark parody. Not surprisingly, all these defendants lost in court.

Plaintiff	Defendant Trademark
Coca-Cola Company	"Enjoy Cocaine" (used, on a poster, in a script and color identical to those used for the COCA-COLA® logo)
Anheuser-Busch, Inc.	"Where There's Life . . .There's Bugs" (for a combination floor wax-insecticide, in a parody of the Anheuser-Busch slogan "Where There's Life . . .There's Bud")
General Electric Company	"Genital Electric" (used, on men's underwear, in a script monogram similar to the GENERAL ELECTRIC® script logo)

| Johnny Carson | "Here's Johnny" (used, as the name of a line of portable toilets, in a parody of the phrase associated with the famous comedian; no trademark infringement was found, but the court found that Mr. Carson's right of publicity had been violated) |

Not every trademark parody is ruled a trademark infringement. For example, the use in a florist's ad campaign of the slogan "This bud's for you" was held not to infringe the trademark rights of Anheuser-Busch, Inc. In its ruling, the court specifically mentioned the innocuous and pleasant nature of the florist's slogan. As a practical matter, all this tells us is that *sometimes* parodists win in court. Since paying to defend a lawsuit is almost as much a misfortune as losing it, this is really no encouragement to would-be parodists. The best thing to do with famous trademarks is to steer clear of them, especially if your parody is smutty or would associate a famous mark with an unsavory product.

More than one trademark infringement lawsuit has been brought simply because the trademark owner was angry and felt like doing something about it. If this doesn't scare you, consider the fact that owners of famous trademarks have whole squads of trademark lawyers who have to justify their existence by periodically going after evildoers. If they are short of true malefactors this month, you and your ad may look like very good targets. When it comes to using someone else's famous trademark in an ad without permission, discretion really is the better part of valor.

The Etiquette of Trademark Usage

The only thing left to say about using other people's trademarks is that you should do so carefully. This boils down to the following four rules:

1. **Trademarks are proper adjectives; remember to use them as such.** It is a "Kleenex® tissue," not just a "kleenex," and you wear "Levi's® jeans," not just "levis."

2. **Trademarks should never be used as nouns or verbs.** You do not "Xerox®" a document, you make a photocopy of it, and it *is* a "photocopy," not simply a "xerox."

3. **Spell it right.** Most importantly, capitalize trademarks; it is "Coke®," not "coke," and "Cuisinart®," not "cuisinart."

4. **Give a mark its due.** If it is a registered mark, use the ® symbol in conjunction with the mark in at least the two or three most prominent uses of the mark in a text or an ad. If it is not registered, use informal trademark notice, i.e., the ™ superscript or subscript, if the owner of the mark does so on its products. (If the mark names a service, the trademark owner may use ˢᴹ to indicate this.)

You can read what the International Trademark Association (INTA) has to say about proper trademark usage in a short but informative little slideshow at http://www.inta.org/Trademark Basics/Documents/INTAProperUsePresentation.ppt#256, or you can read a similar PDF brochure at www.inta.org/TrademarkBasics/Documents/INTATMProperUse.pdf. Print out the slideshow or the brochure and keep it as a reference.

If you are confused about the proper spelling of a trademark or whether it is federally registered and therefore entitled to be escorted by the ® symbol whenever it appears in print, you can research the mark on the International Trademark Association (INTA) website. Compiled to help journalists, proofreaders, and others with proper trademark usage, the INTA's Trademark Checklist exclusively lists trademarks federally registered in the United States (nearly 3,000 marks), along with the generic terms for the products and services they name and indicates proper spelling, capitalization, and punctuation. You can access the INTA's Trademark Checklist at www.inta.org/Media/Pages/TrademarkChecklist.aspx. If you can't find the mark you are investigating, call the INTA Trademark Hotline at (212) 768-9886 for proper-usage information or contact the Hotline at tmhotline@inta.org. The hotline operates weekdays from 2:00 PM to 5:00 PM (EST), except on U.S. national holidays.

Your rights won't be affected if you fail to follow these rules in using other people's trademarks, but theirs may be diminished. A trademark that is used incorrectly can become "generic"; that is, the mark loses its ability to refer to a particular product or service and comes to indicate a whole class of products. If this happens, the original owner of the mark loses the exclusive right to use it. This happened to "aspirin," and "escalator," and "thermos" as well as numerous other once-valuable trademarks. In determining whether a mark has lost its significance as an indicator of *one* company's products or services, courts often consider whether a trademark owner has acted against infringers. You may have no legal *duty* to use the marks of others carefully, but they may have a very good legal reason—the preservation of their rights—to challenge any misuse of those marks.

Because a trademark represents the reputation in the marketplace of the products or services of the company that owns it, it may be that company's most valuable asset. It is understandable that trademark owners pay close attention when their marks are used by people they never met in ways they don't necessarily approve. That's why they spend time writing letters to people who misuse them and money to publish ads to explain proper trademark usage. The way to avoid trouble when using other people's trademarks is to handle them like you would handle other people's money—carefully.

Is It Infringement?

1. **Q.** In an article for a regional business magazine on a local manufacturing magnate, you write "McCarthy knew he had become famous the day he googled himself and the search produced 350 hits." You are pleased with the article. So is Mr. McCarthy, who calls to ask if you'd be available to help his public relations department prepare a longer biography of him. However, you receive a polite but forthright letter in the mail the next week tells you that Google, Inc., the California company that offers GOOGLE™ Internet search services to millions of people all over the world every day, is *not* happy with you and your story. It seems that you have committed a trademark-usage *faux pas*—you turned Google, Inc.'s well-known trademark into a verb when you said that McCarthy "googled" himself.

   You get a little huffy when you read the letter and are still cranky when you have lunch the next day with your old college roommate, who is now a lawyer. You tell him the whole tale, expecting him to laugh at Google, Inc.'s overzealous attitude toward its trademark. You are surprised when he doesn't laugh. You ask him: *Is it infringement?*

   A. No. Not exactly. Your pal tells you that he understands why Google, Inc. objects to your use of GOOGLE as a verb. He even says that if he were house counsel for Google, Inc., he, too, would have written you a letter, except, he says, that he may have been less polite and more threatening. When you ask why, he explains to you that you and every other thoughtless writer and editor who launches an article into the vast river of modern communication are, by ignoring proper use of Google, Inc.'s trademark, actually eroding the company's mark. You bluster that you don't see how one little freelance writer (you) can do anything to harm such a big company.

Your pal tells you that that is just the attitude that helped to transform many former trademarks into ordinary English words that have lost their original function of pointing to the products of a particular marketer. While you are thinking about this, your old roommate tells you that GOOGLE™ for search engine services may be in danger of losing its trademark status *because* it has become such a well-known name and *because* people like you have begun to use it as a verb. He says, "Why do you think the Xerox Corporation has spent so much advertising money encouraging the correct use of its mark? They may have been able to stop enough people from saying, and writing, 'make a Xerox of this' to preserve the function of their mark. Courts look at things like that when they have to decide whether a mark has become generic, you know."

You didn't know, but you do now. And you feel guilty; after all, you are supposed to be a business writer. You promise your buddy that you will reform. He suggests that you go to the website mentioned in the letter from Google, Inc. and familiarize yourself with the rules for proper usage of the GOOGLE trademark. You read what Google, Inc. has to say at www.google.com/permissions/guidelines.html and vow to become more conscious of proper trademark usage. Then you realize that perhaps this is a new area of expertise that you can pitch to Mr. McCarthy when you meet with him—after all, as a businessman, he has to be aware of the worth of his company's trademarks.

2. Q. Before the annual match between the University of Tennessee Vols and the football team at the big university you attend, you and several of your fraternity brothers spend two whole evenings in the basement of the fraternity house working on the shirts you will wear to the game. You bought an orange UT T-shirt for every guy in your fraternity; then you used wide red tape to create an international "prohibited" symbol on top of the UT logo on each shirt, something like a "no smoking" sign. At the game you and the guys—and your shirts—are a hit. Two of your frat brothers sell their shirts to other fans that day, right off their backs, for fifty dollars each. When you return from the game, you are excited even though your team lost. You think you have figured out how to pay your tuition next term.

The following Monday you consult with a local printer. He agrees to print up five hundred orange tees for you, each bearing the UT logo with a big red "prohibited" symbol on top of it. You plan to sell them on the Internet to other UT football opponents and ship them from the frat house basement. The shirts are printed by the end of the week and before the month is out you have had to reorder your shirts, which you sell for twenty dollars each.

Then you get a call from the dean of men, who wants you to come and visit him, *immediately.* You figure that he's heard about your entrepreneurial acumen and that he wants to congratulate you, maybe even give you some kind of award. But he isn't happy when you go to his office. In fact, he calls you "bone-headed" and tells you that you are going to be sued by the University of Tennessee if you don't give up moonlighting as a T-shirt mogul. You're puzzled. You ask him "What did I do? Is it possible—could it be? *Is it infringement?*"

A. The dean tells you that for answers to your questions you need to see somebody in the university counsel's office and that you have an appointment there in five minutes. You figure that's as good a reason as any to cut your afternoon chemistry lab and you rush to the appointment that you didn't know you had with the lawyer for the university. He doesn't have much time for you, either, but he listens for a few minutes to your account of how your brilliant idea came about— the tale about the UT shirts and the red tape and the popularity of your homemade "anti-UT" shirts at the UT game. But he doesn't listen for even one minute to your claims that your shirts are just an example of harmless parody.

It seems that you have been guilty of trademark infringement, that your use of the UT logo on your shirts violates the valuable rights of the University of Tennessee in its trademark. He tells you that after you buy a shirt with a trademark on it, you can do whatever you want with it, including destroying it, except duplicate it. The red-tape shirts didn't violate anybody's

207

rights and *were* a permissible parody. However, your manufacture and sale of the printed "anti-UT" shirts did violate UT's trademark rights, because you duplicated—and altered—the UT logo without permission and the only reason the shirts sold was that they bore a version, albeit altered, of the UT logo.

He tells you that you are a "young idiot" and that he will be expecting you to turn over all your unsold T-shirts by nine o'clock the following day and that if you have any real business sense, you'll do whatever you can to make UT happy with you. Further, he says that you probably owe UT every nickel of the money you made from sales of the shirt and that if UT will accept that amount as damages for your infringing action, you'll be lucky. Then he tells you he has more important things to do than to instruct young upstarts like you and tells you that you should come back the next day to sign the settlement agreement that he is almost sure UT will fax to him after he pleads your case—and your ignorance—to their university counsel.

You thank him and leave. You don't feel as grateful as he seems to think you should, but you do decide, privately, that you probably have to abandon your plans to ship some shirts to your brother at the University of Oklahoma before their big game with another "UT," the University of Texas. Ah, the vicissitudes of capitalism.

3. Q. You are a member of the board of directors for the local humane association and in charge of planning the publicity for the association's annual "Adopt-A-Pet" drive. You come up with a great idea to encourage local citizens to pick out a pet at the association's

animal shelter. You get a local grocery store to donate free pet food for a year to the winners of a drawing; everyone who adopts a stray dog or cat during the "Adopt-A-Pet" drive is eligible to win. You prepare a big ad to publicize the prizes and run it four consecutive weeks in the local newspaper. Nearly fifty stray dogs and cats are adopted during the drive and one dog owner and one cat owner are awarded the free food.

You feel like a marketing genius until you get a message from one of the humane association staffers to call a lawyer in Chicago who is, in the words of the staffer, "like, really bent out of shape, man." You call the lawyer, even though you think that he must have confused you with someone else. But you find out he wasn't mistaken when he tells you that he represents Purina Mills, which is unhappy with you—specifically with the newspaper ad you wrote and designed. It seems that a Purina brand manager spotted the ad and passed it on to the Purina legal department, which forwarded it to the Chicago lawyer, who tells you that you are in trouble for trademark infringement.

Your use of the PURINA® PUPPY CHOW®, DOG CHOW®, KITTEN CHOW®, and CAT CHOW® trademarks in your ad has irritated Purina, partly because of the reproduction of those marks and partly because the entire ad is designed in such a way as to leave the impression that Purina Mills was the sponsor of your free pet food contest. You thought you were very clever when you scanned the pet food logos into your computer to reproduce in your ad; now, when you take a look at the ad again, you see that readers could easily believe that Purina sponsored the contest or was directly associated with it. Now the Chicago lawyer is mumbling about suing the humane association. You tell him that you'll get back to him after you consult with another board member, who is a real estate lawyer. He hands you off to a trademark lawyer in his firm. You ask the dread question: *Is it infringement?*

A. Yes. Under most circumstances, you would have a lawsuit on your hands. When the trademark lawyer sees the ad you fax to him, he tells you that the mere prominence of the Purina trademarks in your ad, along with the line of copy beneath them reading "Free Purina pet food for a year!" is enough to make Purina's complaint legitimate. He explains that in your effort to create awareness of your pet-adoption drive you have committed the commercial sin of trademark infringement by trading on the excellent, well-established reputation of Purina Mills for quality pet food. He tells you that it makes no difference that you meant only to publicize your drive and the associated free-pet-food contest—an inadvertent infringement is still an infringement.

He also tells you that it is immaterial that the humane association is a nonprofit corporation and that you were acting for it without pay—apparently trademark infringement is trademark infringement and there is no exception for charities or civic organizations or amateur advertising copywriters. However, after you tell him that your ad ran only four times in only one newspaper that has a circulation area of only two counties and that nobody made any money off the ad or the contest and that, like most nonprofits, the humane association has very little money, he says that he can get you off the hook. He makes you promise never to run the ad again or use it in any way. You promptly agree.

Later that day he calls back to say that he has talked to Purina's lawyer and explained the situation, that Purina is being a good sport and won't sue or ask for any monetary settlement, and that it has promised to donate the pet food for next year's "Adopt-A-Pet" drive if you will agree to let it review any ad you create to publicize the drive. You quickly agree, hang up the phone, shred the ad that got you in trouble, and vow never to buy any kind of food for your cat but Purina.

4. Q. You are certain that your laundry and dry cleaning shop gets men's shirts cleaner than Shirts to Go, a similar business two blocks over. You know this because you have at least one businessman in your shop every week with a shirt laundered there that still shows food or ink stains. These poor guys always ask, "Can you can do anything to save my shirt?" Usually, you can fix their problem with a little extra attention before running the shirt through your usual laundry process.

One day when a Shirts to Go customer brings in a stained shirt still in the Shirts to Go wrapper and asks the familiar question, you decide to seize the opportunity and take "before" and "after" pictures of his shirt, which is much improved by being laundered by your process. Then you make the shirt photos the centerpiece of an ad. The shirt is anonymous, but you name your competitor in the ad, in a headline that tells it like it is: "Two Pictures Are Worth a Thousand

Words—Mack's Laundry Outcleans Shirts to Go."
Under the headline you print a photo of the stained
shirt still in the Shirts to Go wrapper and one of the
same shirt, minus the ink stain on the breast pocket, in
a Mack's wrapper. There is no other copy except the
name, address, and phone number of your shop.

You get a handful of new customers every day for
the next month—most of them are former Shirts to Go
customers who bring in their dingy and stained shirts
to see if you can return them to wearability. But one
result of the ad is a nasty phone call from the Shirts
to Go owner, who also saw the ad and who threatens,
loudly, to sue you for trademark infringement. You tell
him you'll have to get back to him; then you call your
lawyer, whom you ask: *Is it infringement?*

A. No, it's not. When you show your lawyer the ad and
tell him the circumstances that led to it, he tells you
that you have nothing to worry about, despite the
threats of your competitor. You have simply told the
truth in your ad. There is no basis for any complaint
for trademark infringement because the ad doesn't
trade on your competitor's name or attempt to imply
some association with the business it names. Rather,
anyone who sees the ad can quickly determine that
Shirts to Go is not associated with you but is, rather,
your competitor and that your ad distinguishes between that business and your own by contrasting the
quality of the service offered under each name.

Your lawyer says that because the ad creates
absolutely no likelihood of confusion between the two
businesses, there can be no infringement. Further, he
says there isn't even any argument that your use of the

Shirts to Go name dilutes that name because the name
is not famous enough to qualify for the protections
of the Trademark Dilution Act. He says that your
competitor's threats must stem from mere anger and
jealousy because there is no legal basis for a lawsuit.
You are relieved. You buy space to run the ad every
Monday for the next six months and you don't hear
from the Shirts to Go owner again, probably, you sur-
mise, because *his* lawyer told him the same thing you
found out from yours.

5. Q. You run an Italian restaurant in the small town where
you've lived all your life. It's a profitable business,
but you have to watch expenses. As an economic measure, you fire your ad agency and hire your nephew,
who has a degree in marketing. You figure that, unlike
the ad agency, he'll follow your instructions, won't cost
an arm and a leg, and will be at your beck and call
every day, all day. The first project you give him is the
Christmas card you send every year to your customers.
Over the years people have come to value receiving your
Christmas cards—partly because the cards are always
attractive, partly because you enclose a coupon good for
a spaghetti dinner for two with every card.

Your nephew has the idea of printing a photo of
your restaurant on this year's card. He takes several
photographs of the restaurant but you know the one
you want to use as soon as you see it. It is an exterior
shot taken at dusk on a Saturday night from the roof
of the hardware store across the street. It's a good
view of the front of your restaurant, the sign that says
"Roma Ristorante," and the line of people waiting for
a table on the benches in front of the restaurant. You

like the fact that the photo includes the front of Tony's Spaghetti House two doors down where *no one* is waiting for a table.

You approve the photo for your Christmas cards and tell your nephew to build an ad campaign around it. You also frame an enlargement of the photo and hang it over the hostess station in the entryway of your restaurant. The Christmas cards go out, the ads begin running in local publications, people are asking for posters of the photo, and it's harder than ever to get a table at Roma. You think about giving your nephew a raise until the day you get a call from your lawyer, who has received, as registered agent for The Roma Corporation, the complaint in a lawsuit filed by Tony, the proprietor of Tony's Spaghetti House. He tells you that you have been sued for trademark infringement for using the photo you like so well in your ads and on your Christmas cards because that photo also includes a view of Tony's establishment.

You ask your lawyer whether Tony has a valid claim, but your lawyer tells you he doesn't know because he knows almost nothing about trademark law. Then he gives you the name of another lawyer in town who may be able to help you. You consult her as soon as you have a copy of the complaint in the lawsuit. Of course, you want to ask her: *Is it infringement?*

Your trademark lawyer is a nice young woman named Gina who looks like your sister and isn't wearing a wedding band. You wait anxiously for her to read the complaint and look at your Christmas card and newspaper ad. When she offers you some coffee, you think she's trying to make you comfortable before she tells you that you're in a lot of trouble. But instead, she hauls out some biscotti she says her mother made, tells you that Tony is her cousin but no one in her family likes him, and assures you that he has absolutely no ground at all for a trademark infringement suit and that she thinks she can get the suit dismissed on summary judgment.

You ask her "But what about the fact that you can see Tony's Spaghetti House in the photo we used? We did use the photo in an ad and that is his trademark, the name of his business." "Not to worry," Gina says, "You have the right to use a picture of your own business in advertising and the fact that Tony's restaurant is two doors down from yours makes it almost inevitable that it would be pictured in some of your advertising materials." She says that there's nothing in your Christmas card or ad that otherwise refers to Tony's—both are clearly promoting your Roma Ristorante—and that the inclusion in the photograph of Tony's is simply an "incidental" depiction of a business on the same street as yours.

"But," you say, "maybe the ad is some kind of defamation of Tony's. Anybody who sees the photos is bound to notice that there are two Italian restaurants practically next door to each other and that one has a lot of customers and one doesn't. Isn't that slander or something?" Gina tells you that there is such a thing as trademark disparagement, which is saying something derogatory and untrue about a product or service by name, but that this is not such a case. She says that you have a right to depict your business in your advertising and a right to publicize its success.

You just can't say or print something negative *and* untrue about Tony's. Since you haven't done that, he cannot sue you—and win—just because he doesn't like your ad.

Then she asks, "Did you get releases from any of the people in your photo?" and says that someone whose image is used in advertising without permission can sue. You tell her you didn't because you didn't know releases were necessary and that you'll check into it. Then you tell her to take care of the suit, that no one in your family likes Tony either, and you ask her for two of her business cards. You give one to your nephew and suggest that he invite Gina to lunch at Roma to find out about photo releases for advertising. You also tell him that if he were to marry a nice Italian girl—say, a lawyer—you'd have to give him a big raise.

I'll See You in Court

The following are thumbnail accounts of actual trademark disputes between the owners of established trademarks and people who used identical marks for *unrelated* products or services. These accounts are proof that the owners of famous trademarks are serious—some would say over vigilant—about protecting their marks. Sometimes the owners of the famous marks won their suits against the accused interlopers, sometimes the courts sided with the junior user of the mark—either way, being the object of a lawsuit filed by a rich plaintiff is a memorable misfortune.

- The giant cereal manufacturer, the Kellogg Company, sued Toucan Golf, Inc., which marketed golf clubs and other golf products by using a depiction of a toucan and the words "Toucan Golf." Kellogg claimed that Toucan Golf infringed on Kellogg's Toucan Sam cartoon trademarks used to market cereals. The court did not agree.

- The online auction giant eBay has been active in challenging similar and parody names for unconnected trading sites. It sued BidBay, a rival auction site, sent a letter to AlternaBay, a gay auction site, and complained about a parody site called eGray.org, which was run by opponents of (then) California governor Gray Davis. A Lego-trading site named BrickBay.com changed its name to BrickLink. com after eBay said that BrickBay infringed eBay's trademark rights. The famous eBay has staked its claim to a large hunk of cyberspace and intends to keep it.

- The World Wrestling Federation (WWF) wrote a letter to the independent record label that marketed the recordings of Wesley Willis, asking it to stop the sale and distribution of an album called "The Wesley Willis Fiasco Live E.P." The album cover featured a logo similar to the WWF logo. The WWF letter claimed that the album logo infringed upon and diluted the WWF trademark and asked that all copies of the album be recalled and destroyed or surrendered to the WWF.

- The World Wildlife Fund sued the World Wrestling Federation to compel it to live up to a 1994 agreement not to use the WWF abbreviation, which the World Wildlife Fund registered when it was formed in 1961. The wildlife group wants the wrestling group to stop using any domain name that includes the WWF mark and to stop selling merchandise bearing it.

- The large online merchant Amazon.com sued Amazon Cosmetics and Tan Products, the owner of Amazontan. com, saying that the beauty products company was infringing its rights; the suit was dismissed on jurisdictional grounds. It also sued the operator of Amazon.gr, which called itself "Greece's Biggest Bookstore"; the Greek business was ordered by the court to stop using the Amazon name.

- The OCLC Online Computer Library Center, Inc. sued The Library Hotel, a boutique New York hotel near the main New York Public Library, for trademark infringement. It claimed that The Library Hotel was using the DEWEY DECIMAL CLASSIFICATION® trademarks without permission. The hotel features theme-based rooms and each room is stocked with books that relate to its specific DEWEY DECIMAL® theme. The suit was settled; the hotel was granted permission to use the OCLC's trademarks in its hotel and marketing materials and the hotel made a charitable contribution to promote children's reading.

Chapter 10
Trademarks in
Cyberspace

Like all frontiers, cyberspace is largely populated by mavericks and rebels who like the cyber-atmosphere of "if you can imagine it, you can do it." Unfortunately, the very dearth of rules that makes cyberspace so intriguing to everyone who has something to say or sell electronically is also causing problems. Americans often complain about overregulation by local, state, and federal governmental agencies and authorities. But many who are familiar with the problems that have arisen as the Internet becomes more and more indispensable, would agree that, in some corners of cyberspace, more rules are needed.

One aspect of cyber-commerce has produced disputes since the very early days of the Internet; this is the ownership of domain names. A domain name is the heart of an email address. In the email address johnjones@jonesventures.com, "jonesventures.com" is the domain name. Domain names tell Internet users where to find companies and individuals in cyberspace. They function like ZIP codes do for "snail mail"; they direct email and other communications to the right cyberspace neighborhood to find the person or entity named in the first part of the email address. They allow Internet users to visit World Wide Web pages.

Internet addresses are actually a series of numbers. However, because people who want to locate an Internet merchant are much more likely to remember a verbal address than a series of numbers, domain names are alpha and/or numeric names that a computer can convert to numeric addresses. This means that the best domain names look like the names of the companies that own them; this sort of domain name creates an expectation as to who is at the Internet address it names. If you are familiar with a company and its domain name resembles the name of the company, you know what you will find at its address on the Internet. Such Internet addresses are easy to guess and easy to remember. For example, because ibm.com is the heart of the Internet address for IBM, anyone can guess that that address belongs to that company.

And although multiple companies engaged in different sorts of business can share a business name, or elements of their names, without confusion because people shopping for tires won't look for them in grocery stores, the same is not true for Internet addresses that are very similar. Because cyberspace isn't a physical space but is, rather, a conceptual place, the physical attributes of a product, such as where it is manufactured and in what stores it is sold do not mitigate any similarity between product or company names. That is, the Internet—the information superhighway—lines up businesses, along with other entities, *only* according to their addresses. And no factor besides addresses determines the accessibility of those businesses and other entities.

To understand this critical distinction between company names and domain names, consider the Johnsons. There are many Johnson companies in the U.S. and they offer everything from paint to accounting services. The products of two of them can be found in literally nearly every household in the country; they are the S.C. Johnson Company and Johnson & Johnson, which is really a family of companies. The S.C. Johnson Company manufactures and markets WINDEX®, ZIPLOC®, PLEDGE!®, and GLADE® products, among many others. Johnson & Johnson manufactures BAND-AID®, MOTRIN®, MYLANTA®, NEUTROGENA®, and SPLENDA® products, among many others, including JOHNSON'S® baby products. We distinguish one giant Johnson company from the other because we shop for WINDEX®, ZIPLOC®, PLEDGE!®, and GLADE® products in different aisles of the supermarket from the ones in which we buy BAND-AID®, MOTRIN®, MYLANTA®, NEUTROGENA®, and SPLENDA® products, and JOHNSON® baby products.

Further, because of the reputations of the different brands owned by these two companies, we shop for the brand names *themselves* rather than specifically for the products of one Johnson company or the other. This sort of differentiation is not possible in cyberspace. Neither company can use the dominant verbal element of its name—Johnson—*alone* in its name for its web address, so the S.C. Johnson Company uses www.scjohnson.com as its web address and Johnson & Johnson's web address is www.jnj.com. (The domain name www.johnson.com is the address for yet *another* Johnson company, the company that manufactures Johnson outboard motors.) In cyberspace you can't stand in front of a store, look through the front window, and see that home-cleaning products or over-the-counter medications and cosmetics are sold there. Instead, you have to depend on the domain name or Internet address for that business.

The system of categorizing Internet user addresses according to type is familiar to most net surfers. They are the generic Top Level Domain names, or gTLDs. The original major non-military domains were .com for commercial entities, .gov for governmental bodies, .edu for educational institutions, .org for organizations, and .net for networks. ICANN, the Internet Corporation for Assigned Names and Numbers (found at www. icann.org), later introduced seven new domain-name categories: .biz, .info, .aero, .museum, .name, .pro, and .coop. Not just anyone can use these domain-name categories; .biz is restricted to businesses; .aero is reserved for the use of airlines and similar organizations, .museum is limited to museums; .name is for personal names, .pro is reserved for licensed professionals like doctors, lawyers, and accountants; and .coop is only for cooperatives. More domain-name suffixes have followed in the nearly thirty years since the advent of the domain-name system. There are currently twenty-two generic domain-name extensions and 240 country and territory suffixes.

That may be about to change. ICANN announced in 2011 that additional domain-name categories will be expanded. Companies and groups may now apply to register their own domain-name suffixes—almost any word in any language will be eligible, including domain names based on common words, brands, company names, cities, and proper names. These new domain names will be available only at considerable cost—at least $185,000 to apply with an additional $25,000 annually. The chairman of ICANN predicted that the expanded system will "usher in a new Internet age." For any company with enough money to obtain a registration, the expanded system may open up an additional avenue for extending its brand—big companies like Coca-Cola and Apple will almost certainly come up with domain names that sport their own, exclusive extensions, such as .coke or .apple. UNICEF, Paris, New York, Canon, and Hitachi have already announced plans to file for the domain name suffixes .unicef, .paris, .nyc, .canon, and .hitachi. ICANN announced that it would begin to accept applications for domain names with the new suffixes during the first half of 2012 and that the new domain-name extensions would be in use by mid-2012.

Unless ICANN bows to the objections of numerous U.S. and international corporations who want ICANN to drop or postpone the introduction of so many new domain names. These business interests worry that the proposed onslaught of new domain names could force businesses to register their own domain names to avoid registration by others. The executive director of the Association of National Advertisers said, "Opening the name spigot is extraordinarily radical and reckless."

So what does the proliferation of Internet domain names mean to the average person who markets products or services on the Internet? Mostly it means that the Internet is going to continue to be a crowded place. It may be harder than ever to choose a domain name that distinguishes you from the enlarging crowd of other website owners and marketers. And there are going to be even more toes to step on in the most crowded part of cyberspace, the commercial district. Fortunately, you can avoid these two problems by judicious consideration of the dilemmas when you pick and register a domain name.

Choosing a Domain Name

All the same considerations inherent in choosing a new trademark apply to the task of selecting a good domain name. (See chapter 4 for the list of the Ten Deadly Sins of Trademark Selection.) However, one of these considerations is particularly germane if you want your domain name to function as a trademark. This is the question whether the domain name is "merely descriptive" of the product or services offered on your website. If the domain name you choose *is* "merely descriptive," it is said to be "generic"—that is, it merely describes what it names and cannot function as a signpost to *your* particular products or services because it applies equally as well to those of others.

This is what the Trademark Manual of Examining Procedure (the TMEP—the rule book used by the examining attorneys of the Trademark Office to decide which trademarks are allowed to be registered) has to say about domain names and their registrability:

Domain Names

A mark comprised of an Internet domain name is registrable as a trademark or service mark only if it functions as an identifier of the source of goods or services. Portions of the uniform resource locator ("URL"), including the beginning, ("http://www.") and the top-level Internet domain name ("TLD") (e.g., ".com," ".org," ".edu,") function to indicate an address on the World Wide Web, and, therefore, generally serve no source-indicating function. . . . The TLD typically signifies the type of entity using the domain name. For example, the TLD ".com" signifies to the public that the user of the domain name constitutes a commercial entity, ".edu" signifies an educational institution, ".biz" signifies a business, and ".org" signifies a non-commercial organization. TLDs designated for types of entities using the TLDs must be treated as non-source-indicating. As the number of available TLDs is increased by the Internet Corporation for Assigned Names and Numbers ("ICANN"), or if the nature of new TLDs changes, the examining attorney must consider any potential source-indicating function of the TLD and introduce evidence as to the significance of the TLD. . . .

Because TLDs generally serve no source-indicating function, their addition to an otherwise unregistrable mark typically cannot render it registrable.

In re 1800Mattress.com . . . MATTRESS.COM [was held to be] generic for "online retail store services in the field of mattresses, beds, and bedding," and applicant "presented no evidence that ".com" evoked anything but a commercial internet domain");

In re Hotels.com, . . . HOTELS.COM [was held to be] generic for "providing information for others about temporary lodging; [and] travel agency services, namely, making reservations and bookings for temporary lodging for others by means of telephone and the global computer network");

In re Reed Elsevier Properties Inc., . . . LAWYERS. COM [was held to be] generic for "providing an online interactive database featuring information exchange in the fields of law, legal news and legal services");

In re Oppedahl & Larson LLP, . . . PATENTS.COM [was held to be] merely descriptive of computer software for managing a database of records and for tracking the status of the records by means of the Internet);

In re Eddie Z's Blinds & Drapery, Inc., . . . BLINDSANDDRAPERY.COM [was held to be] generic for retail store services featuring blinds, draperies and other wall coverings, sold via the Internet);

In re Microsoft Corp., . . . [The court said] "[t]he combination of the specific term and TLD at issue, i.e., OFFICE and .NET, does not create any double entendre, incongruity, or any other basis upon which we can find the composite any more registrable than its separate elements. The combination immediately informs prospective purchasers that the software includes 'office suite' type software and is from an Internet business, i.e., a '.net' type business.");

In re CyberFinancial.Net, Inc., . . . [The court said] "[a]pplicant seeks to register the generic term 'bonds,' which has no source-identifying significance in connection with applicant's services, in combination with the top level domain indicator ".com," which also has no source-identifying significance. And combining the two terms does not create a term capable of identifying and distinguishing applicant's services."); . . . Only in rare instances will the addition of a TLD indicator to a descriptive term operate to create a distinctive mark. There is no bright-line, per se rule that the addition of a TLD to an otherwise descriptive mark will never, under any circumstances, operate to create a registrable mark. If the TLD is capable of indicating a source, the addition of the source-indicating TLD to an otherwise unregistrable mark may render it registrable. . . .

Thus, when examining domain name marks, it is important to evaluate the commercial impression of the mark as a whole to determine whether the composite mark conveys any distinctive source-identifying impression apart from its individual components.

In discussing the problem of generic domain names, the TMEP sets out a two-part test for determining whether a name is generic: "(1) What is the genus of goods or services at issue? and (2) Does the relevant public understand the designation primarily to refer to that genus of goods or services?" If the public thinks your name is generic, it is. What you *intend* when you choose a domain name is less important, when it comes to whether the domain name is registrable as a trademark, than what the public *thinks* it means.

Often marketers think that a generic name for a product or service or website is better than a more imaginative name because it says what the product or service or website is or does. But, of course, that is the problem. If the generic name describes the product or service or website, there is nothing to distinguish your website from others like it. Your generic website domain name can disappear you into the deep reaches of the Internet on a fat cloud of anonymity unless it serves to point people to you and only you.

The practical import of all this is to beware of calling the website where you sell your custom-printed T-shirts "online-tees.com" or the website that sells your new online accounting services "bookkeepers.com." Call it "originali-tees.com" or "meningreeneyeshades.com" and you are much more likely to be granted federal trademark protection for the name of your website. Not only will you be able to build your own unique web presence, you will be able to stop those whose website or business names infringe yours.

227

Whatever domain name you select to name your website, remember that even if it doesn't really serve the functions of a trademark, it can certainly still infringe an established trademark by creating a false association between your domain name and the existing trademark to which it is similar or by "diluting" a famous mark. Which is the second big problem online marketers and website owners face: stepping on the toes—if not the reputation—of other marketers, online or offline.

Signing Up and Signing On

The best tool for eliminating any unavailable website domain name is, of course, right at your fingertips: Google. Use Google or another major search engine to search to figure out whether the domain name is already in use and, therefore, unavailable. Let's say you want to name your mail order basketball-equipment store "toughontheboards.com." A Google search tells you that there is, currently, no such address, so you approach a domain-name registrar to buy the domain name. (You can find a directory of accredited registrars, the countries in which they operate, and the TLD categories for which they grant registrations on the ICANN website at www.icann.org/registrars/accredited-list.html.) Any problem with a conflicting, existing name *should* be cleared up by your purchase of your name, since, presumably, no registrar will grant a registration for an existing name. This is, to some extent, true. But remember that your website name doesn't have to be identical to an existing domain name or trademark in order to infringe it.

228

Obstacles on the Superhighway

So far, trademark disputes have been one of the biggest impediments facing Internet marketers. The gist of trademark law is that every marketer is entitled to his or her own reputation in the marketplace. Any interference with this—any act that causes consumers to confuse the products or services of one marketer with those of another—is trademark infringement. Anyone who understands trademark law would agree that domain names are more than just virtual street addresses.

Problems with domain names have usually arisen when one company registered a domain name identical or similar to the name of another company. It is reasonable that a company whose name had been adopted as the domain name of another enterprise would feel that its rights in its trademark—the embodiment of its commercial reputation—had been infringed. One variety of trademark infringement is confusion of sponsorship or affiliation. If, on account of similarities between a domain name and the name of an unrelated company, consumers are likely to believe that there is some relationship between the owner of the domain name and the company, the company's trademark rights have been infringed.

Superhighway Robbery

Trademark disputes have, in recent years, resulted when competitors and pranksters have registered domain names that are logically related to the names of established companies. Many such domain-name registrations were apparently made for the purpose of extorting fat buyouts from rich corporations. In the early days of the Internet, a journalist registered the domain name mcdonalds.com as a part of his research for an article for *Wired* magazine. Needless to say, McDonald's was chagrined to find that the most obvious domain name it could choose had already been registered. Some overeager capitalist at Sprint Communications registered mci.com; not surprisingly, MCI Telecommunications objected. The Princeton Review, a leading test-preparation company, registered kaplan.com, a domain name based on the name of its competitor, Stanley Kaplan Review, and planned to set up a website that compared the two companies' products, presumably showing the alleged inferiority of the Kaplan products. The domain name mtv.com was registered and used by a former MTV employee. The domain names windows95.com and nyt.com were registered by people who were not connected with Microsoft and the New York Times. Although several of these early "land grabs" resulted in lawsuits, all four disputes were settled out of court.

    Similar problems have arisen when companies have registered domain names they had no intention of using. This has been done in the hope that some company that does want to use one of the registered domain names will buy it from the original registrant. This sort of kidnapping has been fairly common.

Superhighway Patrol

The Internet grew—and grew big—before there were enough systems to control its growth. However, it may be that domain-name disputes will soon become merely a relic of the early, lawless days when the Internet was new and land grabs were still possible. In late 1999, ICANN acted to settle, if not obviate, most domain-name disputes. ICANN adopted the Uniform Domain Name Dispute Resolution Policy. (You can read the short, clearly written Policy at www.icann.org/en/ dndr/udrp/policy.htm.) The Policy has now been adopted by all ICANN-accredited domain-name registrars and by some managers of country-code top-level domains. This is what ICANN (at www.icann.org/en/udrp/udrp.htm) has to say about its Uniform Domain-Name Dispute-Resolution Policy:

230

> All registrars must follow the Uniform Domain-Name Dispute-Resolution Policy (often referred to as the "UDRP"). Under the policy, most types of trademark-based domain-name disputes must be resolved by agreement, court action, or arbitration before a registrar will cancel, suspend, or transfer a domain name. Disputes alleged to arise from abusive registrations of domain names (for example, cybersquatting) may be addressed by expedited administrative proceedings that the holder of trademark rights initiates by filing a complaint with an approved dispute-resolution service provider.

> To invoke the policy, a trademark owner should either (a) file a complaint in a court of proper jurisdiction against the domain-name holder (or where appropriate an in rem action concerning the domain name) or

(b) in cases of abusive registration submit a complaint to
an approved dispute-resolution service provider

Among other important innovations, the Policy, which is
employed by domain-name registrars, states that, in applying
to register a domain name, a would-be domain-name registrant represents that:

1. the statements made in the registrant's Registration Agreement are complete and accurate;
2. to the knowledge of the registrant the registration of the
   domain name will not infringe upon or otherwise violate
   the rights of any third party;
3. the registrant is not registering the domain name for an
   unlawful purpose; and
4. the registrant will not knowingly use the domain name in
   violation of any applicable laws or regulations. (The registrant is responsible for determining whether the domain
   name infringes or violates someone else's rights.)

231

Despite these requirements to keep domain-name registrants honest, any entity that believes its rights are being harmed
by the use of a particular domain name has the right to complain to the registrar. Any registrant accused of using a domain
name to which it is not entitled must submit to a mandatory
administrative proceeding conducted by an approved arbitrator.

All would-be registrants are required to submit to a mandatory administrative proceeding if a third party complains that:

 (i) the would-be registrant's domain name is identical or
     confusingly similar to a trademark or service mark in
     which the complainant has rights; and
 (ii) the would-be registrant has no rights or legitimate
     interests in respect of the domain name; and
(iii) the would-be registrant's domain name has been regis-
     tered and is being used in bad faith.

In the administrative proceeding, the complainant must prove that each of these three elements is present.

To prevail, a complaining entity must prove to a registrar that a registrant's name is identical or confusingly similar to a trademark or service mark in which the complaining entity has rights, that the registrant has no rights or legitimate interests in the domain name, and that the domain name has been registered and is being used in bad faith. Under the Policy a registrar may cancel or transfer any domain-name registration if a court, administrative body, or arbitrator determines that the registrant is not actually entitled to the domain name.

Bad faith on the part of a would-be domain-name registrant is judge by the following criteria:

Evidence of Registration and Use in Bad Faith. For the purposes of Paragraph 4(a)(iii) [of ICANN's Uniform Domain Name Dispute Resolution Policy], the following circumstances, in particular but without limitation, if found by the Panel to be present, shall be evidence of the registration and use of a domain name in bad faith:

(i) circumstances indicating that you have registered or you have acquired the domain name primarily for the purpose of selling, renting, or otherwise transferring the domain name registration to the complainant who is the owner of the trademark or service mark or to a competitor of that complainant, for valuable consideration in excess of your documented out-of-pocket costs directly related to the domain name; or

(ii) you have registered the domain name in order to prevent the owner of the trademark or service mark from reflecting the mark in a corresponding domain name, provided that you have engaged in a pattern of such conduct; or

(iii) you have registered the domain name primarily for the purpose of disrupting the business of a competitor; or

(iv) by using the domain name, you have intentionally attempted to attract, for commercial gain, Internet users to your web site or other on-line location, by creating a likelihood of confusion with the complainant's mark as to the source, sponsorship, affiliation, or endorsement of your web site or location or of a product or service on your web site or location.

You can read the decisions under the UDRP at www.icann. org/en/udrp/Detail128.htm. They are informative, often resulting in the transfer of the infringing name to the complaining party, as was the case with the dispute over the dailymail.biz domain name, owned originally by a U.S. company named DomainsInvest.net. The London newspaper, the *Daily Mail,* sued, asserting that

The Respondent registered the disputed domain name solely for the purpose of selling, renting or otherwise transferring the domain name registration to the Complainant or a competitor of the Complainant for valuable consideration in excess of the Respondent's out-of-pocket costs related to the domain name.

The Respondent intended to capitalize on the repute of the DAILY MAIL mark by registering the domain name. On the Complainant's initial contact, the Respondent requested the extortionate sum of US$15,000. This sum was increased by a further US$5,000 within a day of receiving the Complainant's enquiry. Reference to another bidder for the name is an attempt to put pressure on the Complainant to purchase the name and an excuse to raise the price demanded.

The intended purpose for the dailymail.biz domain name to advertise web design services means that the Respondent is showing an intention to attract, for commercial gain, Internet users to its website by creating a likelihood of confusion with the Complainant's DAILY MAIL trade mark, as to the source, sponsorship, affiliation or endorsement of the Respondent's website or products or services thereof. It is difficult to see any other reason for the choice of the Daily Mail name for web design services.

The Panel that heard the case ruled:

234

(a) the domain name registered by the Respondent is identical to trademarks in which the Complainant has rights;

(b) the Respondent has no rights or legitimate interests in respect of the domain name; and

(c) the Respondent has registered and is using the domain name in bad faith.

Accordingly, the Panel ordered the transfer of the disputed domain name dailymail.biz to the London newspaper whose name was hijacked.

The Uniform Domain-Name Dispute-Resolution Policy should all but eliminate domain-name hijacking, at least after the hijacked party complains against the hijacker. In addition, the UDRP will reduce disputes between legitimate businesses by requiring a registrant to figure out, in advance of trying to register a domain name, whether the name will infringe the rights of anyone else. This would seem to make a trademark search a prerequisite for applying to register a domain name.

Work in Progress

The Uniform Domain-Name Dispute-Resolution Policy isn't exactly international law, but it is like a treaty between various domain-name registrars and it is likely to have far-reaching and beneficial effects. Maybe cyberspace isn't totally civilized yet, but it's on its way to being a more orderly place that is less hospitable to outlaws than it once was. Read the relatively short and clearly written Policy on the ICANN website (at www.icann.org/en/udrp/udrp-policy-24oct99.htm.), try to stay on the right side of it, and if you think someone is using a domain name that infringes your trademark rights, see a lawyer.

There are two misconceptions about cyberspace and the law. The first is that there *is* no law in cyberspace. The second is that our old, boring, existing laws don't apply in cyberspace. Neither assumption is true. "Cyberspace law" is mostly just 235 all our old laws that apply to activities that are carried out on or through the Internet. Any new activity, including marketing on the Internet, that is within the scope of existing law is regulated just like the behavior that the laws were designed to regulate. The courts must apply old laws to new activities and sometimes there is a gap between the behavior and the application, but the law is still there and new law is being written to cover gaps in existing law. This is a good thing. Sometimes individual freedom is hampered, but not much, and a society where the rule of law prevails over force or despotism or disorder is the reward for submission to the law. Like most modern innovations, the Internet can be used for good or evil ends. The growth of protocols for its use and for the protection of its users is a benign and desirable development.

Appendices

Appendix A
Trademark Cease
and Desist Letter

ROMANO AND TORTELLINI, ATTORNEYS
205 Waterman Street
Belmont, CA 52245

October 6, 2012
Mr. Robert Wilson
Mountain Properties, Inc.
729 East Mountain View Drive
Williamsville, CO 72984

Via Certified Mail
Dear Mr. Wilson:

This firm represents Brown Management Corporation of Blair, Colorado. Brown Management which owns three resort hotels in Colorado: the Brown House Hotel in Denver, the Greenview Hotel in Blair, and the Brownstone Inn in Hopewell, which is, as you know, just over the county line from Williamsville. It is with regard to the Brownstone Inn that I am writing.

Brown Management Corporation has owned and operated the Brownstone Inn since 1994. Over the years, Brown Management has expended a great deal of money to advertise the Brownstone Inn and to ensure that the services and facilities there are the finest available. Consequently, the Brownstone Inn has an excellent reputation, both within Colorado and nationally, as a luxury hotel. Brown Management is the owner of two service marks, both of which have been registered in the United States Patent and Trademark Office. These service marks are the famous name BROWNSTONE INN, which is the subject of federal registration 1,985,065, and the well-known Brownstone Inn script logo, which is the subject of federal registration 1,985,094. Copies of these two registrations are attached to this letter.

It has come to the attention of our client that your corporation has begun construction on a Williamsville time-share condominium development that you intend to call and, indeed, are already calling in advertisements in national travel magazines and in publicity of other kinds, "the Brown Stone Community." Your use of the name "Brown Stone Community" for your resort condominium development constitutes infringement of our client's registered service marks and unfair competition, since consumers may mistake your condominiums for our client's famous hotel or mistakenly believe that your condominiums and our client's hotel have the same owners or that your development is sponsored by or affiliated with Brown Management Corporation or the Brownstone Inn. Furthermore, your use of the "Brown Stone Community" for your development dilutes the strength of our client's famous marks and damages the business reputation and diminishes

239

the good will of the Brownstone Inn, all of which were developed and acquired by our client at great expense and effort.

You should be aware that the United States trademark statute (15 U.S.C. 1051 *et seq.*) provides in part that:

> When a violation of any right of the registrant of a mark registered in the Patent and Trademark Office shall have been established in any civil action arising under this chapter, the plaintiff shall be entitled . . . to recover (1) defendant's profits, (2) any damages sustained by the plaintiff, and (3) the costs of the action.

The law also allows the court to award treble damages and reasonable attorney's fees to the prevailing party. In addition, the court may order that all labels, signs, packaging, and advertisements in the possession of the defendant that bear the registered mark or a colorable imitation thereof be delivered up and destroyed.

Therefore, on behalf of our client, we hereby demand that you immediately cease any uses of the name "Brown Stone Community" or any other imitation or version of our client's registered marks in connection with any present or projected condominium development. Our client will require destruction of any printed advertising or promotion materials bearing the infringing name, including brochures and signage. In addition, your corporation must agree to cease giving out any news stories or causing any advertisements to be published or promulgating any materials connected with the offering of your condominiums that contain any reference to those condominiums as the "Brown Stone Community" development.

Due to the serious nature of your infringing conduct, we require your response to our demands not later than ten days after your receipt of this letter. If you agree to our terms, we will forward an appropriate settlement agreement for execution by an officer of your corporation. If we do not hear from you within ten days or if you refuse to comply with our demands, we are authorized by our client Brownstone Management Corporation to commence an action in federal court on its behalf seeking an injunction, damages, your profits, our costs and attorney's fees, and all other relief allowed by law, without further notice to you.

Although we are hopeful that we can obtain satisfaction for our client without litigation, this letter is written without prejudice to our client's rights and remedies, all of which are expressly reserved.

Sincerely,

Romano and Tortellini, Attorneys

Hubert Tortellini

HT/tb

attachments: copies of federal trademark registration certificates 1,985,065 and 1,985,094

Appendix B
Basic Facts about
Trademarks

The U.S. Patent and Trademark Office publication *Basic Facts about Trademarks* can answer lots of your questions about trademarks and trademark registration. You can read it below, where it is reproduced, or access it online (at www.uspto.gov/trademarks/basics/BasicFacts_with_correct_links.pdf) in order to utilize the links in the electronic version.

Trademark, Copyright, or Patent

What is a trademark or service mark?

- A **trademark** is a word, phrase, symbol, or design, or a combination thereof, that identifies and distinguishes the source of the goods of one party from those of others.
- A **service mark** is the same as a trademark, except that it identifies and distinguishes the source of a service rather than goods. Throughout this booklet, the terms "trademark" and "mark" refer to both trademarks and service marks.

Do trademarks, copyrights, and patents protect the same things?
No. Trademarks, copyrights, and patents protect different types of intellectual property. A trademark typically protects brand names and logos used on goods and services. A copyright protects an original artistic or literary work. A patent protects an invention. For example, if you invent a new kind of vacuum cleaner, you would apply for a patent to protect the invention itself. You would apply to register a trademark to protect the brand name of the vacuum cleaner. And you might register a copyright for the TV commercial that you use to market the product.

For copyright information, go to www.copyright.gov. For patent information, go to www.uspto.gov/patents.

Should I Register My Mark?

Is registration of my mark required?
No. You can establish rights in a mark based on use of the mark in commerce, without a registration. However, owning a federal trademark registration on the Principal Register provides several advantages, including:

- Public notice of your claim of ownership of the mark;
- A legal presumption of your ownership of the mark and your exclusive right to use the mark nationwide on or in connection with the goods/services listed in the registration;
- The ability to bring an action concerning the mark in federal court;
- The use of the U.S. registration as a basis to obtain registration in foreign countries;
- The ability to record the U.S. registration with the U.S. Customs and Border Protection (CBP) Service to prevent importation of infringing foreign goods;

- The right to use the federal registration symbol ®; and
- Listing in the United States Patent and Trademark Office's online databases.

When can I use the trademark symbols TM, SM, and ®?

If you claim rights to use a mark, you may use the "TM" (trademark) or "SM" (service mark) designation to alert the public to your claim of ownership of the mark, regardless of whether you have filed an application with the United States Patent and Trademark Office (USPTO). However, you may only use the federal registration symbol "®" after the USPTO actually *registers a mark*, and **not** while an application is pending. You may only use the registration symbol with the mark on or in connection with the goods/services listed in the federal trademark registration. Note: Several foreign countries use ® to indicate that a mark is registered in that country. Use of the symbol by the holder of a foreign registration may be proper.

244

What Does the USPTO Do?

The USPTO reviews trademark applications and determines whether the applied-for mark meets the requirements for federal registration. USPTO employees will answer questions about the application process free of charge.

What Does the USPTO Not Do?

The USPTO does not decide whether you have the right to use a mark (which differs from the right to register). It is not mandatory to obtain a federal registration in order to acquire rights in a mark. The USPTO does not enforce your rights in the mark or bring legal action against a potential infringer. In addition, USPTO employees cannot:

- Conduct trademark searches for the public;
- Comment on the validity of registered marks;

- Answer questions prior to filing on whether a particular mark or type of mark is eligible for trademark registration; or
- Offer legal advice or opinions about common law trademark rights, state registrations, or trademark infringement claims.

How Do I File a Trademark Application?

Is there a form for filing my application?

Yes. You can file your application directly over the Internet using the Trademark Electronic Application System (TEAS) at www.uspto.gov/teas. Two options are available: regular TEAS and TEAS Plus. Both options allow you to pay by credit card, electronic funds transfer, or through an existing USPTO deposit account. Electronic filing has many advantages over filing on paper, including:

245

- **On-line help.** Hyperlinks provide help sections for each of the application fields.
- **Validation function.** TEAS checks information to help avoid the omission of important information.
- **Immediate reply.** The USPTO immediately issues an initial filing receipt via e-mail containing the assigned application serial number and a summary of the submission.
- **24-hour availability.** TEAS is available 24 hours a day, 7 days a week (except 2 AM to 6 AM Sundays when you cannot pay by credit card, although you can create forms and save them for later filing). You can receive a filing date until midnight Eastern Standard Time on any date.
- **Lower filing fees.** The filing fee for using TEAS is lower than the fee for filing on paper. **If you use the TEAS Plus form, the fee is even lower than the regular TEAS application.**

- **More accurate filing receipts.** Most of your information is transferred directly from what you enter into the database and is generally not re-entered by hand at the USPTO.

If you do not have Internet access, you can access TEAS at any Patent and Trademark Depository Library (PTDL) throughout the United States. Many public libraries also provide Internet access.

What is the difference between the regular TEAS and the TEAS Plus application options?

The filing fee for a regular TEAS application is $325 per class of goods/services. The TEAS Plus application has a lower filing fee of $275 per class of goods/services, and you must meet certain additional requirements. For example, you must be able to select an entry or entries from the USPTO's *Acceptable Identification of Goods and Services Manual* that accurately describe your goods/services. Additionally, you must file communications regarding the application through TEAS, and receive communications concerning the application by email. If you fail to meet the TEAS Plus requirements, the USPTO will require that you pay an additional fee of $50 per class.

Are there other ways to file than by the Internet?

Yes. We recommend using TEAS, but you may file a paper application. To obtain a printed form you can call the USPTO's automated telephone line at 1-800-786-9199. Our mailing address is Commissioner for Trademarks, P.O. Box 1451, Alexandria, VA 22313-1451. You may NOT submit an application by facsimile.

246

Is a search of the USPTO database necessary before filing?

It is advisable to conduct a search of the USPTO database before filing your application to determine if there is a registered or pending mark that is similar to yours. You may search the USPTO's Trademark Electronic Search System (TESS) database free of charge before filing or you may wish to hire an attorney to perform the search and assess the results for you. The USPTO cannot search your mark for you prior to filing. After filing, the USPTO will conduct a search and will refuse to register your mark if there is another registered mark or pending mark similar to yours for related goods/services.

The USPTO database is available through www.uspto.gov under "Search Marks". Alternatively, you can search the database at a Patent and Trademark Depository Library (PTDL). Information about PTDL locations is available through www.uspto.gov.

Information on how to search the database (including some search strategies) is available through www.uspto.gov.

247

Do I have to hire an attorney?

No. You are not required to hire an attorney, but if you decide to prepare and submit your own application, you must comply with all requirements of the trademark statutes and rules and may be required to respond to legal issues raised by the USPTO. Because the application process can be complex, many applicants choose to appoint an attorney to represent them. If you choose to appoint an attorney, we will only communicate with your attorney. The USPTO cannot help you select an attorney. However, the American Bar Association website includes information on how to find local attorneys who practice trademark law.

What Is the Filing Date and How Is the Filing Date Determined?

If you transmit your application over the Internet, the filing date is the date the transmission reaches the USPTO server, in Eastern Standard Time. If you file on paper, the filing date of an application is the date the USPTO receives the application. The USPTO relies on a filing date to assess priority among applications.

Receiving a filing date does not mean that you have satisfied ALL registration requirements. To obtain a registration, you must comply with all application requirements and overcome any refusal(s) issued by the USPTO during examination.

What Information Should Be Included in the Application?

- OWNER OF THE MARK (APPLICANT)
- NAME AND ADDRESS FOR CORRESPONDENCE
- DEPICTION OF THE MARK ("THE DRAWING")
- GOODS/SERVICES
- APPLICATION FILING FEE
- BASIS FOR FILING
- SPECIMEN FOR USE-BASED APPLICATIONS
- SIGNATURE

Except for payment information, all data you submit to the USPTO, including your phone number, e-mail address, and street address, will become part of a public record and will be viewable through the Internet.

OWNER OF THE MARK (APPLICANT)

The application must be filed in the name of the owner of the mark. The owner of the mark is the person or entity who controls the nature and quality of the goods/services identified by the mark. The owner is not necessarily the name of the person filling out the form. The owner may be an individual, corporation, partnership, LLC, or other type of legal entity.

Must I be a U.S. citizen to apply?
No. You are not required to be a U.S. citizen to apply for and obtain a federal registration.

Name And Address For Correspondence

The applicant's name and street address is required for the USPTO to send communications concerning the application. If the applicant also provides an email address and authorizes the USPTO to correspond electronically, the USPTO will send notices regarding the application by e-mail. Applicants who file using the TEAS PLUS form are required to authorize e-mail correspondence.

Applicants who reside outside the United States may include the name and address of a domestic representative on their application. A domestic representative is a person residing in the U.S. upon whom notices or process may be served for proceedings affecting the mark.

Changes of Address: You must keep your mailing address and/or email address up to date with the USPTO. Changes of address should be filed using the Change of Correspondence Address form on TEAS at www.uspto.gov/teas. If you send a change of address on paper, please include the applicant's name, the mark, and the application serial number and mail to: Commissioner for Trademarks, P.O. Box 1451, Alexandria, VA 22313-1451.

Depiction Of The Mark ("The Drawing")

Every application must include a clear image of the mark ("the drawing"). The USPTO uses the drawing to upload the mark into the USPTO search database and to print the mark in the *Official Gazette* and on the registration certificate. There are two types of drawings: "standard character" and "special form."

What is a "standard character" drawing?

A standard character drawing is commonly submitted when the mark you wish to register consists solely of words, letters, or numbers. A standard character mark protects the wording itself, without limiting the mark to a specific font, style, size, or color and therefore gives you broader protection than a special form drawing.

A standard character drawing must have the following characteristics:

250

- No design element;
- No stylization of lettering and/or numbers;
- Any letters and words in Latin characters;
- Any numbers in Roman or Arabic numerals;
- Only common punctuation or diacritical marks.

The USPTO has created a standard character set that lists letters, numerals, punctuation marks, and diacritical marks that may be used in a standard character drawing. The set is available on the USPTO's website at http://teas.uspto.gov/standardCharacterSet.html.

How do I file a standard character drawing?

When you file electronically, TEAS generates a standard character drawing for you, based on the information you enter on the form under "enter the mark here."

When you file on paper, you must use standard letter-size paper and include these elements at the top of the "drawing page" as part of your application: applicant's name; correspondence address; and the following statement: "The mark is presented in standard character format without claim to any particular font style, size or color." The representation of the mark must appear in the middle of the page.

What is a "special form" drawing?

If your mark includes a design or logo, alone or with wording, or if the particular style of lettering or particular color(s) is important, you must select the "special form" drawing format.

How do I file a "special form" drawing?

When you file electronically, you must upload an image of your mark into the TEAS form. The mark image must be in .jpg format and should have little or no white space appearing around the design of the mark. Mark images should not include the trademark, service mark or registration symbols (TM, SM,®). Unless a color image is being submitted for a mark wherein color is claimed as a feature of the mark, the mark image should be pure black-and-white. When you file on paper, you must use standard letter-size paper and include the applicant's name and correspondence address at the top of the drawing page as part of your application. The mark must appear in the middle of the page.

Should I submit a color drawing or a black-and-white drawing?

Generally, you may submit a black-and-white drawing even if you use your mark in color, because a black-and-white drawing covers use of your mark in any color. To claim a specific color(s), you must submit a color drawing of your mark.

What are the requirements if I submit a color drawing?
You must submit the following: (1) a "color claim" naming the color(s) and stating that the color(s) is a feature of the mark; and (2) a separate statement describing the mark and stating where the color(s) appears in the mark.

Goods/Services

What is the difference between goods and services?
Goods are products, such as bicycles or candles. Services are activities performed for the benefit of someone else, such as bicycle rental services or catering.

The difference between goods and services may be confusing. Are your customers paying for a product or paying you to perform a specific activity? If your customer is paying you for a product, such as a candle or bicycle, then you have goods. However, if your customer is paying you to perform an activity, such as catering or bicycle rental, then you have services. You may list both goods and services in an application.

You must list the specific goods/services for which you want to register your mark. If you are filing based upon "use in commerce," you must be using the mark in commerce on all the goods/services listed. If you are filing based upon a "bona fide intent to use the mark," you must have a good faith or bona fide intent to use the mark on all the goods/services listed.

You should check the USPTO's *Acceptable Identification of Goods and Services Manual (ID Manual)* at http://tess2.uspto. gov/netahtml/tidm.html, which contains a listing of acceptable identifications of goods and services. Any entry you choose must accurately describe your goods/services. A failure to correctly list the goods/services with which you use the mark, or intend to use the mark, may prevent you from registering your mark. You will not be given a refund of any fees paid.

If the *ID Manual* does not contain an accurate listing for your goods/services, you must describe them using clear, concise terms that the general public easily understands. If you list vague terms, such as "miscellaneous services" or "company name," your application will be considered void and you must file a new application.

If using the TEAS PLUS form, you must choose your goods/services from the *ID Manual*. Therefore, you should check the *ID Manual* prior to filling out the form. If no *ID Manual* entry accurately identifies your goods/services, you cannot use the TEAS PLUS form. However, you can use the regular TEAS form.

May I change the goods/services after filing my application?
You may clarify or limit the goods/services but you may not expand or broaden the goods/services. For example, if you filed for "shirts," you may limit the goods to specific types of shirts such as "T-shirts and sweatshirts." However, you may not change the goods to "shirts and pants." Likewise, if you file for "jewelry," you may change the goods to specific types of jewelry such as "jewelry, namely, earrings." However, you may not change the goods to a service such as "jewelry stores."

Application Filing Fee

Application filing fees are based on the type of application form used (paper, regular TEAS, or TEAS Plus) and the number of International Classes of Goods or Services in the application. Paper applications have the highest filing fee and TEAS Plus applications have the lowest filing fee. For current fees for trademark applications, see the current USPTO Fee Schedule at www.uspto.gov or call the Trademark Assistance Center at 1-800-786-9199.

253

Goods and services are sorted into categories called "International Classes." Each International Class requires a separate filing fee. For a listing of the International Classes, see the International Schedule of Classes of Goods and Services at the back of this booklet.

The TEAS and TEAS Plus forms accept payment by credit card and electronic funds transfer or through an existing USPTO deposit account. If you are filing on paper, you can download the form for authorizing credit-card charges from the USPTO website at www.uspto.gov/forms/2038-fill.pdf or pay by a check or money order made payable to "Director of the USPTO."

Filing fees are not refundable. If your application meets the filing requirements but is later refused on legal grounds, the application filing fee will not be refunded.

Basis for Filing

The application must specify your "basis" for filing. Most U.S. applicants base their application on either their current use of the mark in commerce or their intent to use the mark in commerce in the future.

What is the difference between a "use in commerce" application and an "intent to use" application?

Under either basis, prior to registration you must demonstrate that you have used the mark in commerce. The basic difference between these two filing bases is whether you have started to use the mark on all the goods/services. If you have already used your mark in commerce, you may file under the "use in commerce" basis. If you have not yet used your mark, but intend to use it in the future, you must file under the "intent to use" basis. An "intent to use" basis requires filing an additional form and fee that are unnecessary if you file under "use in commerce." For information on the additional form, see the "HOW DO I ESTABLISH USE OF THE MARK IF I FILED AN INTENT TO USE APPLICATION?" section of this publication.

What is a "use in commerce" basis?

For applications filed under the use in commerce basis, you must be using the mark in the sale or transport of goods or the rendering of services in "interstate" commerce between more than one state or U.S. territory, or in commerce between the U.S. and another country. For goods, the mark must appear on the goods (e.g., tags or labels), the container for the goods, or displays associated with the goods. For services, the mark must be used in the sale or advertising of the services.

How do I establish my "use in commerce" basis?

- Provide the date of first use of the mark anywhere and the date of first use of the mark in commerce.
- Submit a specimen (example) showing how you use the mark in commerce. See the "SPECIMEN" section of this publication.

What is the difference between the "date of first use anywhere" and the "date of first use in commerce"?

The date of first use anywhere is the date on which the goods were first sold or transported or the services were first provided under the mark even if that use was only local. The date of first use in commerce is the date on which the goods were first sold or transported or the services were first provided under the mark between more than one state or U.S. territory, or in commerce between the U.S. and another country. The date of first use anywhere must be the same as or earlier than the date of first use in commerce.

What is an "intent to use" basis?

If you have not yet used the mark but plan to do so in the future, you may file based on a good faith or bona fide intent to use the mark in commerce. A bona fide intent to use the mark is more than an idea and less than market ready. For example, having a business plan, creating sample products, or performing other initial business activities may reflect a bona fide intent to use the mark.

Is there any other possible filing basis?

Yes. Under certain international agreements, you may file in the U.S. based on a foreign application, foreign registration, or international registration. See the *Trademark Manual of Examining Procedure (TMEP)* at Chapters 1000 and 1900 for the specific requirements.

Specimen for Use-Based Applications

What is a "specimen" of use and how does it differ from the "drawing"?

A specimen is a sample of how you actually use the mark in commerce on your goods or with your services. A specimen is not the same as the drawing. The drawing shows only your mark, whereas a specimen shows the mark as your purchasers encounter it in the marketplace (e.g., on the labels or on your website).

What is a proper specimen for use of a mark on goods (products)?

Usually, a specimen for a mark used on goods shows the actual goods, or labeling or packaging for the goods. For example, your specimen may be a tag or label displaying the mark, or a photograph showing the mark on the goods or packaging. The specimen may not be a "mock-up" of these items but must be a sample of what you actually use.

Is my website a proper specimen for goods?

A website is an acceptable specimen if the mark appears near a picture of the goods (or a description of the goods) **and** your customers can order the goods from the website. A website that merely advertises the goods is not acceptable.

What is NOT a proper specimen for goods?

Invoices, announcements, order forms, leaflets, brochures, publicity releases, letterhead, and business cards generally are NOT acceptable specimens for goods.

What is a proper specimen for use of a mark with services?

A specimen for a mark used in connection with services must show the mark used in providing or advertising the services. For example, your specimen may be a sign, a brochure about the services, an advertisement for the services, a website, a business card, or stationery showing the mark. The specimen must show or contain some reference to the services, that is, it is not just a display of the mark itself.

For example, if the mark sought to be registered is "T.MARKEY" for retail stores featuring men's sportswear, a specimen that only shows the mark "T.MARKEY" would not be acceptable, but a specimen that shows the mark "T.MARKEY" on the clothing store would be acceptable.

What is NOT a proper specimen for services?

Printer's proofs for advertisements or news articles about your services are not acceptable because they do not show your use of the mark.

When do I file the specimen?

If your application is based on **"use in commerce,"** you must submit one specimen for each class of goods/services when you file the application.

If your application is based on **"intent to use,"** you must submit one specimen for each class of goods/ services when you file the "allegation of use." The allegation of use may be filed prior to publication (Amendment to Allege Use) or after publication (Statement of Use). For more information on the Allegation of Use see the "HOW DO I ESTABLISH USE OF THE MARK IF I FILED AN INTENT TO USE APPLICA-TION?" section of this publication.

How do I file the specimen?

If filing electronically, you must attach an image of your speci-men in .jpg or .pdf format. To show the context in which the mark is used, the image should include as much of the label or advertisement as possible. For specimens consisting of audio and video files, see TMEP Section 904.03(f).

If filing a paper application, Amendment to Allege Use, or Statement of Use, the specimen must be flat and no larger than 8½ by 11 inches (e.g., a label or photograph of the packaging). However, you may submit compact discs, or DVDs, with files in .jpg, .pdf, .wav, .wma, .wmv, .mp3, .mpg, or .avi format.

Signature

Who may sign the application?

A person who is properly authorized to sign the application on behalf of the applicant is:

- A person with legal authority to bind the applicant (e.g., a corporate officer); or

- A person with firsthand knowledge of the facts and actual or implied authority to act on behalf of the applicant; or
- An attorney who is authorized to practice before the USPTO.

How do I sign a TEAS application?

In a TEAS application, you enter an electronic signature on the form by typing your signature between two forward slashes. Examples of acceptable signatures for TEAS applications include */john doe/* or */jrd/*. It is impermissible for one person to enter another person's signature.

What do I have to do after I file the application?

You must be diligent in monitoring the status of your application. This means you must:

- Check the status of your pending application regularly. We recommend that you check your application's status every 3 to 4 months.
- Promptly contact the USPTO and request corrective action when necessary.

How do I check the status?

You may check the status of any pending application through the Trademark Application and Registration Retrieval (TARR) database at http://tarr.uspto.gov. You must have your serial number available (a serial number generally begins with 76, 77, 79, or 85). If you do not have access to the Internet, you can call the Trademark Assistance Center at 1-800-786-9199 to request a status check.

When you check your application status, make sure that you have received all communications sent to you by the USPTO and have taken appropriate action. Also, print a copy of the TARR status page for your records.

259

What Happens After I File My Application?

- LEGAL AND PROCEDURAL REVIEW OF APPLICATION
- PUBLICATION FOR OPPOSITION

Legal and Procedural Review of Application

Approximately 3 months from the date your application is filed, the application is assigned to an examining attorney to determine whether federal law permits registration. The examining attorney will examine the written application, the drawing, and any specimen. Federal registration of trademarks is governed by the Trademark Act of 1946, 15 U.S.C. §1051 *et seq.*, and the *Trademark Rules of Practice*, 37 C.F.R. Part 2. The examining attorney may issue a letter (Office action) explaining any reasons for refusing registration or other requirements. If you receive an Office action, you must submit a response **within 6 months** of the issue date of the Office action. Your filing fee will NOT be refunded if the application is refused registration.

What is the most common reason an examining attorney refuses registration?
The most common reason for refusing registration is a likelihood of confusion with the mark in a registration or prior application. The examining attorney will search the USPTO database to determine whether there are any marks that are likely to cause confusion with your mark. The principal factors considered by the examining attorney in determining whether there would be a likelihood of confusion are:
- The similarity of the marks; and
- The commercial relationship (e.g., channels of trade or class of purchasers) between the goods/ services listed in

the application and those listed in the registration or pending application.

To find a conflict, the marks do *not* have to be identical and the goods/services do not have to be the same. It may be enough that the marks are *similar* and the goods/services are *related*.

What are some other reasons for refusing registration?
Registration may be refused if the mark is:
- Descriptive for the goods/services;
- A geographic term;
- A surname;
- Ornamental as applied to the goods.

For a discussion of these and other possible refusals, see Chapter 1200 of the *Trademark Manual of Examining Procedure (TMEP)* at http://tess2.uspto.gov/tmdb/tmep/.

Publication for Opposition

If no refusals or additional requirements are identified or if all identified issues have been resolved, the examining attorney approves the mark for publication in the *Official Gazette (OG)*, a weekly online publication. The USPTO will send you a Notice of Publication stating the publication date.

What Happens After Publication?

After publication in the *OG*, there is a 30-day period in which the public may object to the registration of the mark by filing an opposition. An opposition is similar to a court proceeding, but is held before the Trademark Trial and Appeal Board, a USPTO administrative tribunal. A third party who is considering filing an opposition may first file a request for an extension of time to file the opposition, which could delay further action on your application. The next step after publication depends on your basis for filing the application.

Registration Certificate Issues for Use in Commerce Application

If no opposition is filed or if you successfully overcome an opposition, you do not need to take any action for the application to enter the next stage of the process. Absent any opposition-related filings, the USPTO generally will issue a registration certificate about 12 weeks after publication, if the application is based upon the actual use of the mark in commerce (Section 1(a)) or on a foreign or international registration (Section 44(e) or Section 66(a)).

Notice Of Allowance (NOA) Issues for Intent to Use Application

If no opposition is filed or you successfully overcome an opposition, you do not need to take any action for the application to enter the next stage of the process. Absent any opposition-related filings, the USPTO generally will issue a NOA about 8 weeks after publication.

A NOA indicates that your mark has been allowed, but does not mean that it has registered. As the next step to registration, within 6 months of the issue date of the NOA you must:

- Submit a "Statement of Use" if you filed based on intent to use (Section 1(b)) and are now using the mark in commerce;
- Begin using the mark in commerce and then submit a "Statement of Use;" or
- Submit a six-month "Request for an Extension of Time to File a Statement of Use" if you need additional time to begin using the mark in commerce.

Forms for filing both the Statement of Use and Extension of Time are at www.uspto.gov/teas.

How Do I Establish Use of The Mark If I Filed An Intent To Use Application?

Notice of Allowance Has Already Issued

If a NOA has already issued, you establish use by filing a Statement of Use (SOU) form that contains a sworn statement that you are now using the mark in commerce on all the goods/services. You may delete goods/services for which the mark is not in use. The SOU must also include:

- A filing fee of $100 per class of goods/services;
- The date of first use of the mark anywhere and the date of first use of the mark in commerce; and
- One specimen (or example) showing how you use the mark in commerce for each class of goods/services.

Once the USPTO issues the NOA, you have 6 months to file the SOU. The 6-month period runs from the issue date shown on the NOA, not the date you receive it. If you have not used the mark in commerce, you must file a Request for an Extension of Time to File a Statement of Use (Extension Request) before the end of the 6-month period, or the application will be declared abandoned. You may request 5 additional extensions for up to a total of 36 months from the NOA issue date, with a statement of your ongoing efforts to make use of the mark in commerce. A filing fee of $150 per class of goods/services must accompany the Extension Request. The form for filing the Extension Request is at www.uspto.gov/teas. The date of the grant or denial of an Extension Request does not affect the deadline for filing the SOU or next Extension Request. The deadline is always calculated from the issue date of the NOA.

263

Notice of Allowance Has Not Yet Issued

If the NOA has not yet issued and the application has not yet been approved for publication, you may file an Amendment to Allege Use, which includes the same information as the SOU (see above). You may not file the Amendment to Allege Use during the "blackout period" after approval of the mark for publication and before issuance of the NOA. In that situation, you must wait until after the blackout period to file your SOU.

Maintaining a Federal Trademark Registration

To maintain your trademark registration, you must file your first maintenance document before the end of the 6th year after the registration date and other maintenance documents thereafter. Your registration certificate contains important information on maintaining your federal registration. The USPTO does NOT send reminder notices when the documents are due. Forms for filing the maintenance documents are at www.uspto.gov/teas.

Rights in a federally registered trademark can last indefinitely if you continue to use the mark and file all necessary maintenance documents at the appropriate times. You must file:

- Declaration of Continued Use or Excusable Nonuse under Section 8 (§8 declaration); and
- Combined Declaration of Continued Use and Application for Renewal under Sections 8 and 9 (combined §§8 and 9).

A §8 declaration is due before the end of the 6-year period after the registration date or within the 6-month grace period thereafter. Failure to file this declaration will result in the cancellation of the registration.

A combined §§8 and 9 must be filed before the end of every 10-year period after the registration date or within the 6-month grace period thereafter. Failure to make these required filings will result in cancellation and/or expiration of the registration.

For further information, including information regarding the special requirements that apply to Madrid Protocol registrations, see "Maintain/Renew a Registration" at www.uspto.gov or contact the Trademark Assistance Center at 1-800-786-9199.

Fees for Filing Trademark-Related Documents

Current fees for all trademark filings are available online at www.uspto.gov (click "View Fee Schedule") or can be obtained by calling the Trademark Assistance Center at 1-800-786-9199.

For the following documents, fees are based on the total number of International Classes that the USPTO assigns to your goods/services. For a listing of the International Classes, see the "International Schedule of Classes of Goods and Services" at the end of this publication.

Initial Application
TEAS Plus application—$275 per international class
TEAS application—$325 per international class
Paper application—$375 per international class

Intent to Use documents
Amendment to Allege Use (AAU)—$100 per international class
Statement of Use (SOU)—$100 per international class
Request for Extension of Time to file SOU—$150 per international class

Postregistration maintenance fees

Declaration of Continued Use or Excusable Nonuse under Section 8 (§8 declaration)—$100 per international class

Combined Declaration of Continued Use and Application for Renewal under Sections 8 and 9 (combined §§8 and 9)—$500 per international class

For More Information:

- **USPTO website at www.uspto.gov, Trademark Basics** *For instructional videos, application processing timelines and frequently asked questions (FAQs)*
- **Trademark Assistance Center 1-800-786-9199 (Trademark AssistanceCenter@uspto.gov)** *For general trademark information and printed application forms*
- **Patent and Trademark Depository Libraries**

Patent and Trademark Depository Libraries (PTDLs) are a nationwide network of public, state, and academic libraries that disseminate patent and trademark information and support the diverse intellectual property needs of the public. The PTDLs have trained specialists who may answer specific questions regarding the trademark process, but they do not provide legal advice. More information on PTDLs, including a list of the PTDLs in your state, is available at www.uspto.gov under "Products & Services."

International Schedule of Classes of Goods and Services
Goods

Class 1 (Chemicals): Chemicals used in industry, science and photography, as well as in agriculture, horticulture and forestry; unprocessed artificial resins; unprocessed plastics; manures; fire extinguishing compositions;

tempering and soldering preparations; chemical substances for preserving foodstuffs; tanning substances; adhesives used in industry.

Class 2 (Paints): Paints, varnishes, lacquers; preservatives against rust and against deterioration of wood; colorants; mordants; raw natural resins; metals in foil and powder form for painters, decorators, printers and artists.

Class 3 (Cosmetics and cleaning preparations): Bleaching preparations and other substances for laundry use; cleaning, polishing, scouring and abrasive preparations; soaps; perfumery, essential oils, cosmetics, hair lotions; dentifrices.

Class 4 (Lubricants and fuels): Industrial oils and greases; lubricants; dust absorbing, wetting and binding compositions; fuels (including motor spirit) and illuminants; candles and wicks for lighting.

Class 5 (Pharmaceuticals): Pharmaceutical and veterinary preparations; sanitary preparations for medical purposes; dietetic substances adapted for medical use, food for babies; plasters, materials for dressings; material for stopping teeth, dental wax; disinfectants; preparations for destroying vermin; fungicides, herbicides.

Class 6 (Metal Goods): Common metals and their alloys; metal building materials; transportable buildings of metal; materials of metal for railway tracks; nonelectric cables and wires of common metal; ironmongery, small items of metal hardware; pipes and tubes of metal; safes; goods of common metal not included in other classes; ores.

Class 7 (Machinery): Machines and machine tools; motors and engines (except for land vehicles); machine coupling and transmission components (except for land vehicles); agricultural implements other than hand-operated; incubators for eggs.

Class 8 (Hand tools): Hand tools and implements (hand-operated); cutlery; side arms; razors.

Class 9 (Electrical and scientific apparatus): Scientific, nautical, surveying, photographic, cinematographic, optical, weighing, measuring, signalling, checking (supervision), life-saving and teaching apparatus and instruments; apparatus and instruments for conducting, switching, transforming, accumulating, regulating or controlling electricity; apparatus for recording, transmission or reproduction of sound or images; magnetic data carriers, recording discs; automatic vending machines and mechanisms for coin operated apparatus; cash registers, calculating machines, data processing equipment and computers; fire extinguishing apparatus.

Class 10 (Medical apparatus): Surgical, medical, dental, and veterinary apparatus and instruments, artificial limbs, eyes, and teeth; orthopedic articles; suture materials.

Class 11 (Environmental control apparatus): Apparatus for lighting, heating, steam generating, cooking, refrigerating, drying, ventilating, water supply, and sanitary purposes.

Class 12 (Vehicles): Vehicles; apparatus for locomotion by land, air, or water.

Class 13 (Firearms): Firearms; ammunition and projectiles; explosives; fireworks.

Class 14 (Jewelry): Precious metals and their alloys and goods in precious metals or coated therewith, not included in other classes; jewelry, precious stones; horological and chronometric instruments.

Class 15 (Musical Instruments): Musical instruments.

Class 16 (Paper goods and printed matter): Paper, cardboard and goods made from these materials, not included in other classes; printed matter; bookbinding material; photographs; stationery; adhesives for stationery or household purposes; artists' materials; paint brushes; typewriters and office requisites (except furniture); instructional and teaching material (except apparatus); plastic materials for packaging (not included in other classes); printers' type; printing blocks.

Class 17 (Rubber goods): Rubber, gutta-percha, gum, asbestos, mica and goods made from these materials and not included in other classes;

plastics in extruded form for use in manufacture; packing, stopping and insulating materials; flexible pipes, not of metal.

Class 18 (Leather goods): Leather and imitations of leather, and goods made of these materials and not included in other classes; animal skins, hides; trunks and travelling bags; umbrellas, parasols and walking sticks; whips, harness and saddlery.

Class 19 (Nonmetallic building materials): Building materials (non-metallic); nonmetallic rigid pipes for building; asphalt, pitch and bitumen; nonmetallic transportable buildings; monuments, not of metal.

Class 20 (Furniture and articles not otherwise classified): Furniture, mirrors, picture frames; goods (not included in other classes) of wood, cork, reed, cane, wicker, horn, bone, ivory, whalebone, shell, amber, mother-of-pearl, meerschaum and substitutes for all these materials, or of plastics.

Class 21 (Housewares and glass): Household or kitchen utensils and containers; combs and sponges; brushes (except paint brushes); brush-making materials; articles for cleaning purposes; steel-wool; unworked or semi-worked glass (except glass used in building); glassware, porcelain and earthenware not included in other classes.

Class 22 (Cordage and fibers): Ropes, string, nets, tents, awnings, tarpaulins, sails, sacks and bags (not included in other classes); padding and stuffing materials (except of rubber or plastics); raw fibrous textile materials.

Class 23 (Yarns and threads): Yarns and threads, for textile use.

Class 24 (Fabrics): Textiles and textile goods, not included in other classes; beds and table covers.

Class 25 (Clothing): Clothing, footwear, headgear.

Class 26 (Fancy goods): Lace and embroidery, ribbons and braid; buttons, hooks and eyes, pins and needles; artificial flowers.

Class 27 (Floor coverings): Carpets, rugs, mats and matting, linoleum and other materials for covering existing floors; wall hangings (non-textile).

Class 28 (Toys and sporting goods): Games and playthings; gymnastic and sporting articles not included in other classes; decorations for Christmas trees.

Class 29 (Meats and processed foods): Meat, fish, poultry and game; meat extracts; preserved, frozen, dried and cooked fruits and vegetables; jellies, jams, compotes; eggs, milk and milk products; edible oils and fats.

Class 30 (Staple foods): Coffee, tea, cocoa, sugar, rice, tapioca, sago, artificial coffee; flour and preparations made from cereals, bread, pastry and confectionery, ices; honey, treacle; yeast, baking powder; salt, mustard; vinegar, sauces (condiments); spices; ice.

Class 31 (Natural agricultural products): Agricultural, horticultural and forestry products and grains not included in other classes; live animals; fresh fruits and vegetables; seeds, natural plants and flowers; foodstuffs for animals; malt.

Class 32 (Light beverages): Beers; mineral and aerated waters and other nonalcoholic drinks; fruit drinks and fruit juices; syrups and other preparations for making beverages.

Class 33 (Wine and spirits): Alcoholic beverages (except beers).

Class 34 (Smokers' articles): Tobacco; smokers' articles; matches.

Services

Class 35 (Advertising and business): Advertising; business management; business administration; office functions.

Class 36 (Insurance and financial): Insurance; financial affairs; monetary affairs; real estate affairs.

Class 37 (Building construction and repair): Building construction; repair; installation services.

Class 38 (Telecommunications): Telecommunications.

Class 39 (Transportation and storage): Transport; packaging and storage of goods; travel arrangement

Class 40 (Treatment of materials): Treatment of materials.

Class 41 (Education and entertainment): Education; providing of training; entertainment; sporting and cultural activities.

Class 42 (Computer and scientific): Scientific and technological services and research and design relating thereto; industrial analysis and research services; design and development of computer hardware and software.

Class 43 (Hotels and restaurants): Services for providing food and drink; temporary accommodations.

Class 44 (Medical, beauty & agricultural): Medical services; veterinary services; hygienic and beauty care for human beings or animals; agriculture, horticulture and forestry services.

Class 45 (Personal): Legal services; security services for the protection of property and individuals; personal and social services rendered by others to meet the needs of individuals.

Appendix C
U.S. Trademark
Office FAQs

A good place to start thinking about trademarks and how they are registered is to read the list of Frequently Asked Questions offered on the website of the U.S. Trademark Office. These questions and their answers are reproduced below. You may want to read then online in order to take advantage of the links included there: www.uspto.gov/trademarks/notices/index.jsp.

Before Filing an Application

What is a trademark?

A trademark is a word, phrase, symbol or design, or a combination thereof, that identifies and distinguishes the source of the goods of one party from those of others.

What is a service mark?

A service mark is a word, phrase, symbol or design, or a combination thereof, that identifies and distinguishes the source of a service rather than goods. The term "trademark" is often used to refer to both trademarks and service marks.

What is a patent?
A patent is a limited duration property right relating to an invention, granted by the United States Patent and Trademark Office in exchange for public disclosure of the invention. For more information, go to www.uspto.gov/patents/index.jsp.

What is a copyright?
A copyright protects works of authorship, such as writings, music, and works of art that have been tangibly expressed. For more information, contact the U.S. Copyright Office (a division of the Library of Congress) [www.copyright.gov/].

What is a certification mark?
A certification mark is any word, phrase, symbol or design, or a combination thereof owned by one party who certifies the goods and services of others when they meet certain standards. The owner of the mark exercises control over the use of the mark; however, because the sole purpose of a certification mark is to indicate that certain standards have been met, use of the mark is by others.

What is a collective membership mark?
A collective membership mark is any word, phrase, symbol or design, or a combination thereof which indicates that the user of the mark is a member of a particular organization. The owner of the mark exercises control over the use of the mark; however, because the sole purpose of a membership mark is to indicate membership, use of the mark is by members.

What is a collective mark?

A collective mark is any word, phrase, symbol or design, or a combination thereof owned by a cooperative, an association, or other collective group or organization and used by its members to indicate the source of the goods or services.

Where can I get basic trademark information?

For information about applying for a trademark, go to Basic Facts About Trademarks www.uspto.gov/trademarks/basics/ BasicFacts_with_correct_links.pdf, and view the trademark videos at www.uspto.gov/trademarks/process/TMIN.jsp that cover important topics and critical application filing tips. To understand what to expect in the overall process, view the timelines at www.uspto.gov/trademarks/process/tm_timeline. jsp for trademark processing. If you still have questions, contact the Trademark Assistance Center at 1-800-786-9199.

Must I register my trademark?

No. You can establish rights in a mark based on use of the mark in commerce, without a registration. However, owning a federal trademark registration on the Principal Register provides several important benefits.

What are the benefits of federal trademark registration?

Owning a federal trademark registration on the Principal Register provides several advantages, including:

- Public notice of your claim of ownership of the mark;
- A legal presumption of your ownership of the mark and your exclusive right to use the mark nationwide on or in connection with the goods/services listed in the registration;
- The ability to bring an action concerning the mark in federal court;

- The use of the U.S. registration as a basis to obtain registration in foreign countries;
- The ability to record the U.S. registration with the U.S. Customs and Border Protection (CBP) Service to prevent importation of infringing foreign goods;
- The right to use the federal registration symbol ® and
- Listing in the United States Patent and Trademark Office's online databases.

Do federal regulations govern the use of the designations "TM" or "SM" or the ® symbol?

If you claim rights to use a mark, you may use the "TM" (trademark) or "SM" (service mark) designation to alert the public to your claim of ownership of the mark, regardless of whether you have filed an application with the United States Patent and Trademark Office (USPTO). However, you may only use the federal registration symbol "®" after the USPTO actually *registers a mark*, and not while an application is pending.

275

Should I have an attorney?

You are not required to hire an attorney, but if you decide to prepare and submit your own application, you must comply with all requirements of the trademark statutes and rules and may be required to respond to legal issues raised by the USPTO. Because the application process can be complex, many applicants choose to appoint an attorney to represent them. If you choose to appoint an attorney, we will only communicate with your attorney. The USPTO cannot help you select an attorney. However, the American Bar Association website, http://apps.americanbar.org, includes information on how to find local attorneys who practice trademark law.

Is registration guaranteed and can I get a refund of money paid?

Registration is not guaranteed and only money paid when not required may be refunded. For information on why registration may be refused, see Basic Facts About Trademarks at www.uspto.gov/trademarks/basics/BasicFacts_with_correct_links.pdf.

Searching for Similar Trademarks

Should I conduct a search for similar trademarks before filing an application?

It is advisable to conduct a search before filing your application. See TESS TIPS [www.uspto.gov/trademarks/process/search/Tess_tips.jsp] for further information.

Where can I conduct a trademark search for trademarks in pending applications and federal registrations?

You may search the USPTO's Trademark Electronic Search System (TESS) [http://tess2.uspto.gov/bin/gate.exe?f=tess&state=4002:lvha0r.1.1] database free of charge before filing or you may wish to hire an attorney to perform the search and assess the results for you. Alternatively, you can search the database at a Patent and Trademark Resource Center (PTRC). Information about PTRC locations can be found at www.uspto.gov/products/library/ptdl/locations/index.jsp.

Will the Office conduct a search for me?

The USPTO cannot search your mark for you prior to filing. After filing, the USPTO will conduct a search and will refuse to register your mark if there is another registered or pending mark similar to yours.

Filing the Application and Other Documents

Where can I find trademark forms?

You can find USPTO forms through the Trademark Electronic Application System (TEAS) [www.uspto.gov/trademarks/teas/index.jsp]. Two forms are available for the initial application: regular TEAS and TEAS Plus. Both forms allow you to pay by credit card, electronic funds transfer, or through an existing United States Patent and Trademark Office (USPTO) deposit account.

If you do not have Internet access, you can access TEAS at any Patent and Trademark Resource Center (PTRC) throughout the United States. Many public libraries also provide Internet access.

We recommend using TEAS, but you may file a paper application. To obtain a printed form, call the Trademark Assistance Center at 1-800-786-9199.

What is the Trademark Electronic Application System (TEAS)?

The Trademark Electronic Application System [www.uspto.gov/trademarks/teas/index.jsp] allows you to fill out and file an application form online, paying by credit card, electronic funds transfer, or through an existing USPTO deposit account. TEAS can also be used to file other documents including a response to an examining attorney's Office action, a change of address, an allegation of use, and post registration maintenance documents.

Where do I send mail or make deliveries?

Although we recommend you file documents online using TEAS, paper mail may be sent to the following address: Commissioner for Trademarks, P.O. Box 1451, Alexandria, VA 22313-1451. Submissions sent using other delivery services such as Federal Express, United Parcel Service, and DHL is not encouraged, but if used, must be delivered to: Trademark Assistance Center, Madison East, Concourse Level Room C 55, 600 Dulany Street, Alexandria, VA 22314.

Who may file an application?

Only the owner of the trademark may file an application for registration. The owner controls the use of the mark, and controls the nature and quality of the goods to which it is affixed, or the services for which it is used. The owner may be an individual, corporation, partnership, LLC, or other type of legal entity.

May a minor file a trademark application?

278

The question of whether an application may be filed in the name of a minor depends on your state's law. If the minor may validly enter into binding legal obligations, and may sue or be sued, in the state in which he or she is domiciled, the application may be filed in the name of the minor. Otherwise, the application must be filed in the name of a parent or legal guardian, clearly setting forth his or her status as a parent or legal guardian. An example of the manner in which the applicant should be identified in such cases is: "John Smith, United States citizen, (parent/legal guardian) of Mary Smith."

Must I be a U.S. citizen to obtain a federal registration?

No. However, your citizenship must be provided in the application. If you have dual citizenship, then you must indicate which citizenship will be printed on the certificate of registration.

What is the difference between "use in commerce" and "intent to use" in commerce?

The basic difference between these two filing bases is whether you have used the mark on all the goods/services. If you have already used your mark in commerce, you may file under the "use in commerce" basis. If you have not yet used your mark in commerce, but intend to use it in the future, you must file under the "intent to use" basis. An "intent to use" basis will require filing an additional form and fee that are unnecessary if you file under "use in commerce."

What is a specimen?

A specimen is a sample of how you actually use the mark in commerce on your goods or with your services. A specimen shows the mark as your purchasers encounter it in the marketplace (e.g., on your labels or on your website).

What is a drawing?

The "drawing" is a clear image of the mark applicant seeks to register. The USPTO uses the drawing to upload the mark into the USPTO search database and to print the mark in the Official Gazette and on the registration certificate. There are two types of drawings: "standard character" and "special form." For more information on the different types of drawings see Basic Facts About Trademarks [www.uspto.gov/trademarks/basics/BasicFacts_with_correct_links.pdf].

Can you register the name of a musical group or band?

A band name may function as a service mark for "entertainment services in the nature of performances by a musical group" if it is used to identify live performances.

What can I do to help the application proceed as smoothly as possible?

1. File the application and all other documents electronically through the Trademark Electronic Application System (TEAS).
2. Carefully review all documents before filing to make sure all issues have been addressed and all the necessary elements are included.
3. Authorize email correspondence and promptly inform the USPTO of any change in correspondence address, including your email address. This can be done through TEAS.
4. Check the status of your application every 3-4 months using the Trademark Applications and Registrations Retrieval (TARR) [http://tarr.uspto.gov/] database. If the USPTO has taken any action, you may need to respond promptly. All USPTO actions are available for viewing using the Trademark Document Retrieval (TDR) [http://tdr.uspto.gov/init.action] database.

After Filing the Application

Is registration of my mark guaranteed?

No. The examining attorney will review the application and may issue refusals based on the Trademark Act of 1946, 15 U.S.C. §1051 *et seq.*, or the *Trademark Rules of Practice*, 37 C.F.R. Part 2.

The most common reasons for refusing registration are because the mark is:

- Likely to cause confusion with a mark in a registration or prior application;
- Descriptive for the goods/services;
- A geographic term;

- A surname;
- Ornamental as applied to the goods.

For a discussion of these and other possible refusals, see Chapter 1200 [http://tess2.uspto.gov/tmdb/tmep/1200.htm] of the *Trademark Manual of Examining Procedure (TMEP)*.

The examining attorney may also issue requirements concerning, for example:

- The goods and services listed in the application;
- The description of the mark;
- The quality of the drawing;
- The specimens.

How can I check the status of my application?

Once you receive a serial number for your application, you can check the status of your application through the Trademark Applications and Registrations Retrieval (TARR) database. If you do not have access to the Internet, you can call the Trademark Assistance Center at 1-800-786-9199 to request a status check. You should check on the status of your pending application every 3-4 months. If the USPTO has taken any action, you may need to respond promptly. All USPTO actions are available for viewing using the Trademark Document Retrieval (TDR) database.

How long will it take for my mark to register?

The total time for an application to be processed may be anywhere from almost a year to several years, depending on the basis for filing and the legal issues that may arise in the examination of the application. You may view the application processing timelines at www.uspto.gov/trademarks/process/tm_timeline.jsp.

How do I file a Statement of Use or Extension Request after the Notice of Allowance is issued?

The Applicant has six (6) months from the mailing date of the notice of allowance to file either a Statement of Use or an Extension Request.

If the applicant is using the mark in commerce on all of the goods/services listed in the notice of allowance, the applicant must submit a statement of use form, specimen and the required fee(s) within 6 months from the issue date the notice of allowance to avoid abandonment. Applicant cannot withdraw the statement of use; however, the applicant may file one extension request with the statement of use to provide more time to overcome deficiencies in the statement of use. No further extension requests may be filed.

If the applicant is not using the mark in commerce on all of the goods/services listed in the notice of allowance, the applicant must file an extension request form and the required fee(s) to avoid abandonment. The applicant must continue to file extension requests every 6 months calculated from the issue date of the notice of allowance until the statement of use is filed. A total of 5 extension requests may be filed.

If I filed based on an "intent to use" the mark, when must I allege actual use of the mark in commerce?

You must file your Allegation of Use either prior to the date the application is approved for publication or within six months after the Notice of Allowance is issued, unless a request for an extension of time is granted.

May I assign or transfer the ownership of my trademark to someone else?

Yes. A registered mark may be assigned and a mark for which an application to register has been filed may be assignable.

Certain exceptions exist concerning the assignment of Intent-to-Use applications. Assignments may be recorded in the USP-TO for a fee. For the guidelines for filing an assignment and the assignment form itself, click on Assignments [www.uspto. gov/trademarks/process/assign.jsp] or contact the Assignment Division at 571-272-3350.

After the Trademark Has Registered

How long does a trademark registration last?

The registration is valid as long as you timely file all post registration maintenance documents. You must file a "Declaration of Use under Section 8" between the fifth and sixth year following registration. In addition, you must file a combined "Declaration of Use and Application for Renewal under Sections 8 and 9" between the ninth and tenth year after registration, and every 10 years thereafter. If these documents are not timely filed, your registration will be cancelled and cannot be revived or reinstated. For more information see Maintain/ Renew a Registration [www.uspto.gov/trademarks/process/ maintain/prfaq.jsp].

Is a federal registration valid outside of the United States?

No. However, certain countries recognize a United States registration as a basis for filing an application to register a mark in those countries under international treaties. See TMEP Chapter 1000 [http://tess2.uspto.gov/tmdb/tmep/1000.htm] and TMEP Chapter 1900 [http://tess2.uspto.gov/tmdb/tmep/1900. htm] for further information.

What if someone else is using my registered mark on related goods and services?

You may challenge use of your trademark by someone else in several ways, depending on the factual situation. You should consider contacting an attorney specializing in trademark law. Local bar associations and phone directories usually have attorney listings broken down by specialties. Time can be of the essence.

My spouse owned a trademark registration and has since died. Do I own it now?

Perhaps. Because this depends on state law, the USPTO cannot provide a definite answer for all factual situations. You should consider contacting an attorney. Local bar associations and phone directories usually have attorney listings.

Other Trademark Questions

What are "common law" rights?

Federal registration is not required to establish rights in a trademark. Common law rights arise from actual use of a mark and may allow the common law user to successfully challenge a registration or application.

What is "interstate commerce"?

For goods, "interstate commerce" generally involves sending the goods across state lines with the mark displayed on the goods or the packaging for the goods. With services, "interstate commerce" generally involves offering a service to customers in another state or rendering a service that affects interstate commerce (e.g., restaurants, gas stations, hotels).

Will my information be public?

All data you submit to the USPTO, including your phone number, e-mail address, and street address, but not your credit card and banking information, is public record and is viewable on the Internet. Do not submit personal identifying information that is NOT required for a filing, such as a social security number or driver's license number.

What are trademark monitoring and document filing services?
You may receive unsolicited communications from companies requesting fees for trademark-related services, such as monitoring and document filing. Although solicitations from these companies frequently display customer-specific information, including USPTO serial number or registration number and owner name, companies that offer these services are not affiliated or associated with the USPTO or any other federal agency.

May a trademark filing company represent me before the USPTO?
Only licensed attorneys may represent you before the U.S. Patent and Trademark Office (USPTO). If you hire someone to represent you, he or she must be an attorney licensed to practice law in a U.S. state and be a member in good standing of the highest court of that state. Attorneys from other countries, except certain Canadian attorneys and agents representing Canadian filers, may NOT practice before the USPTO.

Glossary

actual confusion: When proven in court, actual confusion is prima facie evidence that trademark infringement has occurred. Any event that demonstrates that consumers are confusing one product or service with another is proof of actual confusion; consumers' asking for one product by a name similar to that of the product they actually want or mail misdirected to a company that has a name similar to that of another company that offers similar services are examples of such events. Actual confusion proves that confusion between two marks is no longer merely a likelihood, which is the usual standard for proving trademark infringement, but has become a continuing reality. This is usually sufficient to convince any judge in a trademark infringement lawsuit that the plaintiff's rights are being infringed.

actual damages: The profits a trademark infringer made by the infringement and the money the plaintiff lost because of the infringement. A court deciding a trademark infringement case may award either actual damages or statutory damages.

case law: A law that originates in the decisions of courts as opposed to written laws passed by state legislatures or the U.S. Congress, which are called "statutes."

cease and desist letter: A letter written by the lawyer for the plaintiff in a lawsuit telling the defendant to immediately cease certain specified actions that infringe the plaintiff's trademark and thereafter desist from any further such actions. These letters are usually the first indication that a defendant has that his or her actions may have violated the plaintiff's rights. Depending on the merits of the plaintiff's claims of infringement, a defendant will decide to comply with the plaintiff's demands and try to settle the infringement dispute out of court or to fight the plaintiff's assertions of infringement in court.

constructive notice: The presumption that because a trademark registration is reflected in the records of the Trademark Office, which are public, everyone knows of the claim of trademark ownership that the

registration evidences, regardless of whether any examination of those records is actually made.

contingency fee: A lawyer's fee taken from an award of damages to the plaintiff. Trademark infringement suits are sometimes filed by lawyers who agree to work for a contingency fee; that is, the lawyer agrees that the fee for his or her work is to be taken from and is contingent upon an award by the court in favor of the plaintiff. If the plaintiff loses, the lawyer is not paid a fee. Usually a plaintiff is still responsible for bearing the costs of the suit, such as his or her lawyer's travel expenses, the costs of court reporters for depositions, and the fees of expert witnesses. Lawyers never agree to work on a contingency fee basis for defendants who have no expectation of any awards.

copyright: The set of exclusive rights that are granted, initially to the creators of works eligible for copyright protection, by the various copyright statutes that exist in most countries. In the

United States, copyright protection begins when a work is first "fixed" in a tangible form and endures, in most cases, until fifty years after the death of the creator.

generic trademark: A product or service name that is merely the generic name for the class of products or services it is being used to market. Such marks do not function as trademarks until they have gained enough fame to escape the anonymity inherent in them. That is, a generic mark does not point to one particular source for the product it names and, therefore, does not function as a true trademark. The reverse situation also occurs. That is, when a name for a product comes, through public usage, to indicate a whole class of products rather than one particular product, it is said to have lost its trademark status and to have become generic.

injunction: A court order that directs the enjoined party to do something or, more typically, to cease doing something and to refrain from doing it in future. Plaintiffs in trademark infringement suits typically seek injunctions to stop defendants from continuing to infringe the plaintiff's trademarks. The scope of an injunction and whether a litigant's motion for one is granted is at the discretion of the judge who hears the suit. A temporary injunction is usually granted at the same time a suit is filed and endures only ten days. A preliminary injunction is granted by a judge after hearing arguments for and against the injunction from both the plaintiff and the defendant and usually lasts until the end of the lawsuit, when it may ripen into a permanent injunction by means of a paragraph to that effect in the judge's order rendering his or her decision.

intent-to-use application: Since November of 1989, marketers may file what is called an "intent-to-use" application to register a trademark with the U.S. Patent and Trademark Office, as opposed to a "use-based" application, which was formerly the only sort of registration application that was allowed. Application for registration may be made before actual use of a new trademark, so long as the trademark owner has a "bona fide intent" to begin to use the mark in interstate commerce within six months of the date the registration application is filed. The period of time for beginning use of the mark may be extended, in six-month increments and upon making the proper filings, to a total period of thirty-six months. Registration may then be granted after use of the mark is made in interstate commerce. This system allows a company to claim ownership of a mark by filing an intent-to-use application to register it; when a second company conducts a trademark search to ascertain the availability of the mark, the first company's application will appear in the search report and warn the second company away from the mark. Further, intent-to-use applications confer one other important benefit not formerly available: when a registration is eventually granted to an

intent-to-use applicant, the date the applicant filed the registration application is deemed to be the date the applicant's rights in the mark commenced. This has the effect of "backdating" the applicant's rights to a date prior to the date of actual use of the mark, which was formerly the date ownership rights commenced.

likelihood of confusion: The test courts apply in determining infringing similarity between trademarks. If consumers are likely to confuse the new mark with the older, established trademark because of the similarity of the marks, gauged by comparing the appearance, sound, and meaning of the two marks, likelihood of confusion is said to exist.

overall commercial impression: An important, usually determinative, factor in any evaluation of possible trademark infringement. The term refers to whole impression created by a trademark on the consumer who encounters it in the marketplace. In a proper analysis, the two marks said to be in conflict are not dissected and their minor dissimilarities tallied and totaled; rather, the total effect the marks have on consumers who encounter them in the environments where they are sold is judged.

patent: The rights granted by the federal government to the originator of a physical invention or industrial or technical process (a "utility patent") or an ornamental design for an "article of manufacture" (a "design patent)." Utility and plant patents endure for up to twenty years after the applications for the patents are filed. A design patent lasts fourteen years from the date it is issued. A patent holder earns the exclusive right to make, use, and sell the invention for which the patent was granted. Any unauthorized manufacture, use, or sale of the patented invention within this country during the term of the patent is infringement.

secondary meaning: When a trademark has become widely known through advertising and the popularity of the product or service it names, it is said to have acquired "secondary meaning." Secondary meaning is necessary for an otherwise generic or unregistrable mark to be entitled to registration on the Principal Register and to enjoy the full benefits of federal trademark registration.

service mark: The Lanham Act, which is the federal statute governing unfair competition and trademarks, defines a service mark as "a mark used in the sale or advertising of services to identify the services of one person and distinguish them from the services of others." A word or symbol qualifies as a service mark when it is actually used in commerce to identify the services of one particular provider of services and when it functions to identify and distinguish those services form those of others. In this country, service mark ownership accrues by virtue of use of a service mark rather than by registration, although registration significantly enhances the rights of service mark owners. Roughly speaking, service mark owners acquire ownership of their marks commensurate with the duration and scope of their use of them. Services marks are often considered a variety of trademark and referred to as trademarks, or, simply, as "marks."

statutory damages: A range of money damages the trademark statute allows courts to award a plaintiff in a trademark infringement suit instead of the money lost by the plaintiff as a result of an infringer's actions plus the actual amount by which the infringer profited from the use of the plaintiff's work. Because actual damages can be very difficult, time-consuming, expensive, or impossible to prove during infringement lawsuits, and because infringers often do not profit from their infringements, awards of statutory damages are often desirable.

trade dress: The packaging and labeling of a product, including the non-functional aspects of the shape and design of the product itself and its container.

The combination of these elements creates the whole visual image of the product encountered by consumers and can become a sort of indication of the origin of the product in the same way that trademarks do. Trade dress infringement, that is, the imitation of a product's packaging and container, is a variety of unfair competition; if a defendant's trade dress is likely to cause consumers to confuse the plaintiff's product with that of the defendant, the plaintiff's trade dress has been infringed.

trademark: A word, phrase, sound, or symbol that represents in the marketplace the commercial reputation of a product or service. The Lanham Act, which is the U.S. federal statute governing unfair competition and trademarks, defines a trademark as "any word, name, symbol or device or any combination thereof adopted and used by a manufacturer or merchant to identify his goods and distinguish them from those manufactured or sold by others." A word or symbol qualifies as a trademark when it is actually used in commerce to identify the goods of a particular manufacturer or merchant and when it functions to identify and distinguish those goods from those of others. In this country, trademark ownership accrues by virtue of use of a trademark rather than by registration, although trademark registration significantly enhances the rights of trademark owners. Roughly speaking, trademark owners acquire rights in their marks commensurate with the duration and scope of their use of them.

trademark abandonment: The cessation of use of a trademark by its owner, with intent to permanently cease any such use of the mark. Trademark abandonment makes a mark available for use by another marketer; however, it is dangerous to assume that a mark has been abandoned merely because is has fallen into disuse. A trademark owner may cease use of a marks for a time without abandoning it.

Trademark Dilution Act of 1995: A federal law that formalizes and makes a part of the federal trademark statute a principle of trademark law that had been available as a ground for suit in only about half the states. The act allows the owners of an existing "famous" trademark to ask the court to enjoin the use of the same mark by another company—even if there is no likelihood of confusion between the marks—on the ground that the defendant's use of the mark, even for noncompeting goods or services, "dilutes" the distinctive quality of the famous mark. "Dilution" is defined in the act as "the lessening of the capacity of a famous mark to identify and distinguish goods or services, regardless of the presence or absence of 1) competition between the owner of the famous mark and other parties, or 2) likelihood of confusion, mistake, or deception."

trademark infringement: The use of a trademark without permission of the trademark owner or the use of a trademark that is confusingly similar to a trademark owned by someone else. Trademark infringement is judged by the "sight, sound, and meaning test." That is, the new mark is compared to the established trademark for similarities of appearance, sound, and meaning. If the two marks are so similar that the average consumer is likely to confuse the products or services the marks name, or to believe that they are somehow related, the new name infringes the older mark. Intent is immaterial in evaluating most trademark infringement cases. In other words, use of a trademark that is confusingly similar to an established trademark will create problems whether or not it was an intentional effort to trade on the good commercial reputation of the established mark.

trademark licensing: When a trademark owner allows another marketer of goods or services to use the trademark owner's mark, under terms and conditions specified in a written agreement and for specified products or services within a specified territory, in return for specified royalty payments.

trademark registration: The registration of a claim to ownership of a trademark, made in Washington, DC in the U.S. Patent and Trademark Office, a division of the Department of Commerce. Trademark registration enhances the rights an owner gains by virtue of the use of a trademark but does not of itself create those rights. Among other advantages, a federal registrant is presumed to have rights in the registered mark superior to anyone else except prior users of the mark and is entitled to use the ® symbol (or another prescribed form of federal trademark notice) that signifies federal trademark registration. While it is possible to register a trademark both with the state governments in the states where it is used *and* in the (federal) U.S. Patent and Trademark Office if it is used in interstate or international commerce, federal registration rather than state registration is generally sought by trademark owners who can qualify for it because it confers much greater benefits than state trademark registration. The sort of federal trademark registration that bestows the full benefits of federal registration is registration on the Principal Register. However, if a mark is unable to qualify for the Principal Register, a Supplemental Register registration is also useful; most marks on the Supplemental Register are descriptive, surname, or geographic marks that do not yet function as trademarks in the eyes of the Trademark Office. Marks registered on the Supplemental Register are entitled to use the ® symbol and gain some benefits of federal registration, such as access to federal courts, and are presumed, after a period of five years, to have gained enough fame to qualify for an upgrade (upon request by the registrant) to the Principal Register. Trademark registration is difficult and usually requires the services of a lawyer experienced in trademark law, unlike copyright registration, which is usually readily granted after a registration process that is

simple enough that copyright owners can usually accomplish it themselves.

trademark search: A survey of data on existing trademarks performed by a trademark search service in order to clear a proposed trademark for use or, alternately, eliminate it from consideration because it is determined to infringe an established mark. Most marks are cleared for use by "full" trademark searches, which are searches of United States federal and state trademark registrations as well as of data regarding valid but unregistered marks. The results of trademark searches are reported in trademark search reports and are interpreted in trademark search opinion letters.

unfair competition: Generally speaking, unfair competition is commercial competition by means that are overly aggressive or less than honest, although several forms of unfair competition can result from otherwise innocent blunders. By declaring certain actions "unfair" in commerce, the courts seek to promote both free competition *and* fair competition. Among the types of trademark-related commercial conduct that have been held to constitute unfair competition are: trademark infringement; trademark dilution; use of confusingly similar business names; use of confusingly similar literary titles; the unauthorized use of a distinctive literary or performing style; copying a product's trade dress and configuration; and infringement of the right of publicity. Not every action that has been or could be labeled unfair competition is codified, that is, enumerated and written down, in a statute. Judges may add to the list of "unfair" business tactics as new situations are presented that seem to them to entail overreaching by a marketer.

unregistrable trademarks: Names (or design marks) for products or services that, because of certain inherent characteristics, are deemed by the U.S. trademark statute to be unworthy of registration. The ten statutory

grounds for denial by the U.S. Patent and Trademark Office of an application to register a name or design as a trademark are: the mark is confusingly similar to a trademark that is already federally registered; the word or, more usually, symbol for which registration is sought does not function as a trademark, that is, does not act in the marketplace to identify the source of the goods or services to which it is applied; the mark is "immoral, deceptive, or scandalous"; the mark disparages or falsely suggests a connection with persons, institutions, beliefs, or national symbols, or brings them into contempt or disrepute; the mark consists of or simulates the flag or coat of arms or other insignia of the United States of or a state or municipality or a foreign nation; the mark is the name, portrait, or signature of a particular living individual who has not given his or her consent for use of the mark or is the name, signature, or portrait of deceased president of the United States during the life of his or her surviving spouse,

296

unless that spouse has given consent to use of the mark; the mark is "merely descriptive" of the goods or services it names; the mark is "deceptively misdescriptive" of the goods or services it names; the mark is "primarily geographically descriptive or deceptively misdescriptive" of the goods or services it names; and the mark is primarily a surname.

use-based application: An application to register a trademark in the U.S. Patent and Trademark Office based on current use of the mark in interstate or international commerce. Use-based applications were once the only sort of registration application available; since a change in the law that allows registration applications based on "bona fide intent" to use the marks that are the subject of such applications, this is no longer the case.

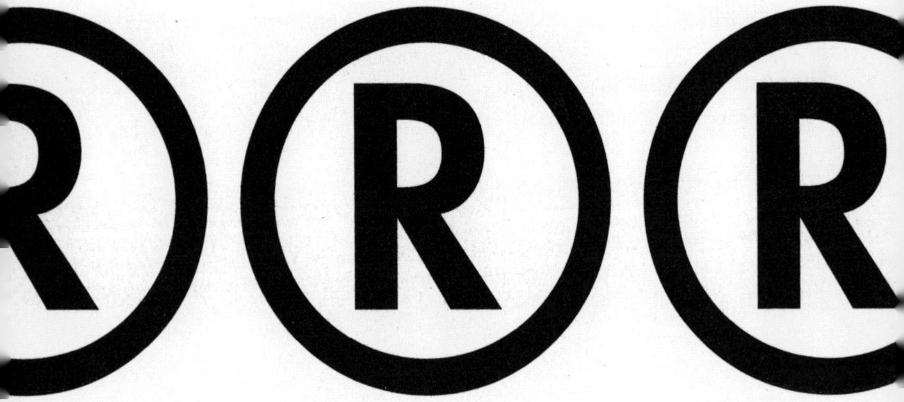

Index

M

N

O

P

 **Books
from
Allworth
Press**

The Pocket Legal Companion to Copyright
by *Lee Wilson* (5 x 7 ½, 320 pages, paperback, $16.95)

Fair Use, Free Use, and Use by Permission
by *Lee Wilson* (6 x 9, 256 pages, paperback, $24.95)

The Patent Guide: A Friendly Guide to Protecting and Profiting from Patents
by *Carl W. Battle* (6 x 9, 224 pages, paperback, $21.95)

Turn Your Idea or Invention into Millions
by *Don Kracke* (6 x 9, 224 pages, paperback, $18.95)

The Pocket Small Business Owner's Guide to Negotiating
by *Richard Weisgrau* (5 ¼ x 8 ¼, 224 pages, paperback, $14.95)

The Pocket Small Business Owner's Guide to Building Your Business
by *Kevin Devine* (5 ¼ x 8 ¼, 256 pages, paperback, $14.95)

Legal Forms for Everyone
by *Carl W. Battle* (8-½ x 11, 240 pages, paperback, $24.95)

Legal Guide for the Visual Artist, Fifth Edition
by *Tad Crawford* (8-½ x 11, 304 pages, paperback, $29.95)

The Law (in Plain English) for Photographers (Third Edition)
by *Leonard D. DuBoff* (6 x 9, 256 pages, paperback, $24.95)

Publish Your Book: Proven Strategies and Resources for the Enterprising Author
by *Patricia Fry* (6 x 9, 256 pages, paperback, $19.95)

Branding for Non-Profits
by *DK Holland* (6 x 9, 208 pages, paperback, $24.95)

The Art of Digital Branding, Revised Edition
by *Ian Cocoran* (6 x 9, 272 pages, paperback, $19.95)

Emotional Branding: The New Paradigm for Connecting Brands to People
by *Marc Gobé* (6 ¼ x 9 ¼ , 352 pages, hardcover, $24.95)

To see our complete catalog or to order online, please visit *www.allworth.com*.